THE STRUGGLE FOR INCLUSION

The Struggle for Inclusion

Muslim Minorities and the Democratic Ethos

Elisabeth Ivarsflaten and
Paul M. Sniderman

THE UNIVERSITY OF CHICAGO PRESS
CHICAGO AND LONDON

The University of Chicago Press, Chicago 60637
The University of Chicago Press, Ltd., London
© 2022 by The University of Chicago
All rights reserved. No part of this book may be used or reproduced in any manner whatsoever without written permission, except in the case of brief quotations in critical articles and reviews. For more information, contact the University of Chicago Press, 1427 E. 60th St., Chicago, IL 60637.
Published 2022
Printed in the United States of America

31 30 29 28 27 26 25 24 23 22   1 2 3 4 5

ISBN-13: 978-0-226-80724-9 (cloth)
ISBN-13: 978-0-226-80741-6 (paper)
ISBN-13: 978-0-226-80738-6 (e-book)
DOI: https://doi.org/10.7208/chicago/9780226807386.001.0001

Library of Congress Cataloging-in-Publication Data

Names: Ivarsflaten, Elisabeth, author. | Sniderman, Paul M., author.
Title: The struggle for inclusion : Muslim minorities and the democratic ethos / Elisabeth Ivarsflaten and Paul M. Sniderman.
Description: Chicago : The University of Chicago Press, 2022. | Includes bibliographical references and index.
Identifiers: LCCN 2021034638 | ISBN 9780226807249 (cloth) | ISBN 9780226807416 (paperback) | ISBN 9780226807386 (ebook)
Subjects: LCSH: Muslims—Cultural assimilation—Europe. | Europe—Ethnic relations.
Classification: LCC D1056.2.M87 I88 2022 | DDC 940.088/297—dc23
LC record available at https://lccn.loc.gov/2021034638

*For Miriam and Eva, a gift to the future,
and Suz, in this as in all else, my lifeline*

Contents

List of Figures ix

Preface xi

1 Introduction 1
    A Note on Methodology and Data 12

2 Demonization and Differentiation 16

3 Respect 35

4 Speech as a Mirror of Dignity 53

5 The Construction of National Identities 70

6 Taking Part: Images of Citizenship 88

7 Liberal Values and Muslim Communities 111
    Appendix: A Methodological Note on the Validity
    of the IMCP Measure 124

8 A New Framework for the Study of Inclusive Politics 128

9 Invitations 143

Acknowledgments 153
Appendix: Documentation of Survey Experiments by Figure 157
Notes 171
Bibliography 185
Data Sources 195
Index 197

Figures

A note on the trial figures: All confidence intervals are 95 percent. All black/white figures show the results from ANOVA-tests. All IMCP figures show the results from probit models. Data source, field period, and *N* for each figure are noted in the appendix.

2.1. An early PEGIDA slogan posted on the anti-Islamic website "Gates of Vienna" (2014) *18*
2.2. Comment made by one of the members of an open Facebook group in Norway entitled "Bring Christian Tybbing-Gjedde into Government" (2015) *19*
2.3. One entry in a discussion on the open white supremacist webforum "Stormfront" in the UK (2015) *20*
2.4. The Differentiation Experiment *32*
3.1. Affirmation of Diversity *41*
3.2. Public Affirmation of Diversity *43*
3.3. Respect for Muslim Culture: First Trial *45*
3.4. Respect for Muslim Culture: Follow-up Trials *46*
3.5. Recognition Respect vs. Appraisal Respect *48*
3.6. Respect Principles by Inclusive Tolerance *51*
4.1. Hate Speech vs. Offensive Speech: First Trial *59*
4.2. Hate Speech vs. Offensive Speech: Evenhandedness *60*
4.3. The May/Should Distinction: The Unreasonable Letters Trial *63*
4.4. The May/Should Distinction: The Contemptuous Speech Trial *65*
4.5. The May vs. Should Distinction by Inclusive Tolerance *68*
5.1. The Textbook Experiment: The First Two-Letter Trial *75*
5.2. The Textbook Experiment: The Second Two-Letter Trial *76*
5.3. The Counterfactual Textbook Experiment *78*
5.4. Continuity vs. Interruption in the Process of National Identity Construction *81*
5.5. The Principle of Continuous Construction: Additional Test *84*
5.6. The Continuity Principle by Inclusive Tolerance *86*

6.1. The Asylum Seeker Sequence: The Pre-Crisis Trial *97*
6.2. The 2015 Refugee Crisis in Norway *99*
6.3. The Asylum Seeker Sequence: The Crisis Trial *100*
6.4. The Asylum Seeker Sequence: The Generalizability Trial *100*
6.5. The Seat at the Table Experiment: Diverse vs. Homogeneous Regional Council *103*
6.6. Preference for Diverse or Homogeneous Regional Council by Inclusive Tolerance *104*
6.7. The Election Day Poll Volunteer Experiment *106*
6.8. Standards for Propriety and Discretion for Christians and Muslims by Inclusive Tolerance *108*
7.1. Conflict between Liberal Values: The Public Rally Experiment *114*
7.2. Opposition to Public Rally by Inclusive Tolerance *115*
7.3. Bad Faith in Muslim Leaders by Inclusive Tolerance *120*
7.4. Bad Faith in Muslim Leaders: Follow-up Trial *122*
7.5. Bad Faith in Muslim Leaders: Final Extension Trial *123*

Preface

A conference in Bergen in 2013 brought us together. On the spur of the moment, we decided on collaboration. We had a conjecture: more ordinary citizens were open to being inclusive than had been recognized. If true, manifestly important. And we had an idea: the willingness of majority citizens to be inclusive depends on what being inclusive asks of them. Yes, a simple idea, but reasoned out, it points to a different way of theorizing about issues of choice in the politics of cultural and religious diversity. A willingness to be inclusive of Muslims partly depends on how positively or negatively citizens who are not themselves Muslim feel about Muslims, how favorably or unfavorably they view them. But the political outcome, in favor of or opposed to inclusion, our results show, depend on the specific substantive options for inclusion on offer and, above all, on their fit with widely shared normative premises of contemporary liberal democracies.

And to turn this from idea to testable hypotheses, we have had the extraordinarily good fortune of being able to use the Norwegian Citizen Panel (NCP) to collect data. We will say a lot about the NCP later. What needs to be said up front is that the NCP gave us the opportunity to introduce a different approach to the study of public opinion. The NCP conducts multiple waves of interviews with a nationally representative sample of Norwegians. That meant that we could take one step, then another, then yet another. That is how the idea of our method, which we call *sequential factorials*, came to us.

The social sciences face a crisis of replication. Too often, if a study is repeated, the second set of results does not match the first. Investigators are forced to choose between two paths. They can do the same study again to see if the third set of results confirms those of either the first or the second.

Alternatively, they can move forward with a different study and attempt to make a new discovery. But since they have limited resources, they (almost always) cannot do both; and learning more (almost always) trumps showing that what was learned was truly learned. This study introduces a methodological innovation to resolve the trade-off between discovery and replication. The key is a repeatable template for randomized experiments: in each trial, we introduce new treatments to take a step forward while, simultaneously, repeating previous treatments to assess the replicability of results from previous steps.

The result has been the adventure of two careers. An adventure is an undertaking that is exciting, in part, because its outcome is not known in advance. But adventures are also exciting because their outcomes matter. So it is here. Our results point to possible paths forward to a more inclusive society.

[CHAPTER ONE]
INTRODUCTION

This book is about whether contemporary liberal democracies are capable of becoming more fully, more truly inclusive. Its focus is the readiness of non-Muslim majority citizens to include Muslim minorities.[1] It is unlike what we, and most other scholars of the politics of cultural and religious diversity, have done before. The aim is *not* to investigate the sources or strength of majority group members' desire to exclude a minority. It is, instead, to identify the conditions under which they are open to inclusion. The difference is not a play on words, not a gambit to substitute one word for another—inclusion for exclusion—in order to say the same thing but the other way around. It is a different undertaking. What are majority group citizens in established democracies willing to endorse, ready to ratify? Where do they draw the line? And why do they draw it there and not elsewhere?

We make three core claims. First, in today's democracies in Western Europe and North America, there are terms on which inclusion of Muslims is widely acceptable. A path forward depends on knowing the difference between the terms that are acceptable and the terms that are not. Second, to see the difference, it is necessary to shift from concentrating on the intolerant, who favor and fight for exclusion, and turn a concentrated light on those who believe in tolerance, who favor the ideals of a liberal democratic society and, at least in principle, are open to inclusion. Third, and ironically, the risk of polarization traps in the struggle for inclusion follows, not from the strength of exclusionary forces, but from the friction between liberal democratic values.[2]

TOCQUEVILLE'S PREMISE

In Tocqueville's account of democracy in America, three factors are fundamental: circumstances, laws, and *les moeurs*. Of the three, *les moeurs*—a society's values, customs, ways of life—is the most crucial. Such is the premise of our study. The habits of the mind and the habits of the heart in contemporary liberal democracies, the broadly shared understanding of what a democracy calls for, are our farthest-reaching concern. "Broadly shared" is key. Left and right, progressives and conservatives, draw different political lessons from these ideals. We fix on what is common ground to the largest number in the mainstream left and right.

Tolerance is at the center of our account. Tolerance is only one of a family of democratic ideals and, until recently, did not bear centrally on the struggle for inclusion. Traditionally, tolerance has meant political tolerance—that is, a willingness to put up with, to tolerate, those you disagree with or dislike. We build on lines of research documenting the emergence of a larger understanding of tolerance:[3] tolerance as affirmative and sympathetic to the prejudice that many minorities confront—*inclusive tolerance* we shall call it.[4] An investigation of the beliefs and concerns of citizens whose outlook is open-minded and inclusive is the core of this inquiry.

About Tocqueville, James Schleifer writes in his landmark work *The Making of Tocqueville's Democracy in America*, "It was in the majority's moral authority that he placed the ultimate power of the many; and it was also in moral limits that he found the best barrier to the abuse of that power."[5] Drawing out what democratic ideals mean for inclusion requires asking what beliefs and what concerns those who affirm them have about inclusion. The ideals of liberal democracies are a primary force in favor of moral arguments for inclusion, but liberal democratic ideals are also the source of the weightiest—and least understood—moral limits on inclusion.

EXCLUSION AND DEMONIZATION

Our focus is on those who believe in inclusive tolerance but not because we discount the force of intolerance. Intolerance, nativism, and political extremism unquestionably remain pressing concerns over a wide array of issues, among them, opposition to immigration and to policies to assist immigrants;[6] prejudice toward immigrants in general and Muslims in particular;[7] the clash of cultural values and group identities;[8] or the surge of support for the far right and populism.[9]

Given this, it would simply be wrong *not* to begin by spotlighting the illiberal strains in today's established democracies. What once—if said publicly—would have ended a politician's career is now a way to make a political career. Geert Wilders, leader of the Freedom Party (PVV) in the Netherlands, is one of a company of established politicians who explicitly argue for exclusion of Muslim minorities and the cultural inferiority of Islam in Europe today: "I am proud to say that our culture . . . is not only better, far better, than what I see as a barbaric Islamic culture" and "#2017in3words No More Islam."[10] And outside the parliamentary and electoral arenas, anti-Islamic groups, websites, and social media networks spill over with appalling illustrations of non-Muslim citizens demonizing Muslims.[11] The Muslim as potential terrorist, a threat to the safety of the country, is a recurring theme. Terror organizations where the leaders and followers identify as Muslims cultivate this notion, precisely because it fuels group conflict and can help enlarge the war of culture and religion that they want to fight.[12] Far-right activists are thriving on what has been called "cumulative extremism—namely, the way in which one form of extremism can feed off and magnify other forms."[13]

To know what hate sounds like, one must hear it; next best is to see it. Hence our presentations, word-for-word, of how some non-Muslims in established democracies regard Muslims. We begin with a showing of posters of PEGIDA (Patriotic Europeans against the Islamization of the Occident / *Patriotische Europäer gegen die Islamisierung des Abendlandes*), a far-right, anti-Islamic activist group that started in Germany, and a sampling of abhorrent Facebook posts.

Our chief resource, though, is the online interviews we conducted with a randomly drawn sample of more than a thousand non-Muslim citizens. We asked them to tell us, in their own words, what comes to mind when they hear the word *Muslim*. Since the interviews were online, participants' anonymity was guaranteed. They were free to say whatever they wanted without fear of presenting themselves in a socially undesirable light; free also to say what they thought without being confined to a choice from among answers predetermined by a researcher. The insults, the contempt, the hostility in the words of many are arresting. We present them, at length and in detail, for readers to see Islamophobia close-up.

But looking for one thing, we also saw another. The overwhelming number of majority group citizens do not see all Muslims as alike. They see differences between young Muslims and old Muslims; between Muslims who are new to their country and Muslims who have grown up in it; between religious Muslims and secular Muslims; between closed-minded and open-minded members of Muslim communities. Demonization and Islamophobia we expected. Differentiation we did not expect. It is humbling to consider that, for all the effort we have put into developing a different approach to the study of public opinion, the finding that may matter most to Muslims is the record of the words that we kept documenting that most non-Muslims see that Muslims, like non-Muslims, do not all follow the same practices, adhere to the same traditions, or share the same outlook on life.[14]

INCLUSIONARY OPTIONS

Turning from a study of exclusion to inclusion changes the focus from those who are intolerant to those who believe in inclusive tolerance. In seeking to account for their concerns and beliefs, some limitations of the standard model of prejudice and politics come into view. The standard model fixes on deep-lying psychological dispositions—authoritarianism,[15] social dominance orientation,[16] or system justification[17]—as long-term drivers of intolerance, compounded by anxieties and animosities generated by intermittent external shocks, most often economic or political crises. To this psychological foundation, we propose to add a political framework spotlighting the pivotal role of inclusionary options.

The core insight is this: the intolerant will throw their weight against inclusion on any terms. All the play is with those who believe in inclusive tolerance. They will not be open to inclusion regardless of what is asked of them. Their openness will depend on the inclusionary options on the table and, more specifically, on the moral premises underpinning those options. They will support inclusion if what they are being asked to support is consistent with their understanding of what a liberal democratic society calls for; they will not support it if what they are being asked to support clashes with this understanding. Our objective is not to pronounce on the validity of their beliefs and judgments. It is to bring out what is and what is not acceptable in the name of inclusion to those who accept the normative premises of contemporary liberal democracies—those who are open to inclusive tolerance.

RESPECT

What should count as being inclusive? At the level of principle, there are two requirements. Respect for the culture of Muslims is one; acceptance of Muslims as a part of the common national identity is the other. Taken by itself, respect for difference tends to favor segregation. Taken by itself, incorporation into a national identity tends to favor assimilation. Inclusion requires both.

A necessary condition of an inclusive society, then, is acknowledgment of the worth of the culture and accomplishments of Muslim minorities. But what does this actually call for? Differences between non-Muslim majority communities and Muslim minority communities over whether women should have equal standing with men are real, not spurious. So, too, are differences over whether the common culture should have a religious temper or a secular one. It is all very well to say that the worth of minority cultures should be acknowledged in a liberal democracy. But what can it mean to say that a person who believes in gender equality and a secular society must acknowledge the worth of Muslim culture and traditions?

In fact, there are two different conceptions of what this may mean. One is that acknowledgment of the worth of Muslims and their faith requires that non-Muslim citizens must evaluate them as commendable, even, possibly, worthy of emulation. This is *appraisal respect*. It is natural and right that those who are part of the community that shares a set of ideals believe that others should see that they are praiseworthy and believe that the larger society should support and help sustain them. But for non-Muslims, including those who are most concerned about prejudice toward minorities, it does not follow that they have a duty to commend the culture and traditions of Muslims; still less that they should accept that the larger society has an obligation to help sustain them or be guilty of intolerance. What is called for is a readiness to appreciate that the ideas and ideals of others are entitled to be taken seriously; to accept that a majority has a responsibility to publicly and privately recognize the culture and traditions of minorities as important to them and therefore worthy of their respect. This is *recognition respect*.

The distinction between recognition respect and appraisal respect speaks to both the opportunities and traps of inclusion. The results of research on a number of fronts converge on a claim that the public in liberal democracies have become progressively more committed to "self-expressive" and "emancipative" values;[18] more supportive of diversity;[19] more aware that the official norms of liberal societies censure prejudice against minorities.[20] Consistent with this research, our results indicate that an ethos of inclusive tolerance is taking hold in contemporary liberal democracies. There is broad acceptance of the need for recognition respect *across the whole of the mainstream political spectrum, right as well as left*—more universally on the left, to be sure, but also widely on the right. But there is not broad acceptance of appraisal respect and the obligations that follow from it to sustain the culture of minorities, *also across the whole of the mainstream political spectrum, left as well as right*.

PUBLIC SPEECH AS A MIRROR OF DIGNITY

Many in Muslim communities, listening to speeches of political demagogues, reading screeds of ordinary citizens, suffering first- or secondhand experience of hate crimes, have concluded, in the words of Tariq Modood, that Muslims are "not respected, that they and their most cherished feelings are 'fair' game."[21] It would be healthy if it were acknowledged all around that a fair share of what now passes as political speech in Western Europe about Muslims is not merely offensive; it is abusive.

Studies of support for freedom of speech focus on the readiness of ordinary citizens to agree that a group they strongly disagree with or intensely dislike has a right, for instance, to hold a public rally to express their ideas. Our responsibility is to bring the issue of speech to bear on the actual everyday challenges that Muslims confront in living in contemporary liberal societies. Hence the investigation of judgments about the propriety of letters to the editor that disparage Muslims or Islam. A preliminary concern is whether ordinary citizens distinguish between offensive speech and hate speech. They do, our results show, condemning letters that threaten Muslims or express hatred or contempt for them overwhelmingly.

Our focus, then, is on how those who believe in inclusive tolerance weigh the concerns of Muslims in questions about speech that does not rise to the standard of hatred and contempt but that Muslims themselves nevertheless find offensive. It turns out that the distinction between what *may* be said and what *should* be said is key. Whether editors *should be allowed* to publish letters that offend Muslims (or Christians) is one question. Whether they *should* publish them is a quite different question. The difference between the two principles is pivotal in questions of offensive speech, once again, not because it matters to the intolerant—they are on board with abusive speech plain and simple—but because it matters to those who believe in inclusive tolerance.

What a person believes *may* be said about Muslims, even if it is offensive, speaks to her beliefs about limits on freedom of expression. What she believes *should not* be said about them and their faith, because it is offensive, speaks to her beliefs about what she owes to Muslims as a matter of common decency. There is overwhelming support both among the tolerant and the intolerant, our results make plain, for newspaper editors having the right to publish letters to the editor even if they are offensive to Muslims. But those who are open to inclusive tolerance stand out precisely because they believe that, although newspapers have a right to publish letters that are offensive to Muslims, they should *not* publish them.

This distinction between what may and what should be said, our studies reveal, is a principled distinction. The same standard is applied to Christians and Muslims, for all intents and purposes; and so far as there is a difference, it takes the form of a greater concern for the feelings of Muslims than Christians among the largest share of citizens, those who believe in inclusive tolerance. On the one hand this pattern is reassuring. The standards for what *should not* be said about Muslims are a mirror of the respect that citizens in contemporary liberal democracies believe is owed to Muslim minorities. They are consistent with the hypothesis of an emerging norm of recognition respect. On the other hand, the pattern points to a challenge for inclusion: non-Muslims' beliefs in what may be said about Muslims—the freedom of speech standard—is what is readily visible to Muslim minorities in contemporary democracies. What non-Muslims think should not be said about Muslims, even though it should be allowed to be said as a matter of liberal democratic principle, is far less so.

BECOMING PART

For Muslims to be included in the larger society, both the larger society and Muslims must take initiatives. Inclusion, not assimilation, is the objective, and inclusion, unlike assimilation, calls for action by both majority and minority. We begin with the question of the readiness of non-Muslims to include Muslim minorities as a part of the national identity.

There is a large research literature on the psychology of national identity—on the degree or intensity with which citizens identify with their country; the diverse forms their identification can take (e.g., patriotism vs. chauvinism); their beliefs about what their country stands for and, by extension, their images of the ideal citizen.[22] Our interest is different.

It is a commonplace that identities are socially constructed. The question we ask is, How does this bear on the prospects for inclusion of Muslim minorities in contemporary liberal democracies? In modern societies, the primary formal institution responsible for the construction of national identities is the educational system. We exploit this to examine a key question in the struggle for inclusion: On what normative premises are citizens who believe in inclusive tolerance open to (re)constructing their country's self-image to incorporate ethnic and religious diversity as an aspect of the national identity?

Following from a long line of scholarship on identity, it is obvious that continuity, in some way or other, is a vital consideration. But continuity of what? Two levels need to be distinguished. Substantive continuity is one.

The issue: quite simply, there is no way of getting around that formally acknowledging diversity as an aspect of the national identity will be a substantive change. So, we focus on continuity of process rather than continuity of substance. An extended sequence of experiments zooms in on changes in school textbooks, contrasting reactions, for example, to textbooks being "written," "updated," "expanded," or "rewritten" to reflect diversity. The pivotal issue, our results show, is not change itself, but continuity of the process of making changes.

TAKING PART

The balance of power may lie in the hands of majorities. But Muslim minorities are not just objects about whom majorities make decisions. On the contrary, on some essential questions, Muslim communities themselves will define who they are and wish to be. These choices—and not all Muslims will make the same choices—will influence how they become part of liberal democracies. Our contribution is to bring into view how and why the practice of shared civic activities is crucial in the struggle for inclusion.

How can Muslims, by their own actions, present themselves to non-Muslim majority citizens as fellow citizens? Previous research has documented that the non-Muslim majority suspects that Muslim immigrants are acting in bad faith when they say that they want to be part of the country they have immigrated to.[23] They believe Muslims still give their loyalty to the countries they came from, not the country they have come to live in. How might Muslims respond?

Symbolic declarations of loyalty are a way to overcome suspicions of allegiance, we reasoned at first. We were wrong. What we believe that others believe is more deeply grounded in what they do or fail to do than in what they say they believe or do not believe. That is one lesson we (re)learned. Another lesson is the role of serendipity in research. It is thanks to colleagues predicting correctly that we had started on the wrong track that an investigation of symbolic politics turned into an analysis of participatory democracy.

Being accepted as a citizen is a matter of behaving like a citizen—not playing a part in political theater but taking an active part in local community affairs. We are not suggesting that Muslim minorities face no barriers in this pursuit. To the contrary, we provide evidence of barriers they confront in making the effort to take part in civic life, for example, by acting as election poll volunteers. Nonetheless, our results show that taking part in civic life is a pathway to becoming part of the larger society.

VALUE CONFLICT AND INCLUSION SETBACKS

Conflicts between the values of societies that have become increasingly liberal and secular and Muslim communities are well documented. We take the next step and bring out conflicts between liberal values. That liberal values can conflict with one another is a commonplace, the textbook example being having to choose between an increase in liberty versus an increase in equality. The conflict between the two can be genuine. It can be a close call. But, ultimately, the choice is not to sacrifice fundamental democratic rights of certain groups in society but rather to have more of the one or more of the other. The conflicts between liberal values we address have different stakes. Our results bring to the surface when conflicts between democratic ideals lead to a sacrifice of the democratic rights of a religious minority, of Muslims.

The most telling example, the Public Rally experiment, gauges the willingness of non-Muslims to allow Muslims to hold a public rally. This experiment is deliberately designed to turn up the heat on the conflict between two liberal democratic principles: gender equality and religious freedom. Sometimes the stated purpose of the rally is to convey Islamic values, sometimes conservative ideas about women in Islam. Sometimes, its mission is to explain, sometimes to preach. We ratchet up the severity of the conflict between freedom of expression and religion on the one hand and gender equality on the other by bringing forward first one opposing consideration, then another, then both at the same time. There is no mystery how those who reject inclusive tolerance will react in all the conditions of the experiment: they will respond, no, Muslims should not be allowed to hold a public rally. The question is, How will those who believe in inclusive tolerance respond?

The first point we make is that those who are committed to inclusive tolerance stand by freedom of expression and religion most of the time. It is only when the conflict between the liberal values of gender equality and religious freedom is fully ratcheted up in the Public Rally experiment that those who believe in inclusive tolerance fail to support the rights of Muslims. But their failure is complete. Those who believe in inclusive tolerance line up right alongside the intolerant to oppose Muslims being allowed to exercise their fundamental democratic rights. The result: overwhelming opposition among majority group members to Muslims exercising their freedom of religion.

What to make of this is subject to debate.[24] A case can be made that advocating religious doctrines that discriminate against women constitutes hate speech and, in established liberal democracies in Europe—but not in the US—hate speech is legally restricted.²⁵ Still, *conservative* ideas (not immediately and directly threatening ideas) and *preach* (not compel) are hardly the most provocative terms. It is not clear what freedom of religion and expression means if conservative Muslims cannot speak on behalf of their faith. At a minimum, the Public Rally experiment brings home what sets the challenge of inclusion of Muslim minorities apart. Out-groups face common risks: illiberal strains in liberal democracies are deeply entrenched. But here and now, Muslims especially face the risk of illiberal choices by those who have liberal ideals precisely because they truly value liberal ideals.

THE POLITICS OF INCLUSION AND POLARIZATION TRAPS

Against a background of the far right gaining electoral ground and amassing political influence by targeting Islam and Muslim minorities as an existential threat, there is a natural concern that efforts to promote inclusion may fan the fires already burning. Hence the importance of identifying which political options are most likely to win broad support for inclusion, and which are most likely to set back inclusion. What we will bring into view is how decisively the answer to this question depends on the normative premises that underpin inclusionary options. A number of specific normative considerations, whose weight and appeal has not been recognized, are pivotal in that they can turn majorities of citizens in contemporary democracies in favor of or against inclusion. A common feature of these pivotal considerations, our results show, is that they matter to the largest share of citizens, to those who are open to inclusive tolerance.

These results reveal, ultimately, a broad willingness to accept paths forward toward more inclusive societies. This claim of broad support for inclusion is modest in one respect, not modest in another. It is modest insofar as it claims not that majority citizens are actively pressing for inclusion of Muslim minorities but, rather, that there is a permissive coalition, a willingness to go along with inclusion—depending, and this is key, on the inclusionary options on offer.²⁶ A claim of broad support is not modest in another respect. It cashes out as a prediction that there is broad agreement *across* the political spectrum, mainstream right as well as left, that the cultures and histories of Muslims should be treated with respect and that cultural and religious diversity should be acknowledged as an aspect of national identity. It is all the more important, then, for us to spotlight the limits on acceptance of inclusion that we identify and the danger of *polarization traps* when they are violated.

It is a standard result that the more policy is shifted to the left of the median voter, the less support it will enjoy, and vice versa. In contrast, the pivotal distinctions we have identified cut the ground out from under support of inclusion across the whole of the mainstream political spectrum left and right. Uniform losses of support are a signature indicator of a violation of widely shared ideas of what is right and what is wrong. It is not a matter of "framing," of the same course of action enjoying more support or less support depending on how it is characterized.[27] The pivotal distinctions we emphasize are substantive in the deepest sense. They turn on what citizens who believe in liberal democratic values understand these values to require, where they draw the line (i.e., what they perceive as inconsistent or optional), and how they negotiate conflicts between liberal values if and when they are forced to do so. The distinction between *recognition* respect and *appraisal* respect is a case in point. Muslims having a right to have their outlook and traditions treated with respect and non-Muslim citizens having to declare that they are commendable are different moral premises.

What we will show is that they are not only analytically distinct, they are also politically pivotal; that is, they can turn majorities in favor of or against inclusion. We emphasize these pivots with some urgency because the failure to recognize them is associated with the risk of polarization traps. A trap is something that nobody wants to fall into and is hard to escape from. A *polarization* trap, as we understand it, is when majorities in favor of inclusion exist, but they are misunderstood as majorities in favor of exclusion because political actors have not recognized that support for inclusion is conditional on the particular terms on which it is proposed.

Recognizing the pivotal distinctions between inclusionary options and the normative premises—the ideas about right and wrong—that underpin them will not take away political conflict over the best paths forward in the struggle for inclusion. Even if we identify distinctions between inclusionary options at large, it does not follow that those who favor inclusion will find sufficient common ground. Leadership matters. But with all the limitations on what our results can teach, and they are substantial, we believe that the insights our results provide can lessen polarization of these political conflicts and provide a more clear-eyed view of the strategic considerations that inclusionary actors confront as well as the constraints under which actors and organizations who still favor and fight for exclusion operate.

A NEW RESEARCH AGENDA ON INCLUSIVE POLITICS

This book reports the results of thirty-four experiments embedded in twenty-four large-scale public opinion surveys of nationally representative samples of adults in eight different countries: Norway, the United Kingdom, the Netherlands, Denmark, the United States, Germany, France, and Sweden, totaling to interviews with more than twenty-seven thousand respondents. We believe the results of the studies make a case for launching a new research agenda focusing on the normative premises on which the tolerant negotiate conflicts between democratic values. This requires going beyond the standard psychological model of prejudice and politics.

Political theories of inclusion are necessary. The distinctions we have found—between recognition respect and appraisal respect; between what may be said and what should be said; between fixed identities assigned by history and the continuous process of their construction and reconstruction; between inclusionary options that pit liberal democratic values against each other and those that do not—are a start. They are, manifestly, not the end. It is simple to ask what is acceptable. It is hard to answer—harder than we had appreciated. The struggle for inclusion of Muslim minorities is bound up with both the moral authority and the moral limits of liberal democratic ideals.

A NOTE ON METHODOLOGY AND DATA

According to one model of how a study must proceed in order to be scientifically valid, the researchers' ideas, measures, plan of analysis, and predictions must be specified in advance. In a maximalist version of this view, a necessary condition is an overarching theory, from which hypotheses are rigorously deduced, then the ancillary requirements of measurement and the analysis plan are exactly specified. We follow another idea about how science is done. To take advantage of John Maynard Smith's rendering, "There is no planned, logical and inevitable attack on the problem. Instead there are false starts, insights which turn out to be wrong, and periods where the problem is dropped altogether because there is no obvious way forward."[28]

We are calling for research to turn in a new direction, to go beyond fixing attention on the intolerant to focus on the tolerant, to move beyond social psychological and rational choice models of group conflict and develop political theories of the politics of inclusion. This requires exploration, experimenting with how to think about the problem as well as doing experiments.

To get underway, our starting point has been hypotheses suggested by previous empirical studies or prompted by studies in political theory. But our strategy, as well as our method, is experimental. Learning as we go. More formally, this study introduces a new approach to survey experiments—*sequential factorials*.[29] The idea is to conduct iterative sequences of survey experiments, learning at each step the next step to take. A repeatable template is the key. For each line of experimental trials, a standardized wording is developed and repeated over a sequence of experimental trials. Only the "fills" in a textbox are randomly varied.

Discovery by following an iterative progression of steps, each small but cumulating over the full sequence, is the strategy. Typically, you learn at each step the next step to take to extend a line of inquiry; to refine your reasoning; to rule out alternative explanations. But from time to time, what you learn is that you missed a step. What seemed an unbroken chain of reasoning is missing a link. Then you must double back and do an experiment to work through the reasoning properly. We present the results of experiments in their logical order. However, the specific study in which they were conducted is always identified, by its number in the iterative sequence of surveys, to make clear when we had to double back to fill in a hole in our reasoning.

Sequential factorials offer another benefit. The social sciences, though not only the social sciences, are suffering a crisis of replication. When an experiment is repeated, all too often the results of the second trial do not match the results of the first. To this point the chief remedy has been regulation—preregistration of hypotheses, reasoning, data collection plans, data analysis plans.[30] Sequential factorials make possible an empirical option. At each trial, thanks to a repeatable template, treatment terms from previous trials can be repeated, so an experiment can be done again *exactly* as it was done before. At the same time, new treatment terms can be introduced. Sequential factorials thus offer a way out of the dilemma of having to decide whether to spend limited resources to make a new discovery or to assess the replicability of a previous one.

Table 1.1 shows an example of a sequential factorial design. In this case, the sequence covers six trials. Note that replications appear in the same row. The table also shows that replication trials are conducted across countries as well as within, in order to assess the generalizability as well as the robustness of results. The sequence will be presented in full in chapter 7. What follows is a brief summary to clarify the methodology.

The hypothesis, at the start, is that majority citizens are even more likely to suspect the sincerity of the commitment of leaders of Muslim communities than of ordinary Muslims when they declare that they want to be part of their new country. So they are. The question then becomes, who are majority citizens thinking of when they think of the leadership of Muslim communities? The second trial tests the obvious hypothesis, that "leaders of Muslim communities" means "Muslim religious leaders." The third and fifth trials test the hypothesis that Muslim religious leaders are distrusted

TABLE 1.1. AN EXAMPLE OF A SEQUENTIAL FACTORIAL SURVEY EXPERIMENT

Trial # (Country)	1 (Denmark)	2 (Denmark)	3 (Netherlands)	4 (Norway)	5 (Norway)	6 (Great Britain)
Target group fill 1	Muslims	Muslims	Muslims	Muslims	Muslims	Muslims
Target group fill 2					Female Muslim leaders	
Target group fill 3						Muslim business leaders
Target group fill 4					Muslim local politicians	Muslim local councilors
Target group fill 5	Muslim leaders	Muslim leaders	Muslim leaders	Muslim leaders		
Target group fill 6		Muslim religious leaders		Muslim religious leaders	Muslim religious leaders	Muslim religious leaders
Target group fill 7			Muslim fundamentalists			
Target group fill 8					Muslim extremists	

Repeatable template: How much do you trust or distrust [TARGET GROUP FILL] when they say that they wish to be a part of our society?

Example: How much do you trust or distrust Muslim religious leaders when they say that they wish to be a part of our society?

because, in the minds of majority citizens, they are Islamic fundamentalists or extremists. The fifth and sixth trials test the hypothesis that suspicions of bad faith are distinctively attached to Muslim religious leaders, not Muslim secular leaders, though in the absence of counter-indicators, Muslim leaders are presumed to be Muslim religious leaders. Finally, the six trials in the Bad Faith sequence, taken together, assess the generalizability of the core hypothesis that Muslim leaders / Muslim religious leaders are doubly suspect, once for being Muslim and once again for being a Muslim leader, comparing results in four countries: Denmark, the Netherlands, Norway, and Great Britain.

As a result of our good fortune to have access to a research infrastructure like the Norwegian Citizen Panel, we have been able to conduct more and longer sequences than would otherwise have been possible. An example of an insight that emerged rather late is the role of recognition respect versus appraisal respect, reported in chapter 3. It was only after having employed variations on the respect template and discussing the nature of the results so far with colleagues that we realized what the crucial distinction likely was. We then proceeded to field experiments, using the same template, but in a way that targeted that specific distinction.

Since our claims are not about the Norwegian context specifically but rather about established Christian-heritage democracies more generally, we have made extensive efforts to test major claims in multiple countries. Thanks to old and newly established research collaborations with colleagues in Denmark, the UK, the US, the Netherlands, France, Germany, and Sweden, we were able to field many of the key trials in these countries. The results are not always exactly the same, but we have been struck time and again by how often the patterns of direct effects that we have found in one country are repeated in another.

We want to underscore the importance of and the need for more detailed comparative work. The templates we provide are repeatable and adaptable, and we invite further scrutiny of the main propositions put forward in the chapters that follow, as regards both the quality of the ideas and their generalizability across countries. This is a beginning, and if we have done our work well, we have come a fair bit down the road of a program of study of inclusive politics.

[CHAPTER TWO]

DEMONIZATION AND DIFFERENTIATION

At first slowly, then with a steadily increasing velocity, scholars have been building a systematic body of research on Islamophobia. Consistent with studies of prejudice against other out-groups, Islamophobia is defined as a set of "indiscriminate negative attitudes or emotions directed at Islam and Muslims."[1] The more readily the majority of citizens dislike, derogate, reject, or react punitively toward Muslims because they are Muslims, the more Islamophobic they are. A readiness to systematically stigmatize and reject Muslims by virtue of their being Muslims is the most useful conception of Islamophobia for most purposes. But not for all. From the start, we want to call out the sheer virulence of the feelings of some native citizens toward Muslim minorities. Demonization is the right word, the risk of sensationalism notwithstanding.

Demonization has been described as an evolving view that "begins with doubt, thrives with suspicion, ends with certainty, and aims at decisive militant action."[2] Abusive stereotypes share a family of characteristics: (1) hostile beliefs and suspicions about the intentions of members of the out-group; (2) generalization—the belief that all, or nearly all, members of the group, with little distinction, share these negative characteristics; and (3) threat perception—the belief that the out-group causes danger or is dangerous. But sharper characterization is needed to capture the virulence of demonization. It is not merely that some native citizens dislike and disdain Muslims; not even that they dislike and disdain Muslims intensely. The root of demonization is the Greek word *daemon*. A daemon is wicked, evil; but wickedness, even evil, are not in isolation terrorizing. It is terrorizing when it is fused with a propulsive—or as one should say, a demonic—force.

HOW ANTI-ISLAMIC ACTIVISTS DEMONIZE MUSLIMS

Anti-Islamic groups, their websites, and their social media groups offer an overabundance of demonstrations of non-Muslim citizens demonizing Muslims.[3] A recurring theme is that of the Muslim as lurking terrorist, a threat to the safety of the country. Unlike traditional far right and white supremacist groups in Europe and the US, the anti-Islamic far right has been ascendant broadly since September 11, 2001. Whereas the traditional far right is highly fragmented according to national boundaries, the newer anti-Islamic community is more transnational.[4] They use Facebook as their primary channel of organizing and disseminating material. A network analysis revealed an online, transnational network of 4,000 groups, half of which are explicitly anti-Islamic. The largest individual groups had approximately 150,000 online members in the fall of 2016.[5] In the electoral arena of Western European countries, populist parties on the far right followed the lead of Pim Fortuyn in the Netherlands and picked up some of the anti-Islamic agenda.[6] In the US, anti-Islamic messages were, until the presidential campaign of Donald Trump, mainly carried by activist groups outside party politics.

Scholars have, so far, identified three significant cycles of diffusion of anti-Islamic activism in Europe and the US. The first cycle came with the rise of the online Counter-Jihadi community in the wake of the terrorist attacks on September 11, 2001. Blogs like *Gates of Vienna* and *Atlas Shrugs* were the most prominent. The "Mohammed Cartoon Crisis" sparked the second cycle in 2006.[7] It was characterized by real world activism by the Counter-Jihadi community and the creation of the umbrella organization *Stop the Islamization of Europe* (SIOE). The rise of *PEGIDA* (*Patriotische Europäer gegen die Islamisierung des Abendlandes* / Patriotic Europeans against the Islamization of the West) marks the third cycle of anti-Islamic activist diffusion. By January 2015, PEGIDA had established itself in most Western European countries, revitalizing the anti-Islamic extreme right with more than two hundred groups.[8] In addition to these cycles, it appears that the 2016 election campaign and the resulting presidency of Donald J. Trump energized anti-Islamic and white supremacist groups, who themselves wish to be labeled the alternative right or identity movements, across the US and Europe.

Anti-Islamic activists and far-right and white supremacist organizations are united in the core belief that Western civilization today is fundamentally threatened by Islam and Muslims. Any societal movement in Europe or in the US in the direction of cultural and religious pluralism that in some way benefits Muslims is in their reasoning a step in the direction of weakening or undermining Western civilization. Their preferred term

FIGURE 2.1. An early PEGIDA slogan posted on the anti-Islamic website "Gates of Vienna" the day after the first PEGIDA demonstration in Dresden on October 27, 2014.

for this undesirable process is "Islamization." The two main anti-Islamic organizations in Europe put this term front and center when naming their organizations—Stop the Islamization of Europe (SIOE) and Patriotic Europeans against the Islamization of the West (PEGIDA).

The importance of the term "Islamization" to anti-Islamic organizations is instructive. It calls out a particular and nonpluralist way of reasoning about society and about the inclusion of Muslims. For the idea of "Islamization" to make sense, the presumption is not only an idealized non-Muslim— often, but not always, Christian—homogeneous cultural starting point ("the West," "Europe," "the United States of America," "France," "Germany," etc.), it is also a homogeneous end point—either a society that has been conquered by Muslims and has become "Islamized" or a society that has successfully resisted "Islamization" and remains "Western," "French," or "American." In this view of the world, the inclusion of Muslims into Western societies is an existential threat. Any attempt to accommodate the customs and traditions of Muslims is seen as a sign of naivete, weakness, or even treason.

One of the most striking features of the anti-Islamic views that we canvassed in our research for this book is the lack of any attempt to *distinguish* among Muslims. We are not just observing the common social psychological pattern of members of an in-group having trouble telling members of an out-group apart. In these anti-Islamic accounts, Muslims are not strangers who look alike because their faces are featureless. Rather the opposite. They look alike because the face of each is as barbarous as the face of every other. All Muslims are categorically viewed as mortal enemies. They have

jeg vil jage alt av muslimer ut av europa stikk eller dø burde det stå på hvert av hjemmene til muslimene

Like Reply 1h

FIGURE 2.2. Comment made by one of the members of an open Facebook group in Norway entitled "Bring Christian Tybbing-Gjedde into Government" (2015). Translation [Capitalization and punctuation as in original]: "i want to chase all sorts of muslims from europe get lost or die should be posted on each of the homes of the muslims." Nouns that describe religious groups are not written with a capital letter in Norwegian (so, unlike in English, it is not a mistake in the Norwegian to write "muslimer").

infiltrated Europe and the US for the purpose of taking over and ruining Western civilization. For the anti-Islamic far right, terrorists who identify as Muslim, fundamentalist Muslim organizations, ordinary Muslims, moderate Muslims, and refugees from predominantly Muslim countries are one and the same.

WORDS MATTER: OPEN-ENDED ASSOCIATIONS IN A RANDOMLY SELECTED SAMPLE

The main methodology employed in this book is survey experiments. The innovation is the deliberate use of iterative sequences of experiment trials, each step dedicated both to replicating and to going beyond the results of previous steps simultaneously. This is a strategy with many strengths, which we discuss in the chapters that follow. Nevertheless, a well-known limit of this strategy, shared with all large-scale studies of public opinion, is in conveying the pitch of emotion in beliefs and feelings of majority citizens about Muslim minorities. Words matter. What native citizens say (or refuse to say) brings out particularities in the emotional tone of their feelings and frame of mind about Islam and Muslim minorities. Words, not numbers, bring into view two signature features of the beliefs and feelings of majority citizens toward Muslim minorities—demonization and differentiation.

WHAT COMES TO MIND

In November 2016, the refugee crisis that peaked in Europe a year earlier was, from a Northern European perspective, becoming less severe. More than one million refugees made their way to Europe during a few winter months in 2015. As a share of its population, Norway was among the top four recipient countries, even if well behind the two countries that received the most asylum applicants, Germany and Sweden.[9] The thirty thousand

FIGURE 2.3. One entry in a discussion on the open white supremacist webforum "Stormfront" in the UK (2015). The text states: "ALL moslems must be regarded as potential terrorists and mind twisters. We haven't just got a deluge of them its a landslide of Islamic soldiers ready & equipped to destroy white Europe!"

asylum seekers, mainly fleeing from the wars in Syria and Afghanistan, who showed up in Norway in a few busy winter months was highly unusual for this country of five million. Many of the refugees who arrived were likely, and were at the time believed to be, Muslim. This means that at the time when we asked respondents in a Norwegian survey for their associations with the word "Muslim," both principles and practical issues associated with asylum policies and the integration of refugees, immigrants, and Muslims were high on the public agenda.[10]

Furthermore, people identifying as Muslim in Europe had executed many acts of terror during the preceding years, and these attacks had received much attention in Norwegian media, as elsewhere in Europe.[11] In this context, we asked respondents in the Norwegian Citizen Panel the following question: "What comes to mind for you, personally, when you hear the word "Muslim"? Please write down the first thing that comes to mind. We are interested in both long and short answers."

Nearly all who were asked to share their thoughts did so. We received 1,125 unique responses. Some wrote just a word or a couple of words, but many wrote much more. Several aspects of these responses are striking, but first and foremost is how few respondents were indifferent or unengaged. Some expressed a fully formed summary of their thoughts about Muslims, some briefly expressed very negative views, many more expressed some of both. There are examples of lexical definitions of the sort that you learn in religious studies, but most replied in more involved ways.

Some responses indicate lack of familiarity with and sometimes a wish to know more about Muslims and Islam. Others express certainty. Some tell quite personal and detailed stories. Others relate stream-of-consciousness reflections. Quite a few are simply lists of words. Many mention the concerns high on the public agenda about refugees, wars, and terror. Many mention concerns about the oppression of women and challenges to integration into Norwegian society. A substantial number express views about religion either in general or with respect to specific illiberal values within Islam. The premise in a majority of the responses is that Muslims grew up in the Middle East, in Asia, or in Africa and have recently arrived in Norway and that they are strangers. Some express a suspicion that Muslims do not want to integrate into Norwegian society or that they have insufficient respect for Norwegian culture and traditions.

DEMONIZATION AND ISLAMOPHOBIA

This material includes examples of demonization every bit as hostile as what one finds on anti-Islamic websites and open social media forums.

One respondent, telling us about what came to mind when he heard the word "Muslim" replied, "Terrorist. An intolerance that kills all other cultures. Radical Muslims overpower those who are peaceful and tolerant. They have shown through history that they do not tolerate other cultures. Therefore, all support for the Islamization of Norway should be stopped." Wrote another, "Fear! Muslims view Christians as third-rate citizens. Christians are infidels in the eyes of Muslims. The Muslim people want to take over governance of the whole world. And the Norwegian government is sitting passively and watching. Muslims have no respect for others, only their own." A third participant wrote, "People from the Middle East who are strongly attached to a dangerous religion that is oppressive and commands memorization of the Qur'an and following sharia in many places. There is a danger that this can lead to Islamization not only in Norway."

After close reading of all 1,125 written responses, 36 of them (about 3%) without doubt demonize Muslims. Considerably more responses express negative stereotypes, focus only on problems, and generalize these to all Muslims. These may be categorized as Islamophobic yet not demonizing, since they do not ascribe evil intentions or threat. Consider one respondent's near exhaustive list of negative stereotypes: "A religious person who often lives by rules that oppress women and judge others. They have limited freedom to choose if they wish to be Muslims, and almost never marry non-Muslims. They have little tolerance for other religions, and people who are not religious. They are not particularly friendly to animals, and do not like dogs. Boys and girls are raised differently, and the boys often have little respect for girls and women."

Such associations were relatively common. As many as 297 responses (26%) could be described as Islamophobic because they express negative stereotypes about Muslims in an undifferentiated manner. Some are a bit hard to interpret in that they contain only one or a few words, such as "extreme religion" or "fanatic," but we made the decision to code responses as Islamophobic if they mention only negatively charged characteristics or problems but make no distinction among Muslims, even if they are brief. When identifying whether responses are demonizing, the shortest answers are most difficult to judge. We coded "extremist who is dangerous" as demonization, while the couple of responses that state only "extreme" we coded as Islamophobic. We could have decided differently, but it would not have influenced our main takeaway, which is that negative stereotypes are much more commonly expressed than demonization.

A common theme in the Islamophobic answers is the conflict with "Western culture." Many respondents mention or focus entirely on discrimination of women or old-fashioned gender norms. Said one, "A person who believes in Allah. People with an old-fashioned view of women. People who often lack tolerance." Many shorter responses also have this focus, "A religion and a lifestyle. Old-fashioned and conservative. Lacking respect for women" or "A religion that oppresses women." Several responses simply state "Burka" or "Hijab." There are also examples of lists of pejoratives, such as the following: "Foreign. Subculture. Old-fashioned. Oppression. Bad attitude toward women. Militant. Aggressive." Another rich and lengthy response raises many concerns but is also particularly concerned about oppression of women:

> I do not have anything against individual Muslims, but the number in Norway is too large. Burka hijab and oppression of women—they reproduce so fast that we can become the Minority. When I am on holiday in Muslim countries, I cover myself to show respect for their customs and culture. I wish we were given the same respect back. If they want to continue living as if they still live in a Muslim country, they should live someplace other than Norway. In my local community, the number of foreigners has grown substantially, and most are Muslim. Often I am the only white person in the store. They do not speak Norwegian, and they wrap their little girls in burka. They should contribute to their own integration too and not just expect the Norwegian state to accommodate. Some Muslims in our country contribute to positively diverse communities and multiculturalism, but the number we have now is a tragedy for our country. We cannot save the world. Far too few who come to Norway choose to return to their home countries. If only they had returned, then we could have helped more. Norway is too naive when it comes to Muslims.

Several wrote about terror, war, and aggression. Said one, "IS, how much . . . [obscenity] they have done in the world. And what they do to their own religion and other Muslims. What that brings about, like anger, fear, and prejudice." Or simply "Religion, terror, ISIS"; or "Suicide bomber, terror, war," or "A bearded man (extremist)"; or "If you look around in the world today it is the Muslims who are at war," "Angry people." Several respondents simply wrote "Terror" or "Terrorism." Some were even more dismissive: "Get them out of here if they only make trouble and complain and do not obey Norwegian laws."

Some focused on what they perceived as an unwillingness to respect Norwegian culture and law specifically. Said one, "I am thinking they are so preoccupied with their own religion, they don't think about the society they live in (Norway) very much. Adaptation to Norwegian culture and learning that the laws of Norway are above Muslim religious laws, has low priority among Muslims." Said another, "A person who puts the religious laws of Muslims above the laws of a country." A third participant simply said, "A slave of religion, refuses integration into Western culture." Others, "Somebody who expects that everybody else should adjust to him and his religion" and "Somebody who dislikes everything we in Norway stand for."

DIFFERENTIATION

Major terror attacks in advanced liberal democracies, where the perpetrators have been identified as Muslims, have in turn often been followed by peaceful demonstrations and calls to remember that most Muslims are not security threats and do not support terrorists.[12] So in the public sphere we have political leaders and activists pointing citizens in opposite directions, some fueling hatred and encouraging demonization, others calling for calm, caution, and differentiation. How majority citizens respond to the events, and how they come to interpret them upon reflection, is important in the struggle for inclusion of Muslim minorities.

Asymmetry is a trademark feature of attitudes toward out-groups.[13] So we found also in the open-ended text responses to the question about Muslims. The Islamophobic sentiments, whether clearly demonizing or not, are not matched by a set of responses that categorically glorify or embrace Muslims. In our material, responses that are not Islamophobic tend to be neutral. Respondents wrote lexical definitions; they expressed distance or difference without negative stereotypes; or they differentiated or subgrouped. A handful talked about individual Muslims or specific people they know, they individuated. Together the responses not expressing Islamophobia or demonization make up about 70 percent of the sample. In these responses, negative stereotypes occur, but the respondent either explicitly stated that they recognize these as such; they offered an example of a person, sometimes a specific person known to them, who is different from the stereotype; or they mentioned other sorts of counter-stereotypical associations.

Some of the differentiating responses explicitly discussed the problem of generalizing about Muslims. One respondent wrote, "Most of them are, I guess, like us. I guess they are different like we are." Another wrote, "Great human beings and work-colleagues that are as different as ethnic Norwegians. They think and behave as differently about their faith as everybody else." Another elaborated further: "This is a person that often is generalized into a group. A lot of stranger anxiety is connected to the term, but I think that is because of lack of knowledge about religion generally and Islam specifically. It is the most visible group of immigrants, and I think that strengthens feelings some have of a division between us. Personally,

I think a multicultural society is enriching and that we learn a lot from dialogue with different groups."

Many reflected on the difference between extremists and ordinary Muslims. Wrote one, "There are many different Muslims. Some are not dangerous and have a balanced take on life. A small share are extreme and dangerous for the world around them." Or, "There are many decent Muslims who suffer because of the terror of the radicalized Muslims." Wrote a third respondent, "Most are good human beings but some extremists make us judge 'Muslims' as evil/ISIS." Another respondent wrote, "Dislike all religion. I think people should get to decide themselves what they believe in, don't dislike Muslims more than for example Christians. Am fully aware that a Muslim is not the same as a terrorist and am not afraid of Muslims."

One of the respondents offered a lengthier reflection along these lines:

> There are many different ways to be a Muslim and many different ways of practicing the Qur'an's rules that Muslims have to live by. We only hear about the extreme, but it is very important that we get to hear about those who manage to live as Muslims in a modern society. It is important to value those Muslim girls who now get a higher education and who have important jobs. That is of course also true of boys. Important to promote good role models and examples for the Muslim part of our society that is growing up today.

Several respondents emphasized the common humanity of all people, regardless of group belonging. Wrote one, "They are human beings like everybody else, and . . . they deserve respect like everybody else here in Norway." A lengthier reflection along these lines reads as follows:

> I think about human beings who have a religious faith. They are human beings like everybody else, and they ought to be met with the same sort of respect as other "groups." I think Muslims receive a lot of bad press, often undeserved. There are Muslims who do horrible things, among others suicide bombers and terrorists, but for me it is important to view these people as individuals instead of treating all Muslims the same. That some Muslims conduct terror does not mean that all Muslims do. There are all sorts of Muslims, just like Christians, Jews, etc. Nobody is exactly the same, and everybody has the same right to be treated as the human being that they are.

Some focused on the obligation to accept diversity. Said one, "A part of the cultural diversity we all have to accept is here to stay." Said another,

"Come on, we have to be able to live together, accept differences, and also see fundamental similarities." A third respondent expressed this sentiment in the following way: "Religion is not my thing, but to each their own desire." Another respondent shared a lengthy reflection:

> Haha. Right. Just today I had a discussion with my dad about Islam and Muslims. He is one of these people who reads Storhaug's book[14] and who could use more balanced and nonpolemical insights into what Islam and Muslims are and do. I tried in the conversation to offer a more nuanced picture of Islam, which definitely is not a cohesive entity. We are talking about large differences between different strands and regional/national. We also discussed the tabloid depictions of Islam that often appear in the media—where the religion as such unfortunately often is equated with violent extremism. I would have wanted a better understanding of the rhetoric in the media and how easy it is to use religion to legitimate political views and actions. That said, I think most Muslims are human beings like everybody else, who are interested in living a good and decent life. It is not the case that in a society there is agreement about what a good and decent life is, but fortunately we have a society where we have the freedom to choose both religion, "spirituality," and nonreligion. Nobody should be discriminated against because of their religion, gender, or sexual orientation—and this is particularly the case in a religiously pluralist society. I think it is important that Muslims themselves (and in particular the many strong young girls) are heard in public debate, and that the terms not always be set by the majority.

Quite a few stated that they do not know enough about Muslims or that they do not know any Muslims. One said simply, "I don't know enough about Muslims, and this makes me insecure." Another said, "A religion I know too little about. A religion that many let themselves be scared of, including me, because of too little knowledge. At the same time, I know that nearly all Muslims are peaceful people." Some expressed that they would like to get to know more Muslims: "A poorly used resource. Somebody I would like to know." One respondent offered a more detailed reflection:

> Unfortunately I do not know many who are Muslim. I think about their religion and culture, and think that I ought to know more. I think about all the religious conflicts that have come and gone—and that we in today's society should know better than to repeat them. Besides I am extra worried on behalf of Muslims and other ethnic groups who are not favorably viewed

by the new president in the US—xenophobia easily flourishes despite the few years that have passed since the second World War. This frightens me. Others' cultures and religions don't, and I hope that curiosity and a compassionate light can show the way forward.

Yet other respondents decided to write about Muslims they know or about encounters with Muslims. Said one respondent, "Probably a lot of people think something negative now, but I myself am particularly fond of one." Said another, "Togetherness. I have traveled the world a bit and have seen how Muslims greet each other even if they do not know their counterpart. We have something to learn from that, we who are afraid of approaching others when we travel."

Quite a few of the differentiating responses are lengthy and offer a mix of many of the themes highlighted above. One of them reads:

> A different culture. Or a different religion is I guess the correct way to put it, since most of the Muslims I know have the same culture as I do. But that depends I guess on definitions. I do not know many Muslims. I grew up in a place where most children were ethnic Norwegians. I also think about exciting countries, places I would like to go one day. I think about good food, beautiful mosques, but also unfortunately about war and the oppression of women, and a large lack of knowledge. I am myself unsure about where to come down on the hijab debate for example because of uncertainty. I think it is difficult to live as a young Muslim in Norway. Both when thinking about pressure from different Muslim groups, but also xenophobia and pressure from school and friends.

Another such rich reflection brings additional insight into how some non-Muslims differentiate:

> A person who is attached to a certain religious conviction. Islam. A large religion with many followers in the world. Africa and the Middle East. A religion that stirs a lot of debate and that I am sure is misunderstood by many. I think about ——, who has converted to Islam and who is married to a fantastic man from Algeria. And their daughter, ——, whom I am very fond of. These people are some of the most enlightened, intelligent people I know. Very compassionate and warm. Thanks to them I know many Muslims, and I always feel very well taken care of when I am together with the Muslims I know. When I think about Muslims, I think about warm human beings who think it is important to take care of each other, of friends, of family. About

people who are used to putting others ahead of themselves. I am saddened that these good people are now suffering from negative stigma, because of terrorists who abuse the word of Islam to fight for their own interests. I also think about my new friends from Syria whom I have been so lucky to get to know through work. They have served me delicious Syrian food, and you would have to search long for more helpful, friendly, and charming people. I also think about Sana from the NRK series *Skam*. She is a fantastic character who challenges prejudices saying that Muslim women are oppressed. When I think about the word Muslim, I think that it is a word that has been met with too much oppression and hatred, and that the word today carries a stigma that is based on misunderstandings and generalizations.

MAKING DISTINCTIONS

A striking difference between the Islamophobic responses and responses that differentiate is the effort respondents made to subgroup or subtype. In the Islamophobic responses, no real such attempts were made. For the anti-Islamic extreme right activists who demonize Muslims, the insistence that there is no difference between "ordinary" Muslims and Muslim fundamentalists or extremists is deliberate. It is a firm conviction on their part about what it means to be Muslim, integral to their view of Muslims as dangerous. They perceive all Muslims as potential extremists. Their view makes impossible the inclusion of Muslims as full members of their democracy because it says that Muslims cannot be trusted with ordinary democratic rights. The conclusion drawn from the point of view of these extreme right activists is, at best, that Muslims must leave the country.

In contemporary right-wing extremist accounts, Muslims prefer to be outside the democratic order but, more than anything, are existential threats to the national order. But the sense of crisis and conspiracy within this ideology extends further. Many also believe that those who work to accommodate Muslims within the democratic order are traitors. Such traitors, they believe, undermine the democratic order either because they are naive or because they deliberately seek to hand over the country to Muslims. Clearly then in contemporary extreme right ideology, the inclusion of Muslims is not a goal. In their view, responsible political leaders and citizens should not include Muslims within the framework of a pluralist democracy, but instead keep Muslims out.

This cursory description of the core anti-Islamic extreme right narrative corresponds to what the British historian Roger Griffin has termed "generic fascism."[15] It is a narrative where an internal and external enemy conspire to bring about a civilizational crisis (an "apocalypse") that legitimizes extraordinary action, such as violence or other forms of norm violation and transgression. As seen above, groups with such convictions exist today, and not only in obscure forums on the internet. These activists march in the streets of Europe and the US, and we have seen several incidents where individuals who subscribe to these views have been responsible for horrific terror attacks that have killed both Muslims and politicians who have called for the inclusion of Muslims.

But how common is this failure to differentiate between ordinary Muslims and Muslim fundamentalists at the heart of these contemporary extreme right conspiracy ideologies? The answers to the open-ended question provide one view. There we discovered a clear preponderance of differentiating responses. They were about twice as common as the Islamophobic ones. Yet the free-text answers are better at capturing the variety of associations and their tone than they are a safe methodology for concluding that differentiation is more common than demonization. Yet the question of where most non-Muslims come down on these questions is important, and it matters in the struggle for inclusion.

To examine it from a more grounded scientific angle, less susceptible to the perils of interpretation and human coding, we ran an experimental test. Survey experiments exploit the power of randomization to ensure that researchers are in full control of what causes differences in outcomes. They are therefore ideally suited to avoiding the potential pitfalls of analysis of open-ended answers coded by humans. In the test at hand, we adapted an experimental design previously used to study tolerance.[16] Thanks to our access to a trial version of the European Internet Panel Study (EIPS) fielded in the spring and summer of 2017 simultaneously in five countries—France, Germany, Norway, Sweden, and the Netherlands.[17] Exactly the same experiment was fielded in all countries. We chose a common situation where ordinary citizens make concrete everyday decisions about a fundamental democratic right. The case in point is the right to assembly, more specifically the right to rent a local community house for a meeting. This is a realistic situation in that neighbors and local organizations often do have discretionary power to decline requests. Yet by law they are not allowed to discriminate based on religion, ethnicity, or race.

The right to assembly is less clearly protected when it comes to transgressive groups. We know from previous studies that ordinary citizens do not readily extend democratic rights to such groups.[18] Transgressive Islamic groups can therefore be used in a differentiation test. Anti-Islamic activists and most contemporary right-wing extremists reject all Muslims just the same, because they believe all Muslims are fundamentalists or potential extremists. The question the survey experiment is designed to answer is whether ordinary people tend to behave in accordance with such a logic of demonization and reject access to the community house for Muslims altogether, or if they instead tend to act in accordance with a logic of differentiation, rejecting the Muslim group described as fundamentalist while accepting the group described only as "a Muslim congregation."

To answer this question, we conducted a between-subject experiment where respondents were randomly assigned to respond to a question about either "a Muslim congregation" or "a Muslim fundamentalist group." In a sample consisting mostly of demonizers, "Muslims" and "Muslim fundamentalists" should both be rejected at about equal levels. In a sample mostly made up of differentiators, "Muslims" should be accepted and "Muslim fundamentalists" should be rejected.

But how can we know if one group has been accepted and the other rejected? One standard often employed in survey experiment research is that of statistically significant difference. By this standard, if the two groups are treated differently outside of the ordinary margins of error, then differentiation is more common than demonization. That certainly has to be a minimal standard. But will we not need a quite large substantive difference in treatment in order to conclude that citizens differentiate? We could eyeball the percentage-point difference and perhaps compare it with other meaningful differences in public opinion research. By this standard, if the percentage-point difference is large, then the tendency to differentiate is strong. Conversely, if the percentage-point difference is small, then the tendency to demonize, to treat transgressive and ordinary Muslim groups the same, is strong. But there are some arbitrary decisions involved in turning response scales into a measure of percentage agreeing or disagreeing,[19] and on top of that there will always be a question as to what should count as a high percentage-point difference. To overcome these potential sources of bias or disagreement about the appropriate standards, we built benchmarks into the design of the experiment.

As a benchmark for acceptance, we included the in-group "a Christian congregation." This is the majority religious group in all countries included in the study. They have historically had, and in contemporary European societies continue to have, a privileged status. This then is our benchmark for the highest reasonable score for granting the right to assembly to "a Muslim congregation." We do not expect similarity, though. Previous research has shown that we are more likely to find that Muslims are discriminated against compared to Christians.[20] What we expect is therefore not that the

Muslim congregation will be treated equally to the Christian congregation (although that would have been an uplifting result). What we expect is that the Muslim congregation should be treated more similarly to the Christian congregation than to the transgressive group, Muslim fundamentalists.

As a benchmark on the side of rejection, we included a Neo-Nazi group. Citizens in Western Europe these days are highly likely to want to exclude Neo-Nazis from ordinary democratic rights, so this group is useful as a benchmark for a high score on exclusion.[21] To be clear, the expectation is not that citizens will treat the Muslim fundamentalist group the same as the Neo-Nazi group, only that they will treat the Muslim fundamentalist group more similarly to Neo-Nazis than to the Muslim congregation. Based on findings in previous research, we expect the difference in treatment of the Christian and Neo-Nazi groups to be very large. It can usefully serve as a benchmark for maximal differentiation. Attention should be directed toward how the difference in treatment of the Muslim and Muslim fundamentalist groups compares to this benchmark of maximum differentiation.

We fielded exactly the same survey experiment in five different European countries— France, Germany, the Netherlands, Norway, and Sweden—at exactly the same time through the European Internet Panel Study in the spring and summer of 2017. This provided a particularly strong design for judging whether patterns are broadly the same in the countries where the study was fielded. While all these countries are advanced Western European liberal democracies, they have chosen different paths when it comes to multicultural policies and regulation of religions. They also have differing degrees of home experience with religious and extreme right terrorism.

Despite these differences among the countries examined, the pattern of how different groups are treated in this question is strikingly similar. As revealed in the five country-by-country panels making up figure 2.4, the overwhelming tendency is to answer according to the logic of differentiation. In all countries, Muslims are treated very much like Christians, Muslim fundamentalists very much like Neo-Nazis. In all cases, a large majority would let the Muslim congregation rent the local community house. Only a small minority would let the Muslim fundamentalists do the same. The demonizing logic that lead far-right extremists to believe all Muslims are dangerous regardless of whether they belong to a transgressive group or not is in other words not a common response among ordinary citizens.

Making use of the benchmark groups, the panels in figure 2.4 further show that the Muslim congregation in all cases is treated more similarly to the Christian congregation than to the Muslim fundamentalists. However,

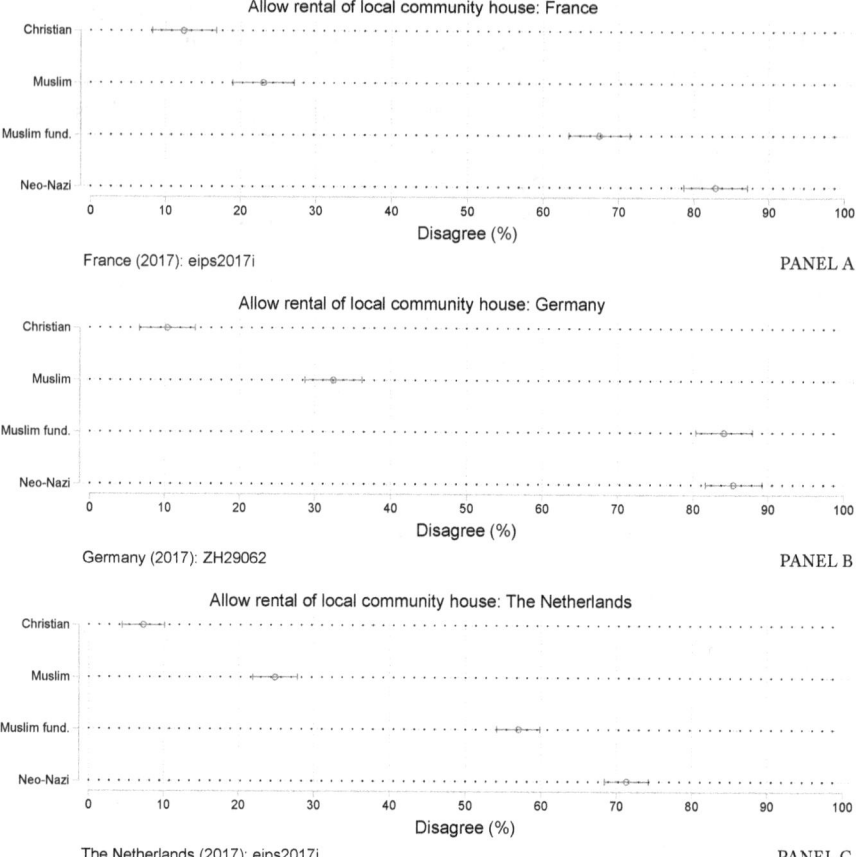

FIGURE 2.4. THE DIFFERENTIATION EXPERIMENT. Rent local community house to Christians/Muslims/Muslim Fundamentalists/Neo-Nazis. Panel A: France, % Disagree. Panel B: Germany, % Disagree. Panel C: Netherlands, % Disagree. Panel D: Norway, % Disagree. Panel E: Sweden, % Disagree.

in only one country—Sweden—do we observe no aggregate discrimination of Muslims compared to Christians at all.[22] The size of discrimination (i.e., the gap in treatment of Muslims compared to Christians) is a bit different in different countries, a finding consistent with previous research.[23] However, as the panels in figure 2.4 all make plain, these differences between countries are rather modest when we consider the big picture. The main tendency across these Western European countries is to make a crucial distinction between a "Muslim congregation," whose democratic right to assembly is supported, and a "Muslim fundamentalist group," which is rejected almost on a par with Neo-Nazis.

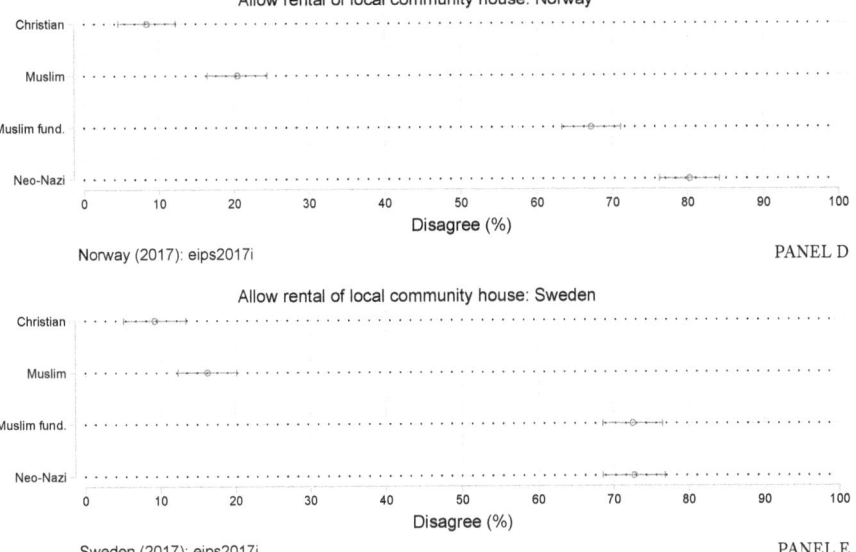

The pronounced tendency among members of the non-Muslim in-group majority to differentiate among Muslims suggests an opening toward the inclusion of Muslim minorities in contemporary liberal democracies in Europe. Even if anti-Islamic activists on the far right demonize Muslims and are increasingly active and visible, one of their central ideas, that all Muslims are transgressive or potentially transgressive, is not widely shared. In the open-ended responses we did observe that negative stereotypes about Muslims—Islamophobia—are fairly common, and we did find in the survey experiment discrimination of Muslims compared to Christians. Intolerance and prejudice remain urgent problems.

Nevertheless, the most pronounced tendency and pattern across the board is for non-Muslim members of the public to differentiate. Importantly, the differentiation test shows overwhelming evidence in multiple countries that most members of the majority public distinguish between Muslims who are part of transgressive groups and Muslims who are not. Most respondents think the latter should be granted democratic rights even if they think the former should not. This pattern means that a core part of the right-wing extremist narrative is widely rejected by the non-Muslim public.

This larger part of the public in contemporary Western Europe, those who differentiate and therefore potentially hold the door open to inclusion of Muslims, we now turn to investigate in greater depth. The intolerant are committed to exclusion. We believe the comparatively tolerant are the key to how far the opening toward the inclusion of Muslims extends. Our claim is that improved knowledge about the principles that matter to those who differentiate, not to those who demonize, will open up a better view of the political opportunities and challenges in the struggle for inclusion.

[CHAPTER THREE]
RESPECT

Becoming accepted as part of a country's identity, its national narrative, is a necessary condition for inclusion. But it is not sufficient. It is necessary also that the majority culture acknowledge that Muslims are worthy of respect as Muslims. To be inclusive, members of the non-Muslim majority must recognize that the culture and traditions of Muslims is integral to their identity as Muslims and therefore should be treated with respect.

Are citizens in contemporary liberal democracies where majorities are not themselves Muslim ready to do this? To focus on the intolerant has no payoff. Their minds are not open to inclusion. The focus must be on the tolerant, but not, or not primarily, because their attitudes toward inclusion are more likely to be positive, other things equal. The key is that other things are not equal inasmuch as the inclusionary options on offer are substantively different. The choices the tolerant make, whether in favor of or opposed to inclusion, hinge on the fit of inclusionary options with the broader set of values that citizens who are tolerant typically hold.

It is, at some level, perfectly obvious that whether non-Muslim majority citizens find inclusion acceptable depends on its fit with widely shared ideas of what is right and what is wrong. The challenge is to identify the pivotal ideas of what is right and what is wrong. In this chapter we concentrate on a distinction that so far has not received the attention it deserves—the distinction between recognition respect and appraisal respect.

RECOGNITION RESPECT VERSUS APPRAISAL RESPECT

Contemporary liberal democracies are committed to value pluralism, in some form and to some extent. Yet, mass societies, even if their ideals are liberal, put powerful pressures on minorities to conform to the values of the larger society, come what may. As Mill strikingly observed, "the tyranny of the majority is more formidable than many kinds of political oppression [and] leaves fewer means of escape, penetrating much more deeply into the details of life, and enslaving the soul itself."[1]

One wall of protection against pressures to conform to the majority's values and practices is a majority's readiness to explicitly acknowledge the worth of diversity and, better still, to specifically affirm the worth of the culture of minorities. Respect makes possible inclusion without assimilation. But what does respect for Muslims require of members of the majority group, who are not themselves Muslim?

Suppose that you are a person who cares about equality for women; you take exception to conservative religious limits on what Muslim women may legitimately do; you do not see counterbalancing considerations. Then you are told that, because yours are liberal democratic values, you should evaluate Muslim culture and traditions positively, even esteem them as one culture among many, each admirable in its own way. You would, we expect, disagree. You are more than likely to be perfectly prepared to agree that the larger society has a responsibility to treat Muslim culture with respect. But you do not accept that you have an obligation to admire it or, even, learn much about it.

But another person, whose values also are democratic, may respond that a dominant culture is under an obligation to do much more. There is a pluralism of values, of outlooks on life. Appreciation of their differences enriches the life of a society and the individuals who make it up. Indeed, insofar as diversity is a value in contemporary liberal democracies, the majority culture has a duty to help minorities sustain their culture and traditions and shield them from outside influence.

Our concern is not to establish which position is morally superior or normatively preferable. It is, rather, to spotlight a distinction between two conceptions of respect, both consistent with liberal democratic values, which require different stances toward the culture and traditions of Muslims. These two conceptions are *appraisal respect* and *recognition respect*. Appraisal respect is owed to "persons or features which are held to manifest their excellence as persons or as engaged in some specific pursuit."[2] Recognition respect is owed because people "are entitled to have other persons take seriously and weight appropriately the fact that they are persons in deliberating about what to do."[3]

It is natural to think of the two types of respect as differing in degree, not kind, as though appraisal respect is a more affirmative form of respect than recognition respect. But the difference between the two types of respect is not a matter of more versus less. The difference is substantive. Appraisal respect calls for a judgment that Muslim culture, taken all in all, represents an achievement of belief and faith that deserves to be held in high regard. A person who believes this may herself value most an outlook on life that is secular, not religious, that is open to change and values diversity rather than prizing tradition and a uniformity of view. But for a person who values diversity, that is just the point. Minority cultures ought to be evaluated on their own terms, as one among many ways of living lives of significance and meaning. To come to this judgment does not require commitment to an extreme relativism. On the contrary, it only calls for an appreciation of the benefits of a pluralism of values and outlooks on life. With this appreciation comes an acceptance of the responsibility of the majority society to help minorities sustain the culture that is the grounds of their identity.

Recognition respect also carries obligations but of a different kind. For Muslims, their outlook on life represents a blending of belief and faith and history that gives meaning and weight to their lives. To fail to appreciate this is to deny them the dignity that a society pledged to liberal democratic ideals has an obligation to honor. There are features of traditional Muslim culture—hierarchy, patriarchy, religiosity—that are at odds with the ethos of a liberal democracy; they are not incidental. Recognition respect does not require those who are not themselves Muslim and may be committed to secular values to have an obligation to praise, admire, or actively help sustain Muslims' culture. They do have a responsibility to recognize the dignity of Muslims and take seriously contributions of their culture and history.

Both recognition and appraisal respect are democratic ideals. Neither demonizes Muslims, neither is exclusionary. But they are not the same. They are different ideas about what one does or does not owe others. Believe that the larger society should actively support the values that Muslims espouse as Muslims, then you must reject the idea that it is sufficient for the larger society to acknowledge that they and their culture have worth. Believe that the values of Muslims deserve to be respected because people "are entitled to have other persons take seriously and weight appropriately the fact that they are persons in deliberating about what to do,"[4] then without self-contradiction, you may reject the claim that the larger society has an obligation to support Muslim communities' culture and outlook on life.

AN ITERATIVE APPROACH

Once the distinction between the two types of respect is put on the table, it is easy to see that one demands more of the majority than the other. But that is not in itself evidence that the distinction is pivotal. Many normative distinctions matter only in books and not to real people in their daily lives. For a distinction between normative principles to be pivotal, it is necessary that large shares of the general public subscribe to the one but not the other—here and now, that a fair share of them are ready to endorse recognition respect but not appraisal respect.

Determining whether this is so, we have learned, is not straightforward. Public opinion surveys have many strengths, but precision is not one of them. But approximations, if recognized as approximations, can point to explanations. The hypothesis that the distinction between appraisal and recognition respect is pivotal was suggested by a point of disagreement between two schools of thought on multiculturalism. In liberal theories of multiculturalism, the state has a duty to acknowledge the worth of minority cultures; in postliberal theories, it has a duty to go further and help sustain them.[5] This point of disagreement between liberal and postliberal theories of multiculturalism prompted our design of an initial trial of experiments. Only subsequently did we make a connection between the initial results and different conceptions of respect.[6] Getting a fix on the distinction between recognition respect and appraisal respect has taken two sequences of survey experiments, administered over a period of six years (2013–2019) as eight individual trials, conducted in three different countries (Norway, the US, and the UK).

A repeatable template is the key to sequential factorial designs. A repeatable template consists of two parts. The first part is the wording of a body of a question which remains exactly the same, from one experimental trial to another, through the whole of a sequence. The second part is a textbox whose content is randomly varied. In our approach, the variation is minimal—sometimes a verb, sometimes a noun, at the most a brief phrase. It is not logically necessary that variation in the textbox is minimal. But if reactions to the variations of only a word or brief phrase differ significantly, it is clear that we have touched a nerve. The textboxes below tables 3.1 and 3.2 show the two templates used in the respect sequences. The first template asks about affirmation of diversity generally. The second template addresses affirmation of Muslim culture and tradition specifically.

We used the affirmation of diversity template in three separate trials in three different countries. We will present the logic of the experimental sequence, why certain fills were included at a particular stage in the sequence, when we lay out the results. This is a departure from the conventional way to present experimental research, where typically theory and experimental design are presented before the results. In what follows, to bring into view the iterative process of our studies, we instead trace the sequence of experimental design choices and results.

TABLE 3.1. THE FIRST RESPECT SEQUENCE

Trial # (Country)	1 (Norway)	2 (United States)	3 (Great Britain)
Respect principle fill 1	Acknowledge	Acknowledge	Acknowledge
Respect principle fill 2		Respect	Respect
Respect principle fill 3			Publicly Recognize
Respect principle fill 4	Celebrate	Celebrate	Celebrate

Repeatable template: How much do you agree or disagree with the following statement?: It is important to [RESPECT PRINCIPLE FILL] the new diversity of [COUNTRY].

Example: How much do you agree or disagree with the following statement? It is important to acknowledge the new diversity of Great Britain.

TABLE 3.2. THE SECOND RESPECT SEQUENCE

Trial # (Country)	1 (Norway)	2 (United States)	3 (Great Britain)	4 (Norway)	5 (Great Britain)
Target group fill	Muslim/ Immigrant	Muslim	Muslim	Muslim	
Respect principle fill 1	Respected	Respected	Respected	Respected	Respected
Respect principle fill 2	Protected	Protected	Protected		
Respect principle fill 3				Supported	Supported
Respect principle fill 4					Helped to keep going

Repeatable template: How much do you agree or disagree with the following statement? [TARGET GROUP FILL] culture and traditions should be [RESPECT PRINCIPLE FILL]

Example: How much do you agree or disagree with the following statement? Muslim culture and traditions should be protected.

Most often we determined the design of a subsequent trial only after having seen the results of a prior trial. We did not know, at the outset, what variation or counter-variation of our initial ideas that the final experiment in the sequence would test. Presenting theoretical reasoning and experimental designs true to the way that we groped our way forward, instead of a showcase presentation of hypotheses first and results afterward as though we knew the answers at the start, has an additional benefit thanks to a repeatable template. For at each step, we could conduct tests of replication and generalizability. The claims we make about pivotal distinctions between inclusionary options do not hinge on the results of a single trial. They came into view, in increasingly sharp focus, as we updated and refined our hypotheses through extended sequences of experimental trials.

THE FIRST RESPECT SEQUENCE

The intuition that launched our study is that the willingness of majority group citizens to be inclusive hinges on what being inclusive asks of them. The null hypothesis that needs to be rejected, then, is that distinctions between inclusionary principles are irrelevant. Is the null hypothesis plausible? We would argue, yes. To take one point at issue, much research on prejudice and politics has been mired in discussions about the problem of social desirability bias in public opinion research. Whenever a piece of evidence has been presented to suggest that public commitment to liberal democratic values has become deeper and more widespread, the reflexive countercharge has often been that what is observed is only social desirability bias: survey respondents tell interviewers, not what they believe, but what they believe interviewers think they ought to believe.

Social desirability effects of course exist, but there is no empirical evidence to show that they are of sufficient magnitude to impeach the validity of systematic studies of prejudice and public opinion. As for the problem before us, a social desirability framework would lead us to predict that members of the majority group do not make distinctions between inclusionary options. Respondents, according to a social desirability framework, are not expressing their true beliefs. What they are voicing is what they believe they should say to an interviewer in order to present themselves in a socially desirable light. The social desirability framework provides a rationale for the null hypothesis that majority group members will not distinguish between inclusionary options. It only requires that they say the politically correct thing.

As table 3.1 shows, the first trial put the null hypothesis to a fair but tough test, where the contrast between two different modes of affirming diversity is maximized. In one condition, respondents are asked if they think it is important to "acknowledge" the new diversity of their country (fill 1). In the other they are asked if they think it is important to "celebrate" it (fill 4). Everything is identical, then, but for the variation of one word. Around the same time, we fielded a similar trial in the US (trial 2 in sequence 1). There, the same template was used, the same terms were repeated ("to acknowledge" and "to celebrate"), but a third treatment term—"to respect"—was added. The reason: to probe the ambiguity of what it means to believe that "it is important to acknowledge" the diversity of one's country. One possibility: it means no more than that one should accept and come to terms with diversity as fact. Another, more positive, possibility: one ought to treat diversity as something deserving respect, in the sense of recognition respect. A third possibility: the different minority cultures that are now part of the national mix are worthy of respect, in the sense of appraisal respect.

One test of which of the three possibilities is closer to the mark is the interchangeability of the responses: the more dissimilar the responses to "acknowledge" and to "respect," the more plausible is a hypothesis that to acknowledge diversity means no more than to accept it as fact. Alternatively, the more similar the responses to the importance of acknowledging and respecting diversity, the more plausible is a hypothesis that majority citizens believe that diversity merits recognition respect. Finally, the more similar responses to "respect" and to "celebrate" diversity, the more plausible is a hypothesis that majority citizens believe diversity merits not merely recognition but appraisal respect.

The results of the first two trials in the initial Respect sequence struck us because the size of the difference that respecting and celebrating diversity makes in the Norwegian setting is remarkable. Panel A in figure 3.1 brings home that, when members of the majority group were asked to *acknowledge* the new diversity, acceptance was as high as 75 percent; but when they were asked to *celebrate* the very same thing, acceptance was as low as 41 percent.[7]

Panel B in figure 3.1 presents the results from the second trial, which was conducted in the US, zeroing in on white Americans since the issue is the

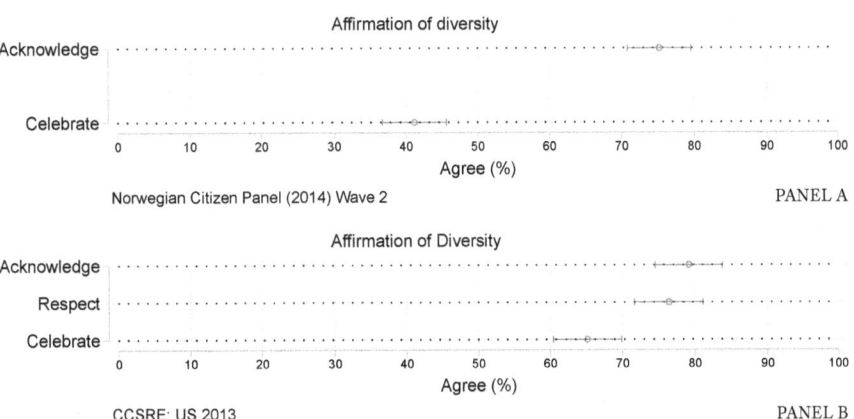

FIGURE 3.1. AFFIRMATION OF DIVERSITY. Panel A: Norway. The new diversity of Norway should be acknowledged/celebrated. % Agree. Panel B: United States (Whites only). The new diversity in the US should be acknowledged/respected/celebrated. % Agree.

willingness of the majority culture to recognize the worth of diversity. Also in this case the results show a substantial difference between "celebrating" and "acknowledging" diversity. Citizens distinguish between inclusionary options. The null hypothesis is rejected in both trials. That said, there is a noticeable difference between the results of the first and second trials. The effect size is statistically significant, but much smaller in the US trial (percentage-point difference: −13) than in the Norway trial (percentage-point difference: −34).

This difference is a warning. It may signal an issue of replicability. If you do the same experiment a second time and do not see similar results,[8] that is evidence of a lack of robustness in the results. From the two trials we know that the distinction between celebrating and acknowledging diversity matters, but how much it matters is a different question. Generalizability may be the problem. Attitudes may be different in the United States than in Norway. More worrisome, the terms "celebrate" or "new diversity" may not have the same connotations in the United States as in Norway. We needed another trial to find out.

The second result that struck us is the similarity of the responses to "respecting" and "acknowledging" the importance of diversity. Panel B in figure 3.1 shows that the responses to "respect" and "acknowledge" are statistically indistinguishable. There is an overwhelming and equal willingness to acknowledge (79 percent) and to express respect for (76 percent) the importance of diversity. Openness to the idea of respecting diversity does not, however, entail support for the idea of celebrating it. There is considerably more widespread approval of the idea of acknowledging and respecting than of celebrating the importance of diversity.

We began to see a pattern, but questions remain and new ones, if one takes more than a moment to think, suggest themselves. Hence a third trial. The first objective of this trial was to test the replicability of the two main results of the first and second trials. The same fills in the same template were repeated. The second objective was to push research forward—to learn something new about the normative distinctions that matter to ordinary citizens. For this reason, we added a new treatment term.

THE THIRD TRIAL: INDIVIDUAL VERSUS SOCIETAL RECOGNITION

Suppose you are asked, Do you agree or disagree that the importance of ethnic and religious diversity should be respected? You answer yes. In answering yes, you might mean that those who make up the majority society should acknowledge that diversity has inherent worth. A widely held belief that people should be willing to do so would be a significant milestone on the way to a more inclusive society. But the respect of an individual as an individual is personal; private. For a society to be inclusive, the willingness to express respect for diversity must be public. What sense would it make to say that a person has respect for diversity were she to think that the larger society should not acknowledge its worth?[9]

Results to this point are consistent with a hypothesis that there is broad-based acceptance of the recognition respect principle. However, they do not speak to whether this extends to a belief that the larger society should acknowledge the worth of diversity. To find out if they do, a third term was added to the fill—should the importance of diversity be *publicly* recognized? The third trial was conducted in Great Britain.

Figure 3.2 displays the results. The idea at this point in the sequence was to ratchet up standards for qualifying as recognition respect, beginning with *it is important to acknowledge*, and then *to respect*, and finally, *to publicly recognize* the new diversity of Great Britain. Figure 3.2 shows that these three terms are interchangeable for ordinary citizens. Similarly decisive majorities are open to *publicly recognize* (70 percent), *respect* (69 percent), and *acknowledge* (71 percent) the new diversity of Great Britain. This result is consistent with the hypothesis of a widespread belief that different outlooks on life are entitled to be treated with respect.

Critical scrutiny of these results counsels caution, though. In this third trial, just as in the first two, agreement that diversity should be "celebrated" is significantly lower. The null hypothesis—that the inclusionary options make no difference to citizens in surveys—can be rejected. However, in Great Britain as in the US, openness to celebrate diversity is not all that much lower. On the order of six in ten respond that they agree that the new diversity should be celebrated.

On seeing this result, and after presenting it to colleagues, we realized that this template had several weaknesses. In the American or British context, it is not clear that "the new diversity" is uniformly understood

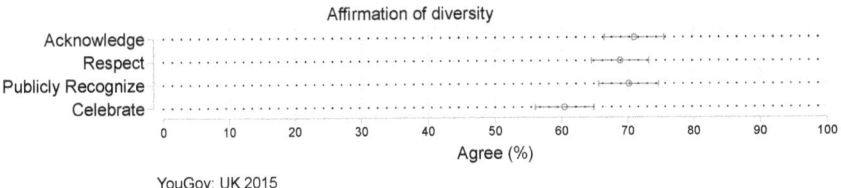

FIGURE 3.2. PUBLIC AFFIRMATION OF DIVERSITY. The new diversity in Great Britain should be acknowledged/respected/publicly recognized/celebrated. Great Britain, % Agree.

as a reference to religious and cultural diversity. It could just as well be understood with reference to the diversity of gender identities and sexual orientations.[10] Perhaps what we see is not an openness to respecting and acknowledging cultural and religious diversity, but to other forms of diversity. In the Norwegian context, furthermore, the expression "celebrate diversity" sounds foreign, like something imported from the Anglo-American cultural sphere. Perhaps what we observed in the first trial, then, was not respondents making distinctions between inclusionary principles but, rather, simply having a negative reaction to a foreign-sounding expression.[11] A more discriminating research design was called for, these criticisms suggested, to determine if the distinction between the two respect principles is pivotal.

REFINING THE DISTINCTION BETWEEN RECOGNITION AND APPRAISAL RESPECT

What must native citizens be willing to endorse or do to satisfy a norm of recognition respect? A guide is the asymmetry in the relation between a duty of (recognition) respect and a duty of care.[12] Acceptance of the latter entails acceptance of the former. But acceptance of the former does not entail acceptance of the latter. The reasoning is straightforward. A duty of care calls for a "benevolent concern," in Darwall's felicitous phrase, a readiness to support policies to see that the disadvantaged have access to better education, housing, employment opportunities—in short, a readiness to back the social welfare policies typically advocated by the left. Such a commitment to improving the welfare of Muslim minorities encourages a duty to respect their dignity as Muslims. But the obverse does not follow. It is not logically self-contradictory to be committed to acknowledging the inherent worth of the culture and traditions of a minority and rejecting a claim that government or the larger society has a duty to help a minority sustain its culture and traditions. A duty of care thus follows from appraisal respect, not recognition respect. This elaboration of the distinction between recognition and appraisal respect informed the design of the second sequence of respect experiments.

THE SECOND RESPECT SEQUENCE

The template we used for the second sequence, summarized in table 3.2, addresses the issue of respect for Muslim culture and tradition head-on. The template zooms in on approval of Muslim minorities' right to have their culture and traditions affirmed. In the first trial, as seen in table 3.2, two parts of the template varied. The minority group whose culture and traditions were supposed to be affirmed is described half the time as "Muslim" and half the time as "immigrant." This we did to test the hypothesis that it makes a difference to ordinary citizens whether the minority group is described as a religious rather than an immigrant minority.

We also, in the first trial, varied the mode of affirmation. In one condition, we asked whether minorities have the right to have their traditions and culture "respected." In another we asked about the right to have their traditions and culture "protected." Our hypothesis, based on findings in the first sequence, was that "respect" would evoke recognition respect and be broadly supported. Our additional hunch was that "protect," because it implies a duty of care, would indicate appraisal respect. If the distinction between recognition and appraisal respect is pivotal, far fewer majority group citizens will approve of the idea of protecting Muslim culture and tradition.

The results of the first trial in the second Respect sequence are remarkable. The distinction between the two terms of inclusion, "respect" versus "protect," makes the difference between widespread approval by a decisive majority of the sample (some 65%) and approval by much less than half the sample (around 35%). This is just the sort of pattern that one should expect from a pivotal normative distinction.

Contrast this sharp difference with the other striking feature of the results on display in figure 3.3. It makes next to no difference to majority group citizens whether the group is described as immigrant or Muslim. Even if there are many immigrants who are not Muslims and vice versa, this piece of empirical evidence suggests to us that, at this point in the progression of history in Norway, the two are interchangeable in the minds of the average citizen. This is important in and of itself, but for the purpose of our sequence of study, the results of the first trial suggested to us that the

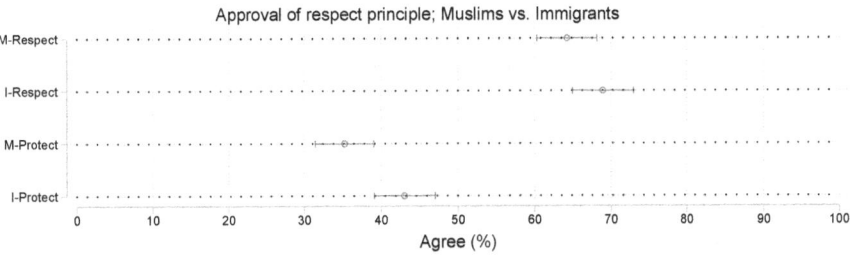

Norwegian Citizen Panel (2013) Wave 1

FIGURE 3.3. RESPECT FOR MUSLIM CULTURE: FIRST TRIAL. Muslim/Immigrant culture should be respected/protected. Norway, % Agree.

all-important next step to take was to establish if the remarkable difference in approval of "respecting" and "protecting" Muslim culture and traditions would replicate.

To test this, we fielded exactly the same template with exactly the same fills (translated, of course, into English) in the same two countries as previously studied, Great Britain and the United States.[13] Panels A and B in figure 3.4 show the results. In both trials, definite majorities agreed that Muslims have a right to have their traditions and culture *respected*—in Great Britain, 70 percent; in the United States, 77 percent. In both countries, significantly fewer agree that they have a right to have their culture *protected*; effect sizes negative and statistically significant in both cases: −15 percentage points and −12 percentage points, respectively. The belief that Muslims have a right to have their traditions and culture respected has the support of a decisive majority. The belief that they have a right to have them protected has the support of a bare majority.

The results are thus consistent with the hypothesis that majority citizens distinguish between recognition and appraisal respect, albeit on a very narrow interpretation of the hypothesis, namely, that a smaller number—though not a small number—of majority citizens agree that the culture of Muslim minorities should be "protected" than agree that it should be "respected."

For this line of reasoning, that the distinction between appraisal and recognition respect is pivotal, to be persuasive, we would have expected a larger difference in public approval in the US and Great Britain, one more

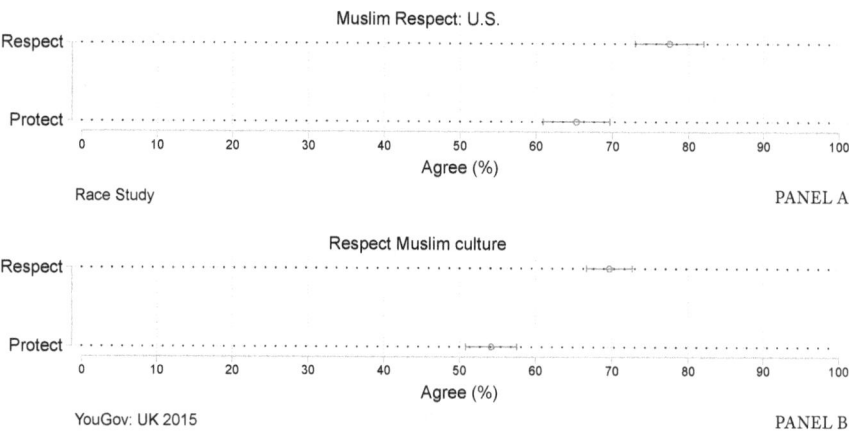

FIGURE 3.4. RESPECT FOR MUSLIM CULTURE: FOLLOW-UP TRIALS. Muslim/Immigrant culture should be respected/protected. Panel A: United States (Whites only), % Agree. Panel B: Great Britain, % Agree.

nearly like the one we saw in the first trial in Norway. This may be evidence that majority citizens do not consistently draw as sharp a distinction between recognition and appraisal respect as we had hypothesized. Alternatively, it may reflect the inadequacy of our indicator of appraisal respect. We had intended a wide interpretation of the word "protect." What we wanted was an indicator of an affirmative commitment to insulating Muslim culture and tradition against forces at work in liberal, secular societies. In retrospect, a narrower interpretation—to protect against persons or groups bent on doing a minority harm—is not implausible.

THE FINAL TRIALS IN THE RESPECT SEQUENCES

Is the problem that the hypothesis is wrong or that the measure is imperfect? Throughout, our experiments were designed with a light touch, aiming to catch reactions to different nuances of meaning. To see a distinction between recognition and appraisal respect, it is, we thought, necessary to emphasize the duty of care less ambiguously. So in the final two trials conducted in Norway and Great Britain, we kept the word "respect," but for "protect," substituted words that more clearly spelled out the duty of care: "support" (in trials 4 and 5) and "help to keep going" (in trial 5). The two trials were conducted at approximately the same time, so we did not know the result of the one before fielding the other.

The challenge in both experiments was to specify terms on which the larger society is, at least implicitly, taking on a measure of responsibility to support Muslims' traditions and outlook on life. There is something presumptuous, we want to acknowledge, about attempting calibration this fine in a public opinion survey. We proceed on the understanding that no one result is dispositive, but a pattern of results can be persuasive.

The first panel of figure 3.5 displays the results of the fourth trial. The top line shows the percentage agreeing that Muslims have a right to have their culture respected. In this trial, 74 percent agreed, on par with the results from the previous three trials in Norway. The question, of course, is whether or not reactions to Muslims having a claim to appraisal respect versus recognition respect significantly differ. So they do, most strikingly regarding whether Muslims have a right to have their culture and traditions supported, with only about half of respondents agreeing with the statement. The difference of about 25 percentage points is both statistically and substantially significant. Again, the results are consistent with a claim that majority citizens accept that the larger society has an obligation to respect the worth of Muslims' traditions and outlook on life, but that there is far less widespread acceptance that it has a duty to admire or support them.

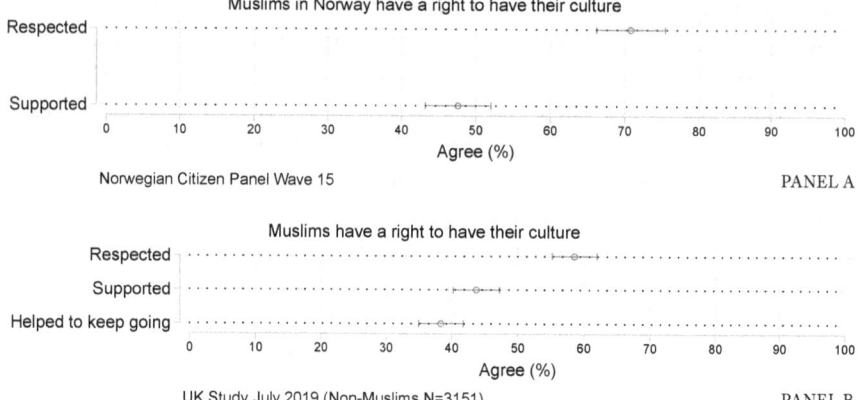

FIGURE 3.5. RECOGNITION RESPECT VS. APPRAISAL RESPECT. Panel A: Norway. Muslim culture should be respected/supported. % Agree. Panel B: Great Britain. Muslim culture should be respected/supported/helped to keep going. % Agree.

Panel B shows our final effort to assess, this time in Great Britain, whether reactions to claims for appraisal respect and recognition respect differ significantly. Again, as a reference point, the "respect" condition was repeated; to enhance comparison with previous trials and to serve as a baseline for comparison within the trial; so, too, was the "support" condition. To assess equivalence, and finally, to introduce a new indicator of appraisal respect, respondents were asked whether they agree or disagree that Muslims have a right "to have help to keep their culture and traditions going."

This time the main pattern of results in the British trial, especially the contrast between the "respect" and the "help to keep going" conditions, matches that seen in the previous trials conducted in Norway. Panel B in figure 3.5 shows that the proposition that Muslims have a right to have their culture and traditions respected was again met with widespread approval (this time at some 60%). If what is being asked is to provide the same culture and traditions with "help to keep going," the drop-off is substantial, on the order of 20 percentage points. The distinction between recognition and appraisal respect turns the majority from being open to inclusion to drawing a line at it. The principle of recognition respect is a widely shared norm. The principle of appraisal respect, when it is clearly evoked, is not.

THE TOLERANT

What we have shown so far is an important part of the evidence needed to demonstrate that the distinction between the appraisal and recognition respect principles is politically pivotal. But additional key pieces of evidence are needed, among them (a) whether the normative considerations make the difference between broad and narrow coalitions of voters being in favor of or against inclusion and (b) whether they make a difference to those who believe in inclusive tolerance. We address the first point in the chapter on political consequences (chapter 8). We address the second point here.

We are calling for a focus on the tolerant when considering which inclusionary options are pivotal and why. The tolerant are the main constituency for inclusionary proposals—they are Muslim minorities' best allies in the struggle for inclusion. Seeing how they negotiate between different normative considerations will give a deeper insight into the politically dispositive conditions on inclusion than seeing how those who favor exclusion do so. A measure of tolerance, accordingly, is needed. Specifically, what we need to measure is not political tolerance, that is, the willingness to put up with ideas or groups that you strongly dislike or disapprove of. Instead, what we need to measure is a readiness to treat out-groups with an open mind, affirmatively, "tolerance plus" if you will, or as we call it, *inclusive tolerance*.

As a measure of inclusive tolerance, we have chosen Internal Motivation to Control Prejudice (IMCP). Developed by social psychologists for the study of prejudice in an American context,[14] political scientists have adapted it and introduced it to the analysis of political behavior and attitudes in contemporary Europe.[15]

Conservative assumptions recommend the IMCP.[16] It recognizes that prejudice against minorities is not an either-or proposition.[17] One reason that some people are sincerely motivated not to be prejudiced against an out-group is because they are aware that they themselves may harbor a bias against it. The bias may be weak, even outside their conscious awareness, but they recognize how difficult it is to be sure that one is entirely free of prejudice. The crucial issue is to what extent do people want to treat a minority as they should, without prejudice, even though they appreciate that they themselves may not be entirely free of prejudice. This is what the IMCP index is designed to measure. So we used it as our indicator of a belief in inclusive tolerance.[18]

Note that we are not making the case that other measures of inclusive tolerance will not show the same thing or will not in some cases be superior. We are making the case that this measure is good enough for our purposes of distinguishing between those broadly committed to a norm of inclusive tolerance and those less so. We are not contending that the results presented here hinge on this specific measure. To the contrary, the results throughout this book should be replicable using any similar measure.

The IMCP measure was included in some, but not all, of the trials presented in this chapter. To strengthen the evidence that the distinction we have introduced is pivotal, then, we need to show that the lower levels of approval of the terms evoking the appraisal respect principle was not driven only by those committed to exclusion. For the normative considerations to be pivotal, as we laid it out in our framework for the study of the politics of inclusion, the normative distinctions should matter also to those who are open to inclusion.

The two panels of figure 3.6 show that this is precisely the pattern we observe when we map out approval of the two respect principles by a belief in inclusive tolerance. In the case of the acknowledge/celebrate distinction (trial 1, sequence 1) seen in panel A of figure 3.6, we see that approval of both principles increases as commitment to inclusive tolerance increases. However, approval of acknowledging the new diversity is very high and indeed complete at the highest levels of commitment to inclusive tolerance. By contrast, approval of the appraisal respect principle is considerably lower and does not cross the 50 percent line until IMCP scores reach very high levels (0.75 on the 0–1 scale). As the distribution of the IMCP shows, this means that there is a considerable share of the public who score quite high on the tolerance measure who do not approve of celebrating diversity.

A second example of the appraisal and recognition respect principles making a substantial difference also among the tolerant can be seen in panel B of figure 3.6. Here approval of the respect versus protect distinction is displayed across different levels of commitment to inclusive tolerance. Again, the pattern among those who score above the midpoint on IMCP is striking. More than half of them consistently approve of the idea of respecting Muslim culture and tradition, while substantially fewer at all levels of support for inclusive tolerance approve of the idea of protecting the very same thing.

ENVOI

The premise of our study is the need to extend the scope of inquiry beyond what majority citizens believe that government ought or ought not to do on behalf of Muslim minorities, vital as this is. How they are treated in their daily lives, in the places they work, in the stores they shop at, on the buses they ride and the streets they walk down—above all, how far they can have a working presumption that they will not be treated with disrespect—goes to the core of the quality of the lives they will lead.

The distinction between recognition respect and appraisal respect opens a new window, we believe, on how to think about terms on which majority citizens are open to inclusion of Muslim minorities. Distinctions

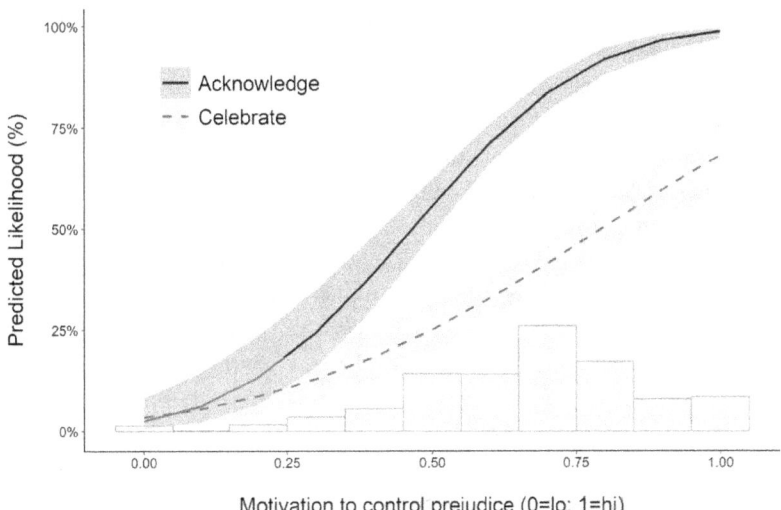

PANEL A

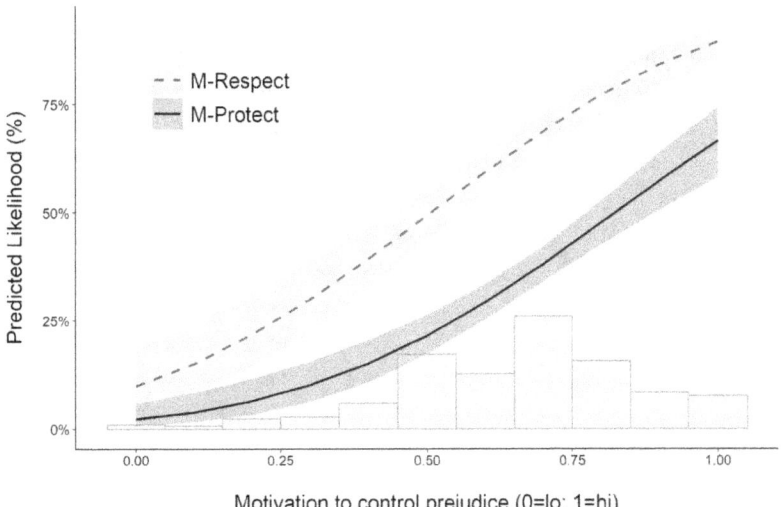

PANEL B

FIGURE 3.6. RESPECT PRINCIPLES BY INCLUSIVE TOLERANCE. Panel A: Affirmation of Diversity. The new diversity of Norway should be acknowledged/celebrated. Norway, Predicted likelihood of approval (%) by IMCP. Panel B: Recognition Respect vs. Appraisal Respect. Muslim culture and tradition should be respected/protected. Norway, Predicted likelihood of approval (%) by IMCP.

are sharper in normative analyses than in real life, to be sure. But the pattern of our results is clear. The largest share of majority citizens accept that the larger society has a responsibility to acknowledge the worth of Muslims as Muslims; they do not accept that it has an obligation to actively support or show admiration for their culture and traditions.

So much is clear, but much remains unclear. Our results show that the "largest share" of majority citizens agree that Muslims as Muslims are entitled to recognition respect. But when we say that a norm of respect is taking hold, it cannot be a matter simply of numbers, as though all that is required is a majority, even a clear majority. A belief that Muslims are entitled to acknowledgment of their inherent worth as Muslims must be broadly held throughout the larger society, not concentrated in a few parts of it. A necessary piece of evidence to sustain this claim, it follows, is an analysis of political patterns. Is it the case that the principle of recognition respect is approved by a wide political base, while the principle of appraisal respect assembles a politically narrow coalition? We will turn to this question in due course.

What should be emphasized here and now is the new light that the distinction between recognition respect and appraisal respect throws on one of our principal themes, namely, the importance of bringing to the surface the specific normative considerations underpinning inclusionary proposals. The distinction between recognition and appraisal respect is one normative consideration that can be pivotal. But it is far from the only one.

[CHAPTER FOUR]

SPEECH AS A MIRROR OF DIGNITY

It is natural to see the challenges Muslim immigrants face in Western Europe as akin to those that other immigrants have faced in other countries; natural because many of the challenges are the same. It is accordingly all the more important to see that Muslim minorities, particularly if they have come recently from countries whose cultures are traditional, patriarchal, religious, face challenges in contemporary liberal democracies that other minorities do not.

Consider the concept of Islamophobia. There is disagreement on how critical must criticism of Muslims or Islam be to count as prejudice.[1] But there is agreement on the heart of the matter. Prejudice, whether toward Muslims or Jews or Blacks, is a systematic, enduring tendency to dislike and disparage members of a group by virtue of their membership in the group. Islamophobia, as we set out in chapter 2, is "indiscriminate negative attitudes or emotions directed at Islam or Muslims."[2]

Muslims do confront prejudice as other minorities have and still do. What sets Muslims apart here and now is that they can, depending on circumstance, be caught up in conflicts with the liberal ideals as well as the illiberal strains in contemporary democracies. We shall show that acceptance of offensive speech about Muslims is a byproduct of tolerance as well as a product of intolerance. Hence the need to investigate sometimes competing, sometimes overlapping normative considerations that weigh on the tolerant on questions of speech.

CONFLICTS ABOUT SPEECH

In many European countries, political mobilization of Muslim minorities *as Muslims* took off following the publication of Salman Rushdie's *Satanic*

Verses (1988).³ This was dramatically the case in Norway, the focus of the Speech sequence of survey experiments that forms the empirical backbone of this chapter. Opposition to the publication of a Norwegian translation was the impetus for the first common committee of Norwegian mosques organized in 1989 under the heading of the Islamic Defense Council.⁴ As elsewhere in Europe, Muslims in Norway read Rushdie's book as a gross provocation: blasphemous and deliberately insulting to devout Muslims. In response, Ayatollah Khomeini, the Muslim leader of Iran, published a fatwa declaring it the duty of Muslims worldwide to kill Rushdie and anybody who aided in the publication of the book.

Muslim minorities mobilized against the book in Norway. In February 1989, the Islamic Defense Council organized a major demonstration in Oslo. Several thousand members of the Muslim minority population took part.⁵ The Islamic Defense Council never officially endorsed the fatwa, but neither did they explicitly denounce it. They did state that every Muslim in Norway should follow Norwegian law. They themselves pursued a legal course of action in suing the Norwegian publisher of the book, Aschehoug, on charges of blasphemy. The suit was unsuccessful.⁶

Several years later, in October 1993, the Norwegian publisher of *Satanic Verses*, William Nygaard, was the target of an assassination attempt, shot three times in the back outside his house. The assassin was not caught, but the incident was widely viewed in Norway as likely related to the fatwa. For his part, Nygaard went on to become a prominent advocate for speech rights and for the publication of Rushdie's novel. Odd Isungset, a respected journalist who worked for the main public television channel in Norway, NRK, and who produced several documentaries and a book about the attempted assassination, stated in his 2010 book, "For the first time since the second world war a Norwegian has been shot because he defends freedom of speech."⁷

In contemporary liberal democracies, speech that mocks, speech that insults, even speech that humiliates, is speech that enjoys protection under the canopy of freedom of speech. The widest scope, consistent with a narrow interpretation of the rights of others, for speech on issues of public concern has been a maxim. Yet, Muslim minorities are especially vulnerable to abusive speech by virtue of their faith. An obligation to defend the integrity of the prophet Mohammed and his teachings and commands goes to the root of their integrity as Muslims, for they are committed in faith to the belief that "the honor and good name of Muslims depends on upholding the honor of the Prophet."⁸ Their faith is their honor; their honor their faith. To belittle, to ridicule, to express contempt for their faith is to belittle, to ridicule, to express contempt for them.

Not that Muslims are peculiar in this respect, we would emphasize. To take one example of many: reactions to Andres Serrano's entry in an arts competition, a strikingly colored photograph of a crucifix immersed in a glass tube of Serrano's urine. Art critics wrote favorable reviews of *Immersion* (or, as it also is known, *Piss Christ*). Seeing an opportunity for outrage, nationally known evangelicals, United States senators, and for good measure, the Catholic Archbishop of Australia denounced the exhibition. Taking pride in their devotion to Christianity, teenagers went after *Immersion* with a hammer. Other worthy citizens, understandably preferring anonymity, issued death threats to Serrano and exhibitors. Putting an end to this edifying spectacle, Christian protesters physically destroyed *Immersion*. An atypical example, snatched out of memory, in a misguided attempt to conjure up an image of moral equivalence between Muslim fundamentalists and Christian fundamentalists? Hardly.

But if both Christians and Muslims sometimes overreact to political or symbolic speech that offends them, there is all the difference between Christians, secure in their standing as an established majority, and Muslims, chronically vulnerable as a minority. As Modood emphatically declares, "From the Muslim side, the underlying causes of their current anger are a deep sense that they are not respected, that they, and their most cherished feelings, are 'fair game.'"[9]

If non-Muslims think Muslims are "fair game" in the Sturm und Drang of contemporary politics, then the principle of recognition respect is gutted. The issue, to be clear, is not whether there should be limits on free speech. There manifestly are: libel is one; hate speech another, threats to public order and individual safety still another; regulations on time, place, and manner yet another. But none of these bear on Modood's concern. What is at issue here is the weight to be given to respecting the dignity of others and appreciating the harm that vilifying or denigrating them does. Our objective, accordingly, is to bring to the surface sometimes competing, sometimes overlapping ideas of right and wrong that majorities who are supportive of inclusive tolerance turn to in weighing the legitimacy of speech that can do harm, and to assess the evenhandedness with which they apply them.

THE SPEECH SEQUENCE

To get an empirical grip, we fix on a form of public speech both familiar and open to the ordinary citizen—letters to the editor. Citizens send letters for newspapers to publish on all kinds of issues: to complain about failures of public services, to excoriate politicians, to rally support for a community project, and not uncommonly, to vent about the times that they—and we—live in, very much including immigrants and citizens who are Muslims.

As the textbox below table 4.1 shows, we again exploited a repeatable template. At its core, the question posed to respondents was whether newspapers should publish letters to the editor that are offensive to Muslims. As table 4.1 lays out, the Speech sequence consists in total of four trials. The versatility of a repeatable template allowed us to pursue several lines

TABLE 4.1. THE SPEECH SEQUENCE

Trial # (Year)	1 (2015)	2 (2015)	3 (2017)	4 (2020)
Target group fill 1	Immigrants	Immigrants		
Target group fill 2			Muslims	Muslims
Target group fill 3			Christians	Christians
Nature of speech	Express negative views			
Nature of speech		Critical	Critical	Critical
Nature of speech			Offensive	
Nature of speech	Express prejudice			
Nature of speech		Unreasonable		
Nature of speech		Inaccurate		
Nature of speech				Mock
Nature of speech				Show contempt for
Nature of speech	Express hate		Express hate	Express hate
Nature of speech	Threaten		Threaten	
Inclusion term		Should publish (editorial decision)	Should publish (editorial decision)	Should publish (editorial decision)
Inclusion term		May publish (legal principle)	May publish (legal principle)	May publish (legal principle)

Repeatable template: Should newspapers [INCLUSION TERM FILL] publish letters that are [NATURE OF CONTENT FILL] to [TARGET GROUP FILL]?

Example: Should newspapers be allowed to publish letters that are offensive to Muslims?

of inquiry simultaneously. Over the four trials, the question was asked in fifteen different ways (as indicated by the number of rows in the table). As importantly, two (sometimes three) of the ways the question was asked repeated previous fills (indicated by the number of times a fill is repeated in each row). This means that the main results we report have been replicated in separate tests, on independent samples, in a sequence of experimental trials conducted over a period spanning five years (2015–2020). At each step in the sequence, we learned we had to take another step to learn still more.

The experimental trials were designed to address, in increasing depth, three conceptually distinct lines of inquiry. Two are well established but empirically underexplored, the third is brought front and center for the first time.

The first line of inquiry investigated boundaries of legal and illegal, acceptable and unacceptable speech. Do non-Muslims draw a clear and distinct line between speech that criticizes or in some other way offends Muslims and hate speech directed against Muslims? Do they distinguish between different ways speech may be offensive to Muslims? How distinct is the line between criticism and prejudice? The large number of unanswered empirical questions motivated the high number of "nature of speech" fills over the four trials listed in table 4.1.

The second line of inquiry also centered on a question addressed in prior research. Are the standards of what is fair and what is unfair, what is right and what is not, applied evenhandedly? Standard practice is to ask whether a group is entitled to a benefit, varying the group that will benefit—for example, black or white, immigrant or native. Our specific focus, of course, is the extent to which the largest cultural and religious minority in Europe today—Muslims—is treated the same as the largest cultural and religious majority—Christians. But here and elsewhere our objective is to pull standard practice closer to real life. In real life, rarely is one and only one standard of right and wrong relevant. Accordingly, the experiments were designed to put more than one normative consideration in play.

The third and final line of inquiry, we believe, goes to the heart of the challenge Muslims face in understanding the standards of right and wrong non-Muslims affirm. It concerns the distinction between what *may* and what *should* be said, written, or published. The distinction is vital in a liberal democracy. If people believe that newspapers should only be allowed to publish what they themselves think newspapers should publish, then freedom of expression is gutted. But if they are indifferent to respecting the dignity of others, simple decency is gutted.

Determining a distinction between *may* and *should* gives one more reason for turning a spotlight on the tolerant. There is little point in distinguishing between what should be and what should be allowed to be published for the intolerant. They are the ones who write the most abusive letters to the editor. Naturally, they believe that newspapers should as well as should be allowed to publish them. For the tolerant, the issue is more complex. On the one hand, insofar as they share the larger family of liberal values, they will favor newspapers having discretion to publish or not publish letters that will offend Muslims. On the other hand, insofar as they are concerned about the harms that prejudice does, they will oppose the publication of letters that offend Muslims. Tensions between democratic ideals are thus our concern.

THE FIRST TRIAL: HATE SPEECH VERSUS OFFENSIVE SPEECH

We began, in chapter 2, by calling out how vile some speech about Muslims and their faith is in societies that pride themselves on tolerance. But offensive speech, even vile speech, is not the same as hate speech. To be sure, experts struggle with the line that separates legally permitted speech from illegal speech. One approach is to distinguish between *what* is said and *how* it is said. "Extreme" speech, one argument runs, is key in distinguishing the two.[10] What is the hallmark of extreme speech? Hatred is an extreme emotion; hence hate speech should be sanctioned. This is less helpful than it may seem. Not all speech that is intolerant or hostile is considered hate speech. Nor should it be. "We *should* be intolerant of injustice and we should dislike the needless suffering of the innocent," it is argued.[11] Intolerance of intolerance is key. Following the European Court of Human Rights, we take hate speech to be "all forms of expression which spread, incite, promote or justify hatred based on intolerance."[12] Taking this pronouncement as a guide, the first point we want to establish is whether ordinary citizens, as irregularly attentive to political principles as they are, draw a clear distinction between hate speech and offensive speech.

Inevitably, there are borderline cases where there are good reasons to debate whether speech is truly hate speech or not. But more commonly, hate speech is hateful on its face. Offensive speech poses a tougher problem, beginning with the legitimacy of criticism. It is not uncommon to contend that speech that expresses a strongly negative view of a minority, for instance, remarking that they are arrested more often than members of the majority, is an expression of prejudice. The negative characteristic attributed to the minority is a stereotype. But again, not uncommonly, it can and is argued that the claim is about base rates, and that characterizing it as prejudice is a strategy to silence honest discussion of the facts.

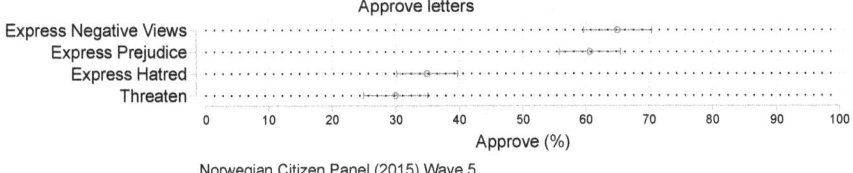

FIGURE 4.1. HATE SPEECH VS. OFFENSIVE SPEECH: FIRST TRIAL. Letters about immigrants expressing negative view/prejudice/hatred/threat. Norway, % Approve.

Accordingly, the first trial of the Speech sequence asked a representative sample of Norwegians about four different forms of speech: Should newspapers publish letters that express negative views of, express prejudice toward, express hatred of, or threaten immigrants? Note that, as seen in the summary of the whole Speech sequence in table 4.1, the two first trials asked about speech about immigrants, the last two about Muslims specifically. As the results are laid out, it will become evident that whether majorities are asked these questions about Muslims or immigrants turn out to be irrelevant in this setting.[13]

Two results stand out in figure 4.1. First, the distinction between offensive speech and hate speech is unmistakable. A clear majority (60–70%) approve of the publication of letters that express negative views and even prejudice about immigrants. Only a minority (30–40%) approve of letters that threaten or express hatred toward immigrants. The second result that stands out in figure 4.1 is the similarity of reactions to letters that express "negative views" and letters that "express prejudice." Clear majorities approve of editors publishing both. Characterizing evaluations of a minority as expressions of prejudice does not rule them out of bounds.

The first trial answers our initial question about whether citizens draw distinctions between forms of negative speech about minorities, in this case immigrants. It makes plain that they distinguish clearly, almost qualitatively, between offensive speech on the one hand and hate speech on the other. This suggests that certain forms of speech are directly related to widely shared ideas about right and wrong. Expressions of hatred and threats are overwhelmingly judged unacceptable. Offensive speech may be acceptable. The next step is to bring to light the conditions under which offensive speech is and is not acceptable.

A FOLLOW-UP TRIAL

That non-Muslims draw a distinction between offensive speech and hate speech about immigrants is evidence that different normative considerations, different principles, underpin judgments about the two forms of speech. It is, however, not evidence that the distinction they draw is a principled one. A test of whether it is principled—not the only one, it should be said, but the one that we can implement—is whether the distinction is applied in the same way to Christians as to Muslims. It is surely not hard to imagine that Christians may be inclined to more often balk at letters that offend Christians being published than equivalent letters that offend Muslims. One of the follow-up trials (trial 3) was explicitly designed to test this idea. The types of potentially objectionable letters were reduced from four to two, offensive speech versus hate speech, to insure that, if there is a lack of evenhandedness, we would not fail to observe it because of a lack of statistical power to detect differences in reactions to Muslims and to Christians.

Trial 3 asked a representative sample of Norwegians whether they agree or disagree that newspapers should publish letters that are either offensive to or express hatred toward either Muslims or Christians. Figure 4.2 displays their reactions.

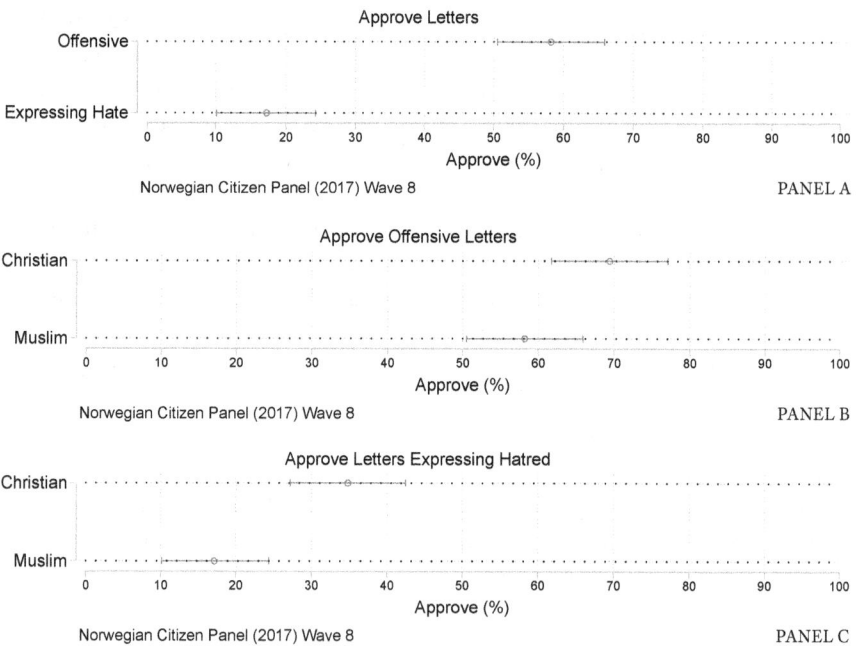

FIGURE 4.2. HATE SPEECH VS. OFFENSIVE SPEECH: EVENHANDEDNESS. Panel A: Letters about Muslims that are offensive/express hatred. Norway, % Approve. Panel B: Letters about Muslims/Christians that are offensive. Norway, % Approve. Panel C: Letters about Muslims/Christians that express hatred. Norway, % Approve.

Panel A makes evident that in the follow-up trials, as in the initial experiment, majority citizens draw a sharp distinction between offensive speech and hate speech. Some 60 percent approve of the publication of the letters that are offensive to Muslims, while some 20 percent approve of letters that express hatred toward Muslims. This replicates the main finding from the first trial, and beyond this, shows that the distinction is drawn similarly whether the speech is about immigrants or Muslims.

What the follow-up experiment adds to the initial experiment is evidence of whether or not the distinction drawn between offensive speech and hate speech is a principled one. The test, minimally, is whether Christians and Muslims are treated the same. This is a minimum requirement, because it can be reasonably argued that more concern should be shown for the dignity of Muslims, who are a minority in a society where a good number are prejudiced against them.

The results on display in panels B and C of figure 4.2 are evidence of evenhandedness. Decisive majorities (60–70%) approve of publication of letters that will offend Christians and Muslims. By contrast, only minority percentages agree that letters should be published that express hatred toward either. What is more, the results in figure 4.2, particularly in panel C, offer a suggestion that an average non-Muslim citizen believes that more concern should be shown for the feelings of Muslims than of Christians. It shows that non-Muslim citizens are markedly more likely (35%) to believe that newspapers should print letters that express hatred toward Christians than letters that express hatred toward Muslims (20%).

Caution is called for. The results suggest (and *suggest* is the right word) that there is some recognition in the larger society that Muslim minorities are in the lion's den. The main pattern across the panels in figure 4.2, however, is not in doubt. Most non-Muslims do not single out Muslims as "fair game" for insults—a result replicated in the fourth trial.

THE SECOND TRIAL: THE DISTINCTION
BETWEEN *MAY* AND *SHOULD*

The first experiment asked whether newspapers should publish abusive letters about Muslims or letters that express hatred toward them. But there is a deep difference between the question What should newspapers be allowed to publish? and the question What should they publish? The first speaks to how citizens may behave in a liberal democracy, the second to how they ought to behave. The great risk is that Muslims who live as minorities among non-Muslims in liberal democracies will take the answer to the first question to be the answer to the second.

Because the distinction between what may and should be said is clear on paper does not mean that non-Muslims hold to this distinction when we ask them about letters to the editor that will offend Muslims. This is all the more reason to go to special lengths to establish whether it is a distinction that ordinary citizens draw in real life. We have put thought into what this requires. It is easy to design an experiment which will show that majorities react differently to questions about what may be said and what should be said about minorities. It is only necessary to make this the only thing that can catch their eye.[14]

Using the Letters to the Editor template, the strategy in the second trial was to introduce a blatantly obvious alternative criterion of when a letter should not be acceptable and observe whether respondents, all the same, also take heed of the difference between being asked whether newspapers should be allowed to print it versus whether they should print it. Specifically, respondents were asked whether newspapers [should/should be allowed] to publish letters to the editor that are intensely critical of immigrants and [unreasonable/ inaccurate/no mention].[15] It was quite conceivable, to us certainly, that knowing that a letter is "unreasonable" or "inaccurate" suffices. The answer is no, newspapers should not print it, period.

Panel A in figure 4.3 first provides a baseline, showing that most non-Muslims believe that newspaper editors should be allowed, if they choose, to publish letters that are intensely critical of immigrants. The further results in panel A show that it matters—it would be bizarre if it did not—whether critical letters are false on their face. The likelihood of their being acceptable is slashed by half or more if they are either "unreasonable" or "inaccurate." We again counsel caution. Respondents were told that the letters are unreasonable or inaccurate. It is another question whether, were they themselves to read the letters, they would judge them to be unreasonable or inaccurate.

Our primary interest is whether the distinction between *may* and *should* matters to how citizens think about the publication of offensive letters. They may believe, without self-contradiction, that free speech requires that newspaper editors have discretion whether to publish or not publish letters to the editor, even though they themselves, were they in charge of making editorial decisions, would not publish them.

Panel B of figure 4.3 compares levels of agreement, in the control condition, that letters intensely critical of immigrants may be published and should be published, respectively. Panels C and D report comparable results for the Unreasonable and Inaccurate conditions. In each condition, considerably more respondents think that the newspaper should be allowed to publish the letters than think that the newspaper should publish them.

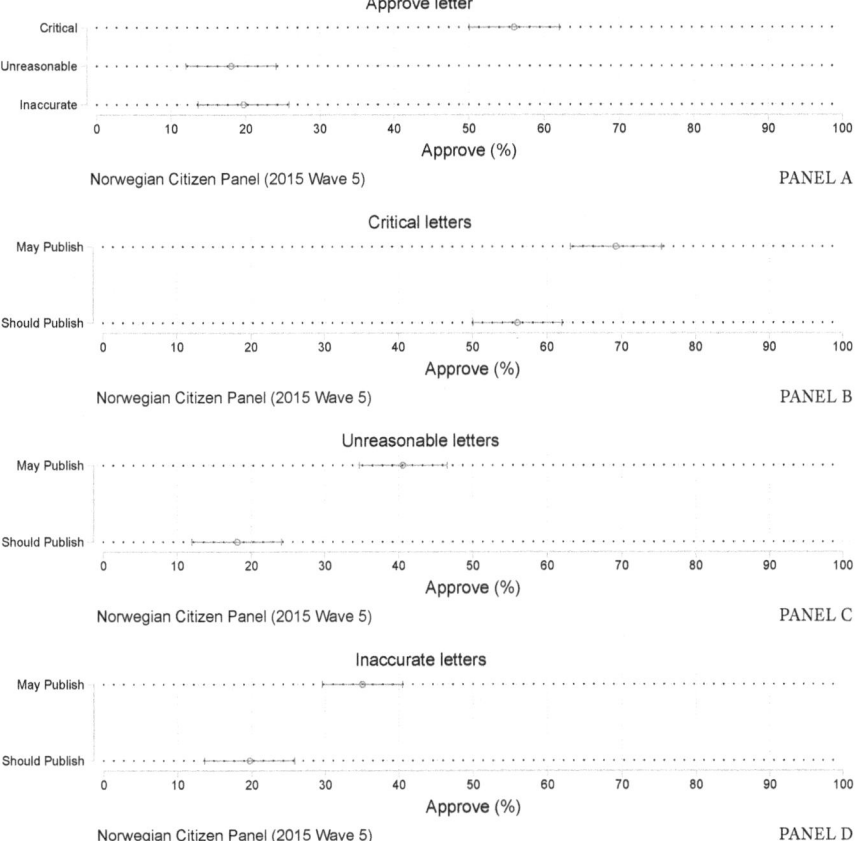

FIGURE 4.3. THE MAY/SHOULD DISTINCTION: THE UNREASONABLE LETTERS TRIAL. Panel A: Letters about immigrants that are critical/unreasonable/inaccurate. Norway, % Approve. Panel B: May/Should publish critical letters. Norway, % Approval. Panel C: May/Should publish unreasonable letters. Norway, % Approval. Panel D: May/Should publish inaccurate letters. Norway, % Approve.

The size of the difference is between 15 and 20 percentage points in each of the three panels. If the letters are described as intensely critical and wrong, either in the sense of being inaccurate or in the sense of being unreasonable, only one in five think that the newspaper should publish the letters. However, twice as many believe that the newspaper should be allowed to do so.

These experiments bring into focus a root challenge members of outgroups face in a liberal democracy—the difference between norms of what may and what should be said about them. The challenge in real life is not the validity of the distinction as a matter of principle. It is the invisibility of it in practice. Insofar as editors give letter writers broad latitude, Muslims will read letters declaring that they are unwelcome. What, unfortunately, they cannot see is that most non-Muslims believe that such letters should *not* be printed. What citizens believe should be allowed to be said publicly is visible publicly; but what they believe should not be said publicly is not publicly visible. Compounding this challenge, everyday life presents Muslims in today's liberal democratic society with in-your-face experiences of the deliberate provocations of anti-Muslim far-right groups, which now includes the burning of Qurans,[16] to advance their exclusionary agenda; and in response to criticism, complain that their right to freedom of speech is being abridged. Hence our desire to probe more deeply the concept of offensive speech.

THE FOURTH TRIAL: CONTEMPTUOUS SPEECH VERSUS OFFENSIVE SPEECH

The first results in the Speech sequence show that majority citizens draw a clear distinction between hate speech and offensive speech but no distinction between letters to the editor that express "negative views" of immigrants versus letters that "express prejudice" toward them. As we progressed through the sequence of experimental trials, we became increasingly struck by the opaqueness of "negative views." Did that category cover, indiscriminately as it were, all fault-finding letters? Or is there another category in play? The distinction we are reaching for is between speech that is offensive and speech that is contemptuous. Is this a distinction that an ordinary citizen makes?

Earlier experimental trials established that non-Muslims draw a sharp distinction between offensive speech and hate speech. Accordingly, the rule we followed is that the greater the similarity between reactions to letters that express hate and letters that are unequivocally contemptuous and insulting, the greater the value of distinguishing between contemptuous speech and offensive speech. Conversely, the greater the dissimilarity between reactions to letters that express hate and letters that are unequivocally contemptuous and insulting, the less the value of distinguishing between offensive speech and contemptuous speech. Accordingly, in the fourth and final trial in the Speech sequence, we randomly varied whether the letter expresses criticism or is unequivocally meanspirited—specifically, mocking or showing contempt for Muslims. In addition, to deepen the analysis of the difference between *may* and *should*, we randomly varied whether newspapers should be allowed, versus whether they should, print these letters. Finally, to gauge the robustness of the evenhandedness of standards of acceptable speech, we randomly varied whether non-Muslims were asked about Muslims or Christians. Figure 4.4 sets out the results.

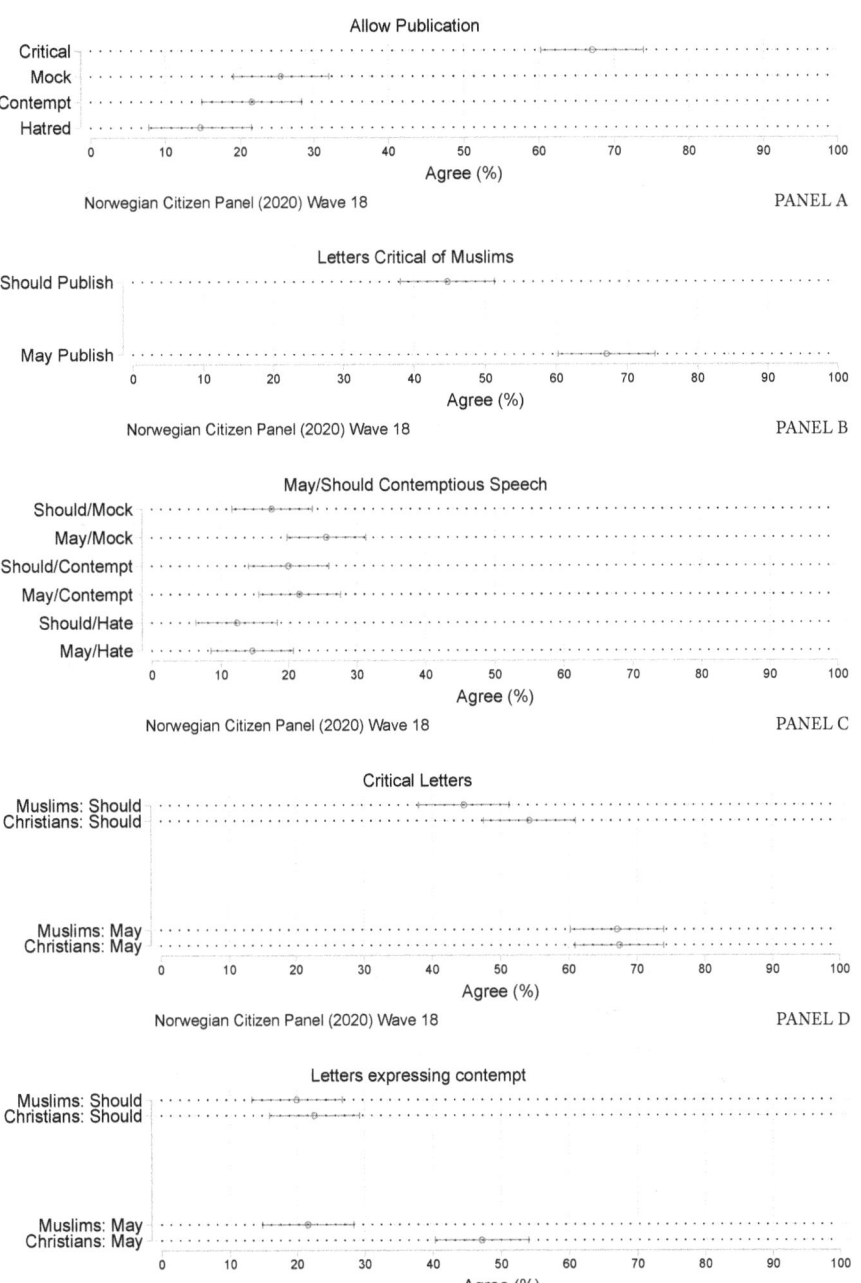

FIGURE 4.4. THE MAY/SHOULD DISTINCTION: THE CONTEMPTUOUS SPEECH TRIAL. Panel A: May publish letters about Muslims that are critical/mock/show contempt/express hatred. Norway, % Approve. Panel B: May/Should publish critical letters about Muslims. Norway, % Approve. Panel C: May/should publish letters about Muslims that mock/show contempt/express hatred. Norway, % Approve. Panel D: May/Should publish critical letters about Muslims/Christians. Norway, % Approve. Panel E: May/Should publish letters that show contempt for Muslims/Christians. Norway, % Approve.

The first thing to note is the sharp difference between critical and contemptuous speech about Muslims. A clear majority (67%) believe that newspapers should be allowed to print letters that criticize Muslims. In contrast, only a small minority (between 20 and 25%) believe that newspapers should be allowed to print letters that mock or show contempt for Muslims.

The next important thing to be learned from the fourth trial has to do with the elasticity of the may/should distinction. Panels B and C show that, consistent with previous results, citizens make the distinction for offensive speech but not for hate speech. It is therefore striking, as panel B in figure 4.4 shows, that the distinction virtually vanishes for letters that mock Muslims and entirely vanishes for letters that express contempt for them—yet more evidence of the importance of distinguishing offensive speech and contemptuous speech. The difference in reactions to offensive and contemptuous letters therefore has the hallmark of a pivotal distinction. Restricting speech that is contemptuous of Muslims is acceptable, restricting speech that is offensive to them is not.

A third thing worth noting has to do with whether non-Muslim citizens have more concern for how speech may wound minority Muslims than majority Christians. Panels D and E lay out these results. At one limit, when the norm of free speech most directly applies, there is evenhandedness. Thus, two-thirds believe that newspaper editors should have discretion over whether to publish letters that criticize Muslims or Christians. At the other limit, when a norm of common decency most directly applies, there also is evenhandedness. Any difference in reactions to the propriety of publishing letters that express hate or contempt for Christians or Muslims amounts to no difference. Otherwise, the pattern is unmistakable: greater concern for Muslims than for Christians, often by considerable margins. As Panel E shows, nearly one in every two believe that newspapers should be allowed to print letters that show contempt for Christians. In contrast, only one in five take the same view of letters that show contempt for Muslims.

AN IRONY OF *MAY* AND *SHOULD*

One reason we undertook this study is a lengthening record of studies documenting the support of ordinary citizens for a wider conception of democratic ideals—of the right of individuals to live their lives by the standards they believe are right rather than having to conform to an orthodoxy of majority opinion; of the legitimacy of differences of ideas and outlook; of a democratic ethos that has become more open-minded, more inclusive. Of all the ways that this ethos might be gauged, and there are many, our choice has been to focus on inclusive tolerance, operationally gauged by the IMCP index. Because we have fixed on one measure, we think it all the more important to repeat that in measuring concern about prejudice, we are simultaneously tracking orientations closely correlated with it. The person who is concerned about the harms that prejudice can do, indeed, is aware that she herself may not be perfectly free of it, is also a person who will favor liberal democratic ideals overall. Freedom of speech and concern about prejudice are not the same. But the person ready to support the rights of others to express ideas that she disagrees with is also very likely to be concerned about the tenacity of prejudice and discrimination.

It is natural and understandable to see offensive speech directed against Muslims as an expression of prejudice. Here and now, for Muslims living in Western Europe, with anti-immigrant political parties enjoying a surge of support and anti-immigrant demonstrations a common occurrence, it is easy to see support for public speech that is critical of them as Islamophobia. And not without reason.

The intolerant are more than willing to support newspapers printing letters that take Muslims to task for this or that supposed offense. For them, there is no difference between *may* and *should* in the question of printing offensive letters. They naturally believe that newspapers should be allowed to print them; and, just as naturally, that they should print them. But the frankly intolerant are a minority, a fifth of the general public we would estimate, perhaps significantly less but not likely significantly more. They can and do poison the public mood from time to time. But they do not have the numbers or the moral weight to alter, by themselves, the trajectory of contemporary democracies. Hence the irony. The pillar of support for speech that offends Muslims, we are suggesting, is the tolerant, not the intolerant, portion of mass publics.

Figure 4.5 displays the results of a test of this reasoning. It shows the likelihood of believing that printing an offensive letter is acceptable as a function of strength of motivation to control prejudice: the farther to the right on the horizontal axis, the more strongly motivated to control prejudice majority citizens are; the farther to the left, the less strongly motivated. The top curve tracks the probability that they agree that newspapers should be allowed to publish these letters; the bottom curve, the probability that they agree that they should publish them.

The striking feature of figure 4.5 is the yawning gap between the two curves as you look from left to right. The intolerant are overwhelmingly, and equally likely, to agree that offensive letters about Muslims may be pub-

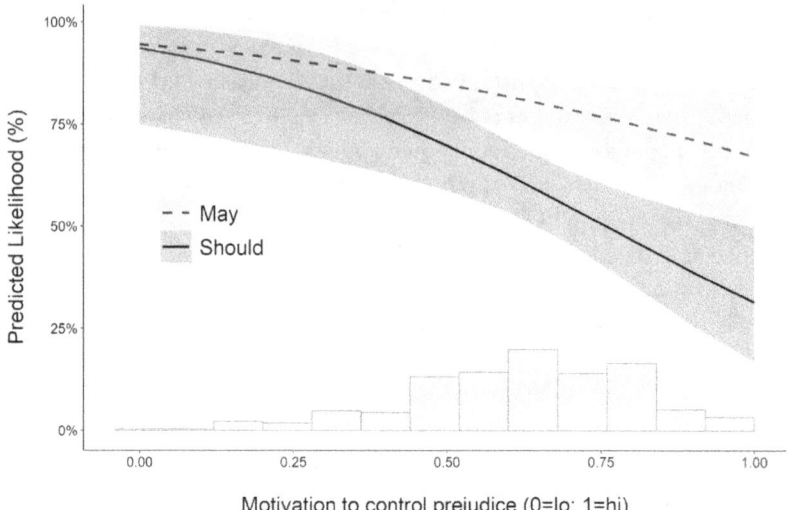

FIGURE 4.5. THE MAY VS. SHOULD DISTINCTION BY INCLUSIVE TOLERANCE. May/Should publish offensive letters about Muslims. Norway, Predicted likelihood of approval (%) by IMCP.

lished and should be published. For the tolerant, they agree that newspapers should be allowed to publish offensive letters about Muslims, supporting freedom of speech. There is a decrease in support the more concerned non-Muslims are about prejudice; however, even those who are most concerned are still decisively more likely to support freedom of speech. It is an altogether different matter when the issue is not whether newspapers may publish offensive letters about Muslims but, rather, whether they should or should not publish them. The lower curve tracking agreement that newspapers should publish them plummets (relative to the upper curve), the more concerned non-Muslims are about prejudice. At the highest levels of IMCP, majorities believe that newspapers should *not* print offensive letters about Muslims.

This is a febrile time. In politics and the media, outbursts of ill will toward Muslims are part of the regular news cycle in Western Europe, some manifestly beyond the pale, but much accepted as part of the tumult of a democratic politics. Hence the irony of *may* and *should*: if Muslim minorities have an impression that the larger society is closed against them, it follows from the acceptance of those who believe in inclusive tolerance that the intolerant, too, have a right to freedom of speech.

ENVOI

It is the view of many Muslims and non-Muslims sympathetic to Muslims that Muslims are singled out for speech that mocks, insults, humiliates. As an actuarial matter, they are correct: Muslims are more likely to be targets of offensive and contemptuous speech than Christians. Then again, it takes only a few to generate a great many posters, blogs, and rallies that attack Muslim minorities. Which is just the point here. For all their limitations, the strength of representative studies of public opinion is that they allow us to tell the difference between what is typical and what is atypical. Our experiments, repeatedly, do not find a double standard in what is and is not acceptable to say about Muslims as compared to Christians. Indeed, insofar as there is a difference, it takes the form of a greater concern for offensive and contemptuous speech about Muslims than about Christians.

Systematic studies of public opinion have another strength. By varying the terms on which a policy is formulated, they can usefully complicate our understanding of how citizens negotiate competing normative considerations. A distinction between recognition respect and appraisal respect is an example of a useful complication. So is a distinction between *may* and *should*. And so, too, is a distinction between offensive speech and contemptuous speech. Together, they provide a finer-grained view of the moral temper of contemporary liberal democracies under stress.

Issues of speech have become a flashpoint. Indeed, the very meaning of public speech is being reconstructed. Unedited media, or self-publication, are experiencing unprecedented growth and popularity globally. Moreover, edited media that practice strict editorial guidelines, not least when it comes to representations of minority groups, are increasingly facing competition from a set of media actors who bill themselves as "alternatives," and who more or less explicitly challenge the editorial codes of conduct followed by traditional media organizations. The supply of unedited, inflammatory public speech about Muslim minorities is exploding. It is not hyperbole to write that the need to bring into view what the largest number by far of non-Muslims believe is out of bounds is urgent.

[CHAPTER FIVE]

THE CONSTRUCTION OF NATIONAL IDENTITIES

What are the components of national identities?[1] How does identification with a country differ from national pride or chauvinism?[2] What do images of exemplary citizens say about a national narrative?[3] These are all ways of asking, What is the social psychology of national identity? In contrast, our question is political. Inclusion of Muslim minorities requires authoritative acknowledgment that they are and ought to be part of a country's national narrative. Accomplishing this requires the use of societal institutions, most notably, the educational system. Under what conditions are majority citizens ready to go along with Muslim minorities formally included in the national identity?[4] And why are they more likely to do so under some conditions, less likely under others? These are the questions that we propose to tackle.

Our starting point is a paradox of identity: you are the same person now as you were a year ago, even though you are not the same now as you were. So, too, with countries or national communities—except for scale, that is. The United States has remained the United States, with the arguable exception of the Civil War period, even though it is now different in every way imaginable than it was in the beginning.

Getting even a bit of a grip on this paradox is a key to catching sight of openings to more inclusive national identities in contemporary liberal democracies. The route we followed—*route* because it was a journey— started with a commonplace observation, then stretched into a sequence of progressive variations of key terms to clarify results and to test our reasoning. The commonplace observation: national identities are presented as though they are assigned by history. But nations, as Benedict Anderson famously remarked, are "imagined communities."[5] Shared images of "who we are" bind together members of groups too large to know one another face-to-face.

Identity, as has endlessly been repeated, is socially constructed. We may act as though "who we are" has been assigned by history. In fact, "who we are" is a social construction. This holds even in the absence of change, since a shared sense of national identity must be renewed as one generation of members succeeds another. What we want to bring into view is how continuity in the *process* of constructing a national identity can provide reassurance of national continuity.

We aim to make a twofold contribution. The first is to show that the idea that national identities are, and should be, constructed is widely accepted by majorities in liberal democracies in Western Europe. The main alternative perspective—that national identities are assigned once and for all at a point in time in history and that the job of institutions is to maintain that conception—is a more narrowly held view, shared by fewer than we, and we believe many others, had appreciated. Even on a hot-button issue like acknowledging diversity, advocates of keeping the status quo with minimal change are concentrated among the limited number of citizens who favor an exclusionary agenda. The second contribution is to bring to light conditions under which non-Muslims are open to enlarging their country's identity to include ethnic and religious minorities. In the struggle for inclusion, we shall show, a pivotal consideration is continuity in the *process* of constructing the national identity.

THE PARADOX OF IDENTITY

The concept of identity is a logical troublemaker, for at its core is a conundrum. A stock example is Sir John Cutler's stockings. Sir John had the good fortune to have a pair of silk stockings. With wear, a tiny hole appeared. Darning was necessary. But only wool was available. So, Sir John patched the tiny hole with wool. With more wear, another tiny hole appeared. Again, Sir John threaded his needle with wool. Then another, then yet another, until the pair of stockings were all wool. But were they then the same stockings?[6]

This is both a deep and a broad problem. Time and sense of self are bound together. Who you are at the moment you are reading this is nothing like who you were your first day of elementary school. Yet, you know yourself to be the same person now as you were then. What is more, everyone who started school with you is different now in endless respects than they were then. There is no exception. Yet, without exception, each one knows that he or she is the same person now as she or he was then. How is this possible? National identity is a deeper mystery still. It is necessary to hold on to a sense that we are who we were, even though "we the people" are quite literally different people as one generation gives way to the next. At each moment in time, part of the past is part of the present; at each moment in time, what was the future becomes the present.

INSTITUTIONALIZED NATIONAL IDENTITY CONSTRUCTION

Transmission of culture in many aspects is informal, a private rather than a public undertaking. Socialization is carried out through one's family, then as one life stage succeeds another, through one's peers, one's associates at work, the media, even, to a limited degree, one's own children. But transmission of national identities is deliberate, focused, strategic. It requires management.

In a modern society, transmission of national identity is a core task of formal institutions. It is through "shared subjection to a common formative context" that members of a culture come to share a lineage of ideals and practices.[7] Schools are the preeminent social institution to transmit a country's self-representation because they are the preeminent institution to enforce "shared subjection to common formative influences."

THE NATIONAL IDENTITY CONSTRUCTION SEQUENCE

Our empirical strategy was to fix on a primary educational instrument regulating a country's representation of itself—school textbooks. School textbooks are commissioned by public agencies and therefore officially authorized; written by (presumed) experts and therefore treated as authoritative; periodically revised in successive editions or replaced altogether, and therefore part of a legitimate process of deliberate construction of a national narrative. All of this is common knowledge—and sufficiently vague to capitalize on.

Accordingly, we developed an experimental template centering on school textbooks. Table 5.1 lays out the template and the main elements of the eight trials that make up the National Identity Construction sequence of survey experiments. Trials were carried out in five different countries over a period of six years (2013–2019). Most treatments (fills) were included in two or more trials so that none of the results we report rely on the outcome of a single trial.

TABLE 5.1. THE CONSTRUCTION OF NATIONAL IDENTITY SEQUENCE

Trial # (Country)	1 (US)	2 (Norway)	3 (Norway)	4 (Norway)	5 (Denmark)	6 (Norway)	7 (Netherlands)	8 (Britain)
Exclusion term			Less emphasis	Less emphasis				
Inclusion term	Written	Written	Written; to reflect	Written; to reflect		Written		
Inclusion term						Updated	Updated	Updated
Inclusion term						Expanded	Expanded	Expanded
Inclusion term					Developed			
Inclusion term					Revised			
Inclusion term			More emphasis	More emphasis				
Inclusion term						New added	New added	New added
Inclusion term						Redone	Redone	Redone
Inclusion term	Rewritten	Rewritten			Rewritten			
Nature of diversity	Ethnic							
Nature of diversity	Cultural							
Nature of diversity	Ethnic and cultural							

Repeatable template: Should school textbooks be [INCLUSION or EXCLUSION TERM FILL] the [NATURE OF DIVERSITY FILL] diversity of [COUNTRY]?

Example: Should school textbooks be rewritten to reflect the ethnic and cultural diversity of the US?

THE TWO INITIAL TRIALS

The first two trials of the sequence were designed to test the elementary hypothesis that citizens care about the process of construction of national identities. A randomly selected half of respondents in the US were asked whether they agreed or disagreed that "school textbooks should be *written* to reflect the diversity of the US." The other half were asked whether they agreed or disagreed that "school textbooks should be *rewritten* to reflect the diversity of the US."[8] Two questions identical in every respect but one, the one being a difference of only two letters, no more.

In addition, since the idea of diversity takes distinct—or, at any rate, distinguishable—forms and, arguably, people respond differently to them, the type of diversity—ethnic, cultural, or both—was also randomly varied in the first trial. Each appeared on its own in one experimental condition, both appeared together in a third. It is not that we anticipated a different reaction to cultural versus ethnic diversity but, rather, we wanted to consider the possibility that "doubling up" on the type of diversity would increase the strength of the treatment. A final consideration: race has defined *majority* and *minority* in America since the country's beginning. Our analysis therefore focuses on the reactions of white Americans.

Figure 5.1 lays out the results. Panel A contrasts reactions of white Americans to textbooks being written or rewritten to reflect cultural and ethnic diversity. That small distinction made a striking difference in reactions. We observe overwhelming support, around 70 percent, for textbooks being written to reflect diversity. There is distinctly less support, around 50 percent, for textbooks being rewritten to do exactly the same thing. Some 20 percent of the majority population are open to textbooks being written to reflect the cultural and ethnic diversity of the United States, but not open to their being rewritten for this purpose. Contrast this stark difference with the null-result in panel B of figure 5.1. Doubling up on the type of diversity made no difference. The process matters to many ordinary citizens, the type of diversity does not, at least in the United States.

But is this, possibly, another example of American exceptionalism? Most countries in Western Europe have had no experience comparable to the American-style hand-to-hand combat to win control of local or state boards of education in order to determine the content of school textbooks.[9] For that matter, inclusion of minorities in the national narrative is a defining feature of the American experience. Immigrants from Ireland became Irish-Americans; those from Germany, German-Americans; from Italy, Italian-Americans. Shared superordinate identity, differentiated

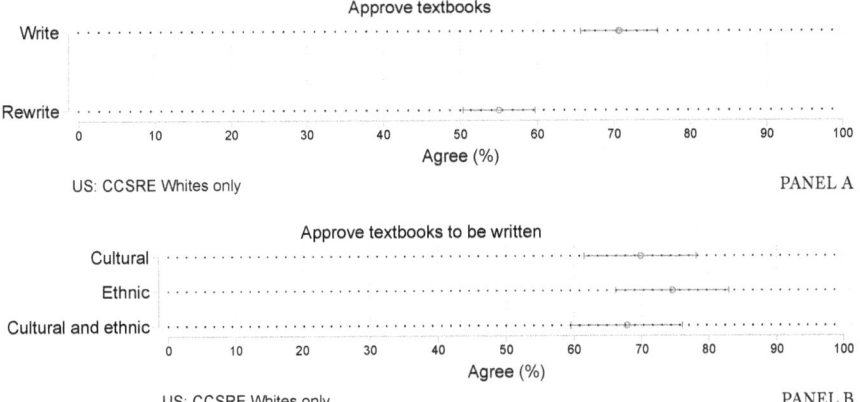

FIGURE 5.1. THE TEXTBOOK EXPERIMENT: THE FIRST TWO-LETTER TRIAL. Panel A: Process of Construction. Textbooks should be written/rewritten to reflect diversity. United States (Whites only), % Agree. Panel B: Type of Diversity. Textbooks should reflect cultural/ethnic/cultural and ethnic diversity. United States (Whites only), % Agree.

subordinate identity, has been the American game plan—not standard practice historically in Western Europe, to say the least.

To test the possibility of American exceptionalism, we replicated the textbook experiment in Norway. A nationally representative sample of adults were asked if they agreed or disagreed with the statement "School textbooks should be [written/rewritten] to reflect the new diversity of Norway."

Figure 5.2 shows the outcome of this second trial. The Norwegian results are interchangeable with the American ones. Again, a sharp distinction is drawn between textbooks being written versus being rewritten to reflect diversity. An overwhelming majority in both countries, nearly three in every four, are open to textbooks being written to reflect diversity. Markedly fewer, on the order of one in two, support textbooks being rewritten to do exactly the same thing. The average citizen in both countries draws a clear distinction between writing textbooks to reflect diversity and rewriting them to do exactly the same thing.

The overall lesson to take away from the results of the first two trials of the sequence is that there appears to be considerable openness to the idea of constructing official national identities so that they include cultural and ethnic diversity, but the process of construction is important. This raises two new questions. First, is our optimistic interpretation of openness to the idea of constructed national identities warranted? Second, what are those citizens who approve of textbooks being written to reflect diversity—but

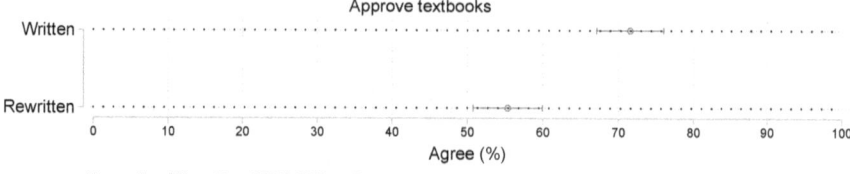

FIGURE 5.2. THE TEXTBOOK EXPERIMENT: THE SECOND TWO-LETTER TRIAL. Textbooks should be written/rewritten to reflect diversity. Norway, % Agree.

not rewritten to do the same thing—reacting to? What, more exactly, is the principle underpinning the process of identity construction that matters to them? We address the two questions in turn.

THE ASSIGNED IDENTITY TRIALS

The results of the first trials show large shares of majority group members agreeing that school textbooks should be written to reflect the diversity of the country. Insofar as this captures what we intended to measure, openness to the idea that national identities are constructed rather than assigned, this result points to an openness to more inclusive identities. But is it possible that, although they agree that textbooks should reflect diversity, this is not as strong a ground for optimism as the results on their face might suggest? Could we have fallen victim, for example, to acquiescence bias?

Reality has changed. Norway is only one of a number of countries in Western Europe that used to be ethnically and religiously homogeneous, or at any rate considered itself so. Norway has changed, indisputably. Moreover, this change in cultural, ethnic, and religious composition has not come as a result of a domestic political, economic, or societal crisis. Quite the contrary. Norway, like many European countries, has become more diverse because, as one of the safest and wealthiest countries in the world, it has attracted increasing numbers of immigrants and refugees, many from fraught circumstances. The question is whether Norwegians, and citizens of other European nations, despite the pride they take in their heritage, nevertheless believe that their national identity should evolve to reflect the new diversity of their country.

School textbooks are supposed to teach students the way the world is. So they should teach students the way it is now—that the country is now ethnically and religiously diverse. This is not open to question. This is no more than facing up to reality. But here is a thought experiment. Suppose that you accept that ethnic and religious diversity is now a fact. But you have mixed feelings. On the one hand, it does no good to put one's head in the sand like an ostrich. One should make the best of things. Yes, the new diversity of the country should be acknowledged, for example, in school textbooks. On the other hand, you feel that some people are putting too much time and energy into lauding the virtues of diversity. Things should be done in the right proportion. At the end of the day, the major lessons school textbooks should teach about the country now are the same lessons they have taught before. Minimally, you have some concerns, you are ambivalent, about acknowledging diversity as an aspect of your country's identity.

The two initial trials were not designed to pick up ambivalence. The more who have mixed feelings about formally endorsing diversity as an aspect of the country's identity, the greater the risk that the impression of openness to inclusion the first round of experimental trials gives is misleading. Accordingly, in this round, the textbook experiment has three conditions. The first is an exact replication of the Written condition in the first round: respondents are asked whether they agree or disagree that "textbooks for primary and lower secondary students should *reflect* the new diversity of Norway." In the second condition, respondents are asked whether school textbooks should "put *less emphasis* on the new diversity of Norway." In the third condition, they are asked whether they should "put *more emphasis* on the new diversity of Norway." The fills are listed in the trial 3 column in the overview of the National Identity Construction sequence in table 5.1.

There is something to be said for researchers sometimes putting on record their level of confidence of success before conducting an experiment. This is one of those times. The results of the initial trials gave us a reason for a measure of optimism about an openness to national identities becoming more inclusive. But given the understandable skepticism about expressions of positive attitudes on issues bearing on minorities, we deliberately designed this version of the textbook experiment to show that optimism is unfounded. All the more reason to put on record that we thought it had a nontrivial chance to do just that.

The first two trials established the robustness of the write/rewrite results. Even so, it is a fair question whether, if the experiment is done a third time, the results will match the first two times. Accordingly, the first thing to note about the third trial, shown in panel A in figure 5.3, is that the percentage agreeing that textbooks should reflect the new diversity of Norway is almost exactly the same as in the first round of experimental trials. The numbers are statistically indistinguishable: on the first trial, 72 percent agreed; on the second, 68 percent. This speaks to both the replicability of the results of the initial round of textbook experiments and the validity of the results of this new round of treatment terms.

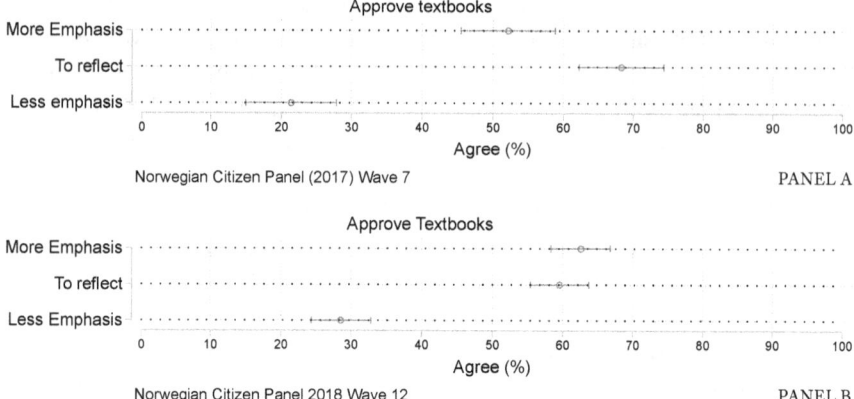

FIGURE 5.3. THE COUNTERFACTUAL TEXTBOOK EXPERIMENT. Textbooks should be written with less emphasis on/to reflect/with more emphasis on diversity. Panel A: First Trial. Norway, % Agree. Panel B: Replication Trial. Norway, % Agree.

The specific question that the second-round variation of the textbook experiment was designed to answer is whether, or rather to what extent, majority citizens have mixed feelings about their national identity being constructed. If offered an opportunity to choose an option that puts some weight on a historically assigned national identity, will they take it? It is surely conceivable that many who go along with textbooks being written to reflect the new diversity of their country nonetheless are going along reluctantly, even grudgingly. The more who have mixed feelings, or who are simply not paying attention to the details of the question, the more who will agree that textbooks should acknowledge diversity but de-emphasize it.

The idea that a large body of majority citizens, though willing to go along with acknowledging diversity, are nevertheless dragging their feet is surely plausible. Plausible but wrong. As panel A in figure 5.3 indicates, barely a fifth endorse the proposal rooted in the idea that national identities are assigned and believe diversity should be de-emphasized.

Wrong is not a term that ordinarily should be used when interpreting results of a single survey experiment. There is always reason for skepticism about the results of public opinion studies. In this case, the results were so remarkable and decisive that they were worth trying to replicate once more on a different sample in the same country. Panel B shows the result of the replication trial. The key result is reactions to putting less emphasis on diversity. There was good reason to suppose that it might be the option that enjoys the most support. However, once again, it demonstrably enjoys the least support. With this assurance we turn to our puzzle: What explains the striking differences in reactions to textbooks being written to reflect diversity as opposed their being rewritten to do exactly the same thing?

A REFLECTION ON PERSONAL AND COLLECTIVE IDENTITIES

Why the objection to textbooks being rewritten? There is a commonsense answer: *rewritten* suggests the possibility of the past being rewritten in Orwellian fashion. Change risks changing what we have stood for and therefore what we now stand for—that is what puts people off. Having textbooks "written" to reflect diversity somehow elides the issue of change. But how? Having textbooks acknowledge the new diversity of the country patently involves making a change.

How does Sir John know his stockings are the same, even though the content of them is not the same as it was? How do we know that we are the same person now, even though we are not the same as we were? The root of personal identity, William James contended, is the stream of a person's thoughts. Every thought we have is our thought and no one else's. In his inimitable style, speaking of the continuity of consciousness of the self, James writes: "When Peter and Paul wake up in the same bed . . . each one of them reaches mentally back, . . . Peter's present instantly finds Peter's past, and never by mistake knits itself onto that of Paul's."[10]

How is this possible? James picks out two mechanisms—similarity and continuity. The two may seem to overlap. Insofar as a person's consciousness is a stream of thought, from instant to instant, similarity has to be the rule. And insofar as similarity is the rule, continuity is a proxy for similarity. James's insight is that continuity is a mechanism for the resolution of dissimilarities in our streams of thought. "Continuity makes us unite what dissimilarity might otherwise separate."[11]

Having school textbooks in countries like Norway or Denmark present ethnic and religious diversity as a feature of the country's identity is a substantive change. The stockings, to continue the metaphor, are mended with a different sort of thread now than they used to be. But Sir John can nevertheless hold on to the idea that his stockings are his stockings. It is the continuity of the process of (re)construction of his stockings that supplies an impression of continuity in their identity. So, too, we hypothesize, with ideas of national identity. A continuous process of construction has been institutionalized. The continuity of process is a key to the continuity of the narrative.[12] The last round of trials in the National Identity Construction sequence was designed to test and refine a hypothesis of process continuity.

THE THIRD ROUND OF TRIALS

Formally acknowledging diversity as part of the national identity is a more abrupt change than most, but change in circumstances is what a modern country must regularly manage in the transition from one generation to the next, and recently, even from one cohort to the next. The idea, then, is that there is already on hand an array of terms for managing transitions in institutionalized settings such as education. Changes in school textbooks are not merely routine; they are routinized. The strategy, then, is to contrast terms that call to mind the routinization of the process with terms that imply a break in the process.

Imply is the operative word. Again, the challenge in selecting treatment terms is keeping a light touch. We want to reiterate that there is something foolhardy about supposing that a public opinion survey has the exactness of measurement to detect citizens' drawing fine distinctions. Hence our strategy: four separate studies, in four different countries, to assess citizens' reactions to a variety of ways of constructing textbooks to reflect diversity as an aspect of the country's identity. What matters is not a specific result considered in isolation, but whether the consistency of the pattern of results across multiple trials suggests that a considerable share of citizens is open to continuous processes of identity constructions but balks at discontinuity or interruptions.

This third and final round of the National Identity Construction sequence, then, took full advantage of the textbook experiment's repeatable template. Across four trials, reactions to six treatment terms were assessed. In two of these trials, terms from the first round were repeated, one evoking continuity and the other, discontinuity (textbooks being written or rewritten) to test for replicability and to provide an anchor to gauge reactions to new terms introduced in the third round. The trials were conducted in four different countries: Denmark, Great Britain, Norway, and the Netherlands. The trial in Denmark was conducted before the others, so the results were known in advance of the final three, simultaneously conducted trials. The trials and fills are included in the summary of the National Identity Construction sequence in table 5.1.

Panel A of figure 5.4 shows the results of the first experimental trial in this final round, conducted in Denmark. It provides an important first clue to the significance of the continuity principle. The mode of construction that accents continuity the clearest—to "develop" textbooks to reflect diversity—attracts the most approval. Those that accent interruption or discontinuity—"redo" and "rewrite" textbooks—attract the least. This is an indication that the drop-off in approval for books being rewrit-

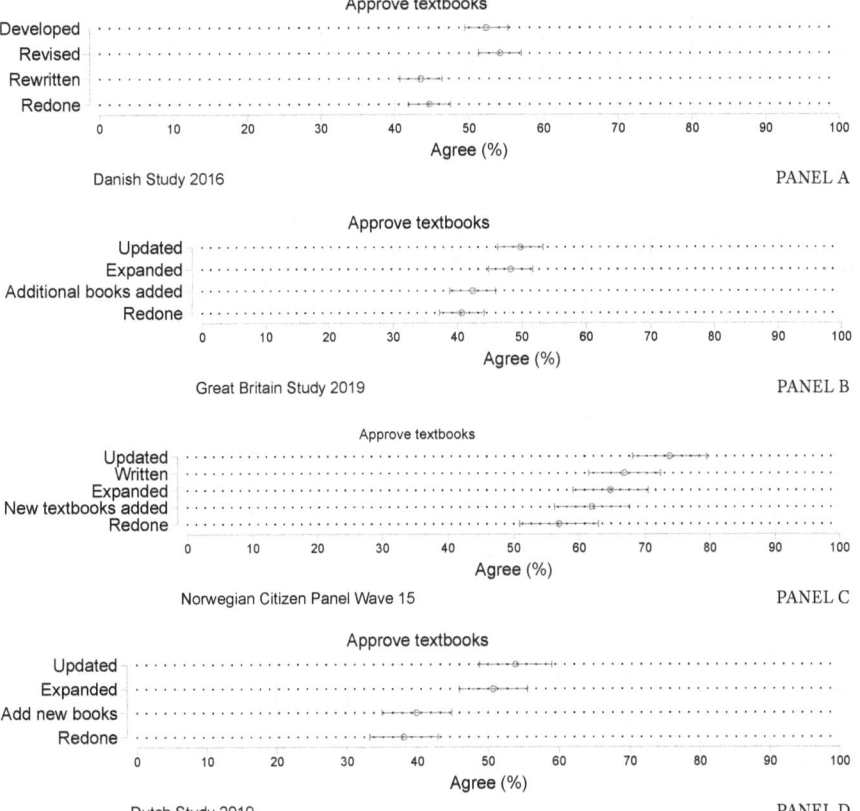

FIGURE 5.4. CONTINUITY VS. INTERRUPTION IN THE PROCESS OF NATIONAL IDENTITY CONSTRUCTION. Panel A: Textbooks should be developed/revised/rewritten/redone to reflect diversity. Denmark, % Agree. Panel B: Textbooks should be updated/expanded/added/redone to reflect diversity. Great Britain, % Agree. Panel C: Textbooks should be updated/written/expanded/added/redone to reflect diversity. Norway, % Agree. Panel D: Textbooks should be updated/expanded/added/redone to reflect diversity. Netherlands, % Agree.

ten has to do *not* with the idea that national identities are constructed but rather with an impression of discontinuity in the process of their construction.

We want to flag one of the results, though. It has to do with responses to "revising" textbooks to reflect diversity. In designing the experiment, the image we had in mind was revising a manuscript, to take the most current example, the manuscript for this book—the seemingly never-ending (in our experience) process of, simplifying, qualifying, trimming, all in an attempt to clarify what we mean to say—a paradigmatic example of a continuous, and continual, process. But, writers aside, the act of revising could be perceived as similar to the act of rewriting. And yet, in this instance at least, *revising* is not a synonym for *rewriting* in the minds of citizens.

The next three trials share the objective of focusing on a pair of terms that reflect the continuity principle in that they highlight the regularity of the processes in which textbooks are changed from edition to edition—namely, whether they should be "updated" or "expanded" to reflect diversity. To provide two points of contrast, we also asked about processes that mark a break—whether textbooks should be "redone" and whether "additional new books" should be written to reflect diversity.

Panel B shows the results of the trial conducted in Great Britain. There is more openness to construction of diverse national identities if the underlying principle of construction is continuous; that is, if it is a question of "updating" or "expanding" textbooks. "Redoing" textbooks, the option that most clearly marks a break, shaves off support. More telling, "adding new books" to acknowledge the country's ethnic and religious diversity elicits the same reactions as having textbooks "redone." A continuous process of construction, the pattern of results suggests, enlarges the coalition open to inclusion compared to interruptions or discontinuities in the process. Panel C shows the results of the final round of textbook experiments in Norway. The pattern of results in this trial are not crisp, though their similarity with the Great Britain results is clear enough. Updating textbooks is the most popular option, redoing them the least. On its own, though, this trial in Norway would not count as strong evidence in favor of the discontinuity hypothesis. In contrast, panel D shows the results of the final round of textbook experiments in the Netherlands. Again, updating and expanding bunch together with the most support; adding and redoing with the least.

A general observation on all four textbook trials is in order—the differences between experimental treatments are more modest than others that we have reported. To say again, this is the price of our design choice of seeking to probe more deeply by making finer and finer distinctions. It is the regularity of the pattern of differences in this final round of the National Identity Construction sequence that is critical. It suggests openness to continuous processes of national identity construction.

A FINAL TRIAL

To this point, we have seen that principles of identity construction that smooth the flow of a country's self-narrative by accenting continuity of process meet the highest levels of openness in the majority population to reflect the diversity of contemporary societies. This is the view looking backward. What, then, about the view looking forward to inclusion as a project rather than a fact to acknowledge?

Continuity and similarity are two means of maintaining a sense of identity. From instant to instant, each tends to reinforce the other. But continuity and similarity are not the same. The difference between the two comes out in coming to terms with inclusion as a project, as an ongoing process. Change projected into the future means difference, necessarily. Similarity cannot do the job. To turn again to James, "Continuity makes us unite what dissimilarity might otherwise separate."[13]

A survey experiment with a different template was used to test this reasoning. The idea was to assess reactions to two ways of presenting change "in what our country stands for." Again, the strategy was to search for fault lines in public opinion by, paradoxically, minimizing the difference between alternative courses of action. When minimal differences make a substantively significant difference, it is evidence of touching a nerve. Specifically, in one experimental condition, respondents were asked whether they agree or disagree that "truly respecting the cultural and ethnic diversity of our country calls for *opening a new chapter* in our country's history about what it stands for." "Opening a new chapter" evokes interruption or discontinuity—but, and this is worth underlining—*not a rejection of the past*. In the other condition, respondents were asked whether they agree or disagree that "truly respecting the cultural and ethnic diversity of our country calls for *fresh thinking* about what our country stands for."[14] Note that both alternatives are frank in licensing a new representation of what the country stands for. The difference is that in one the process is interrupted, albeit very slightly—a new chapter must be opened.

This design was implemented in a study of a nationally representative sample of adults in the United Kingdom. Figure 5.5 shows the results. Despite the minimal variation between conditions, there is a clear difference in reactions. In the Fresh Thinking condition, the condition that does not require interruption or discontinuities in the process of identity construction, a clear majority, on the order of three in five, is open to inclusion as a project. In the Opening a New Chapter condition, where discontinuity is a focal point, a bare majority are willing to do the same.

What is remarkable about this result is not the magnitude of the difference between the two experimental conditions. It is the fact that there is a difference at all. "Opening a new chapter" is as close—at any rate as close as we could think of—to an assurance of the story of a country staying on the same rails, as it were. It is the same book, after all. Then again, it is not a continuation of a country's story. It is opening a "new" chapter in what the country stands for. In contrast, the alternative of "fresh thinking about

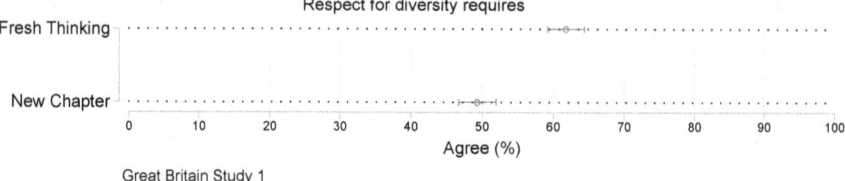

FIGURE 5.5. THE PRINCIPLE OF CONTINUOUS CONSTRUCTION: ADDITIONAL TEST. Fresh thinking/opening a new chapter. Great Britain, % Agree.

what the country stands for" acknowledges that what the country stands for is a construction but assumes continuity in the process of construction. And insofar as this principle of continuity is recognized, we have seen in many different ways that majority citizens are more disposed to the idea that their national identity should be constructed so as to recognize diversity.

THE TOLERANT

This is a picture of how citizens, on average, respond. But of course, citizens differ from one another, and an important way they differ, we have repeatedly seen, is the degree of their support for the value of tolerance. It is not in the cards that the intolerant will throw their weight behind acknowledgement of diversity. But the choices that the tolerant will make are not baked in. They depend on the alternatives on offer. Our starting point, accordingly, is the most obvious illustration of the dependence of choices on the alternatives on offer. One option is that textbooks should be written to reflect the new diversity of the country. Another option is that, yes, they should acknowledge the new diversity but place less emphasis on it. In panel A of figure 5.6, we plot reactions to the two courses of action as a function of strength or intensity of tolerance. The result is a figure that looks like an X. The higher the IMCP score, the higher the probability of agreeing that textbooks should be written to reflect the diversity of the country. And the higher the IMCP score, the lower the probability of agreeing that there should be less emphasis on diversity.

Now, for a harder question. How should differences in the process of textbooks being written to reflect diversity affect the readiness of the tolerant to embrace them? Reasoning from results like those in panel A, our expectation was that the more tolerant majority citizens are, the less sensitive they would be to differences in how textbooks are changed. Perhaps they would slightly prefer textbooks being written rather than rewritten to reflect diversity; perhaps they would not care at all about the difference. But the more they value inclusion, the less importance they would attach to the difference in processes for achieving it. So we reasoned. We were wrong.

Panel B in figure 5.6 displays the responses to the textbook experiment—written versus rewritten to reflect the new diversity of the country—again as a function of scores on the IMCP index. The solid line tracks the probability of support for textbooks being written to reflect the new diversity of the country; the dotted line traces the probability of support for their being rewritten to do exactly the same thing. Naturally, the stronger the support for inclusive tolerance, the higher the level of support for textbooks acknowledging diversity will be. How could it be otherwise?

The vital question is whether the distinction between textbooks being written versus their being rewritten strikes a chord of belief deep enough to matter to the most tolerant. Panel B gives a clear-cut answer. Yes, it matters as much, if not more, to those who are most supportive of inclusive tolerance as to those who are least. The marginal difference at each level of tolerance is not large, but the marginal difference occurs throughout the distribution, including the densest part of the IMCP distribution, where most members of the majority group are concentrated. A measure of the importance of the terms on which inclusion is to be carried out is that they matter even to those who are most strongly in favor of inclusion.

ENVOI

The aim of this chapter was to probe, to look for terms on which non-Muslim majority citizens are open to including ethnic and religious diversity as a feature of their country's identity. In the process, we have followed a new track, employing sequential factorials to investigate their readiness to go along with the quasi-official role of the educational system in identifying who belongs and defining what their country stands for. Each trial in the sequence of textbook experiments is fallible. But the full sequence of experimental trials provides a greater measure of confidence than studies of public opinion commonly can muster. An invaluable measure of confidence, we should add, considering our decision to make minimal variations in treatment terms. The stability of the pattern of responses, over repeated trials and across countries, is key.

There are many ways of going wrong in reporting research, but some are more seductive than others. Among the most seductive is to highlight what is novel in how the research was done at the expense of what is substantively important. We have emphasized the benefits of iterative sequences of experimental trials. But our primary objective is to probe for

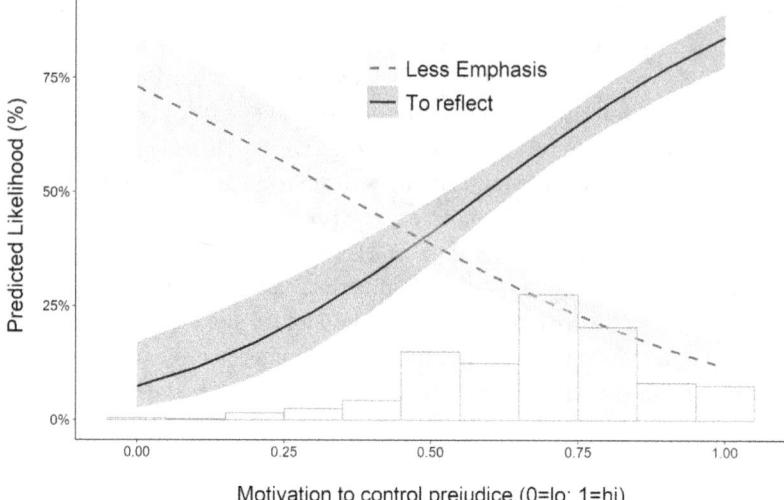

PANEL A

Data source: Norwegian Citizen Panel (2018) Wave 12

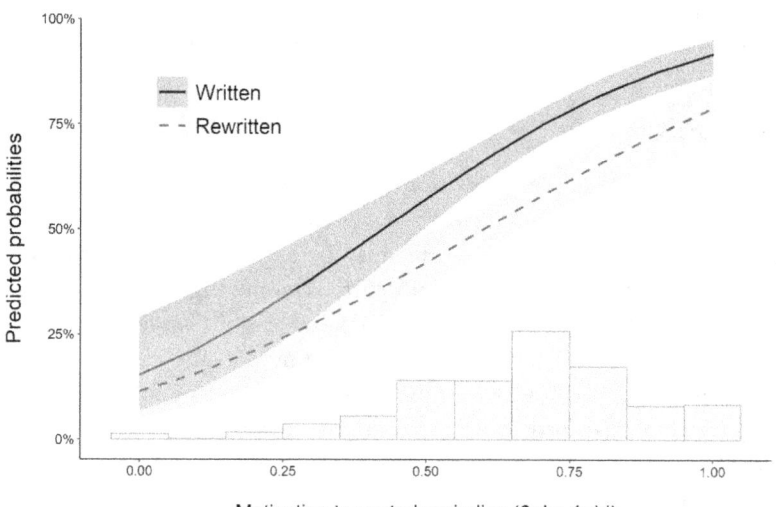

PANEL B

Data source: Norwegian Citizen Panel (2014) Wave 2

FIGURE 5.6. THE CONTINUITY PRINCIPLE BY INCLUSIVE TOLERANCE. Panel A: Assigned vs. Constructed National Identity. Letters should be written with less emphasis on/to reflect diversity. Norway, Predicted likelihood of approval (%) by IMCP. Panel B: Continuity vs. Interruption in the Process of National Identity Construction. Letters should be written/rewritten to reflect diversity. Norway, Predicted likelihood of approval (%) by IMCP.

openings, possible paths forward to more inclusive societies. Hence the importance of the consistency of results over multiple rounds of experimental trials with the overarching hypothesis that continuity in the process of national identity construction provides an opening to a more inclusive national identity.

[CHAPTER SIX]
TAKING PART

Images of Citizenship

Inclusion makes demands on minorities as well as majorities. If the goal is to be included in Sweden or Norway on equal terms with Swedes or Norwegians who are members of the majority group, the challenge for Muslim minorities is to become Swedes or Norwegians without having to give up their identity as Muslims. Citizenship, then, is our concern—citizenship in its broadest sense.

PARTICIPATORY DEMOCRACY

To truly be a part of a democratic politics, citizens must take part in its political life. This is the intuition underpinning participatory democracy. It is not obvious, certainly not immediately obvious, that the idea of participatory democracy is relevant to modern democratic politics. The decisions open to citizens' direct influence are limited. Representative democracy houses the levers of power. This is fortunate, or so many political scientists have concluded, since systematic research has documented how little attention citizens regularly pay to public affairs, how little of consequence they know about them, and how erratic are the positions they take on them.[1] To be sure, recent decades have seen the development of a literature on direct democracy showing that participation, for example in referenda, has an educative effect.[2] But this research has perhaps not had the impact that it deserves—or, to bring the point home, not had the impact on *us* that it deserves. This chapter is an account of how we got on the wrong track at the beginning of our inquiry by not taking to heart recent research on participatory democracy, and how, thanks to the good fortune of a compelling criticism, we were directed to the right one.

Muslim immigrants, here and now, are uniquely at risk of being suspected of choosing to give their loyalty to the countries they came from, not the country they came to live in. The challenge of majority citizens' presuming bad faith on the part of Muslim minorities is well recognized in the literature, and we discuss it at length in chapter 7. The question before us is, how Muslims can demonstrate that their allegiance is to the country they now live in?

Pledging allegiance is a form of political theater—public ceremonies in which citizens salute the flag, recite the national anthem, march in holiday parades, and the like. If Muslims declare their loyalty, we reasoned, then they stand a better chance of being fully included as part of the citizenry. To show that this is so, we designed an experiment to demonstrate the power of symbolic declarations of loyalty. Instead, it brought to light something else entirely—something, we are happy to have the opportunity to acknowledge, that colleagues predicted it would show before we or they learned the results of the experiment. This, then, is a story of research serendipity—a report on how an investigation of symbolic politics turned into an analysis of the participatory citizen.[3]

The argument for participatory democracy is made on many grounds, among them, gains in political equality, legitimacy, the knowledge and enlightened values that citizens acquire by virtue of participating in politics, and not least, the quality of decisions citizens make thanks to the opportunity to discuss, to deliberate, to learn by taking part in civic life.[4] This is a long list. All the same, we propose to add yet one more item: minority inclusion. The challenge for Muslim minorities is to actually be, and not merely show that they want to be, part of their new society.

SYMBOLIC POLITICS

Muslim immigrants are outsiders twice over: once because native citizens categorize them as outsiders and again because native citizens believe that Muslims categorize themselves as outsiders, identifying with the culture and country they have left, not the culture and country they now live in. This stigma of suspect loyalty is a major obstacle to inclusion. What can Muslims themselves do to overcome this stigma? Our initial master idea was the power of political theater and gesture: the strategy, to demonstrate the power of symbolic declarations of loyalty. Hence we started off the inquiry with the Loyalty Declaration experiment.

THE LOYALTY DECLARATION EXPERIMENT

Three principles guided the design of the Loyalty Declaration experiment. One is impact. A report of an action by Muslim immigrants must be capable of attracting the attention of the wider public. To catch the public's attention, an out-of-the-ordinary event is necessary. Novelty and visibility are thus design requirements. A third is the necessity of collective action. A symbolic act of declaring loyalty cannot be the act of an individual Muslim. It must be the act of the community. Novelty, visibility, and community action, then, are the principles that the Loyalty Declaration experiment builds on.[5] The intuition is that, by means of attention-catching symbolic acts, Muslim communities can induce majority citizens to see them as members of a common community sharing common values.

Sweden is the country in which we began our probe. Every country falls short of its ideal self-image, of course. But Sweden falls a shorter distance than most.[6] For decades, Swedes have shown themselves to be consistently more tolerant than citizens from other Western European countries.[7] A belief in equality, broadmindedness, and mutual respect is embedded in the Swedish culture. Not surprisingly, Swedes historically have felt an obligation to reach out to the disadvantaged, to bring them into the life of the larger society. But part of the responsibility for inclusion falls on minorities. As Swedes are asked to value diversity, so immigrants are asked to accept Swedish values—not all its values, but its civic values at least. A commitment to doing so, made publicly by Muslims acting as a community, is the heart of the Loyalty Declaration experiment.

We chose the device of a newspaper story.[8] All respondents read a brief report on a local event that ostensibly had appeared in a recent newspaper. The largest part of the newspaper story was the same for all respondents: "Muslim community leaders and members in Stockholm held a very large meeting Tuesday. The meeting was called to [. . . —diverse reasons were given]. The meeting began at 7:30 p.m. Many people spoke. Many ideas were discussed. At the end of the meeting, the community leaders voted with enthusiasm in support of [. . .]." After reading what the community leaders voted in support of, all respondents were asked "Do you agree (strongly or somewhat) or disagree (strongly or somewhat) that 'Muslims in Sweden have respect for the culture and way of life of others.'"

Respondents were assigned at random to one of three conditions. In the Symbolic Declaration condition, the newspaper story reports that the purpose of the community meeting was to support "a proclamation that it is the responsibility of Muslims to demonstrate that their primary loyalty is to their new country, Sweden." In contrast, in the Accusation condition, the newspaper story reports that the purpose of the meeting is to support "a proclamation that the government of Sweden should increase efforts to protect Muslims from discrimination." Finally, in the control condition, the newspaper story reports that the purpose of the community meeting is to produce "a new draft of the budget"—a phrase deliberately chosen to be uninformative, providing no actual information about why the meeting is being held.

Straightforwardly, the symbolic politics hypothesis holds that a declaration of loyalty will increase the probability of a comparatively positive response to Muslims; while a charge of discrimination and call for government action to combat it will do the opposite. These are commonsense expectations, no more. But the purpose of this first experiment was only to initiate a progression of experimental trials on the power of symbolic politics, beginning at a point where we could be confident about the ground we were standing on.

At this point, the story of the Loyalty Declaration experiment took an unexpected turn. As part of a campaign to call attention to the virtues of survey experiments, we gave a presentation at the University of Southern Denmark. The data had been collected but not yet analyzed. We presented our hypotheses, then described the experimental protocol. Immediately, an objection was raised. The control condition is not a true control condition, colleagues contended.[9] Control conditions are meant to be neutral, neither increasing nor decreasing the likelihood of a positive or negative response. That, of course, was what we had intended. The stated purpose of the meeting in the control condition, to vote on "a new draft of the budget," says nothing about what the budget is for; nothing about who it is supposed to benefit or what community needs it is meant to meet. The budget, deliberately, is a *tabula rasa*.

So we thought. But we were wrong to think so, we were told, because in Sweden a meeting of citizens to create a budget is an example of civic action. It shows people who care about their community coming together to respond to community problems, to achieve community goals. If this reasoning is right, the control condition does not describe a meeting without any real content. Instead, the resulting newspaper story conveys a positive message of Muslims actively participating in community life, coming to decisions together, meeting their social responsibilities to fellow citizens. What we had intended as a content-free story is, in the context of Scandinavian culture, a report of Muslims new to Sweden exemplifying the values of Sweden.

And what did the Loyalty Declaration experiment reveal when the data were analyzed? Native citizens who are told that the purpose of the meeting is to protest discrimination are the least likely to agree that Muslims have respect for the values of others (M = 2.82; SE = .03)—not exactly an electrifying outcome.[10] Nor is it surprising that native citizens who are told that the purpose of the meeting is to have Muslims declare that their primary loyalty is to their new country are more likely to agree that Muslims share the values of the larger society (2.99; .02). What is surprising—certainly, it was to us—is that respondents in the control condition were the most likely to agree that Muslims "have respect for the culture and ways of life of others" (3.06; .03).[11] Yes, the differences between experimental conditions are modest. But this qualifies as a textbook example of when judgment by p values should be put aside. The significance of outcomes is relative to expectations. We had supposed that the control condition was neutral. Our colleagues hypothesized that it conveys a positive message of Muslims being civically engaged. They were right; we were wrong.

Getting the characterization of the control condition of the Loyalty Experiment wrong—for the reason that our critics got it right— switched our focus from a study of symbolic politics to a study of the participatory citizen.

CITIZENSHIP AS PARTICIPATION

Contemporary political science focuses on two roles of democratic citizenship: retrospective, punishing public officials for poor performance by voting them out of office; and prospective, signaling courses of action for which office holders will be rewarded.[12] In contrast, classical political theory spotlights the role of democratic citizenship as educative.[13]

To a modern political scientist, to characterize political participation as educative might be appropriate in a high school civics textbook. It is now broadly (albeit not consensually) agreed that citizens know little about public affairs. Their ideas are put together higgledy-piggledy.[14] Their understanding of democratic principles is shallow. They are all too likely to say just the opposite of what they said the previous time they were asked their political convictions, because a different set of considerations chanced to come to mind. In any case, the high-water mark for political participation for far and away most citizens is casting a vote, once every few years or so.

Curiously, it is commonly supposed that "classical democratic" theorists are so caught up in thinking about the way that things should be, that they can't see what is in plain sight—namely, that the ordinary citizen is only intermittently and minimally interested in politics and public affairs and is therefore chronically minimally informed about them.[15] In fact, if by a "classical democratic" theorist, you have in mind a political analyst like John Stuart Mill, he is admirably clear-eyed about the limitations of ordinary citizens. What does he think? They know too little; care too little; do too little. But, for Mill, the way that citizens are now is the beginning, not the end, of the matter. Must they always be as they are? he asks. And if they can be different, to more nearly live up to the responsibilities of democratic citizenship, how can they achieve their potential?

The question Mill then asks is, What can be done to enlarge regular citizens' understanding and engagement with politics and public affairs so that they are better capable of discharging the duties of democratic citizenship? The standing presumption is that ordinary citizens must get ready first—that they must learn what they do not yet know and form the moral habits of a responsible citizen that they have not yet formed—in order to be fit for democratic citizenship. But for Mill, believing that people must first learn what they need to know to be good citizens gets the problem the wrong way around. The political ignorance and irresponsibility of ordinary citizens is a consequence of a failure to participate in politics. So he writes: "The nation as a whole, and every individual composing it, are without any voices in their own destiny. They exercise no will in respect to their collective interests. All is decided for them by a will not their own, which it is legally a crime for them to disobey. What sort of human beings can be formed under such a regime? What development can their thinking or their active facilities attain under it?"[16]

And the remedy? By participating in politics, citizens become fit to participate in a democratic politics: become, that is, public-regarding rather than self-regarding, informed rather than ignorant, active rather than passive. This may have the appearance of a paradox: How can a person perform the duties of a citizen without first learning how to perform them? On the contrary, Mill maintains, it is common sense. "We do not learn to read or write, to ride or swim, by being merely told how to do it, but by doing it."[17]

This is an idea that Mill thought through. To be educative, participation has to be involving. Voting, certainly, does not qualify as participation in politics. "A political act," Mill notes with some asperity, "to be done only once in a few years, and for which nothing in the daily habits of citizenship has prepared him, leaves his intellect and his moral dispositions very much as it found them" (1963, 229).[18] If voting is not sufficient, what then about the other forms of political participation that modern political scientists have studied?—attending political rallies, joining a campaign, contributing money to a candidate, or writing a representative. They won't do the job either.

To obtain the benefits of participating in politics, one must do the real thing. Local government, Mill maintains, is the school of democratic politics. "It is only by practicing popular government on a limited scale, that the people will ever learn how to exercise it on a larger."[19] Mill—it should be said, then said again—does not have a romanticized conception of the benefits of "practicing popular government." Its capacity to increase the competence of the average citizen is limited. Citizens active in local government, he recommends, should defer to national elites, at least as a general rule. The benefits are acquiring the habits of mind and learning the arts of working alongside others to achieve common goals. Participation in politics provides an "education in public responsibility."[20]

The serendipitous result of the experiment in Sweden—finding that Muslims taking part in a community meeting to achieve common goals evokes a positive response—brought to our minds Mill's ideas about participatory democracy. Civic participation, taking part in community affairs, working together with others to respond to common problems, is a value in the political culture of Scandinavia.[21] How do we learn best what others believe? Not by listening to what they say they believe, but by observing how they behave. Perhaps, we reasoned, our Swedish respondents were more open to believing that Muslims shared Swedish values, not because they said they did but because what they were doing—meeting as a community to meet a community concern—exemplified participatory values.

This is not, to say again, the idea we started with. We had presumed that doubts about the loyalty of Muslims could be eased, to some significant degree, by symbolic declarations of loyalty—by political theater. But far from confirming our reasoning, our experiment cut the ground from under it. A newspaper story of Muslims carrying out what we had supposed was an empty exercise, meeting to agree on a budget for no declared purpose, was the most effective way to persuade native citizens that they share common values.[22] Call this the Participatory Citizen hypothesis.

TAKING PART

The premise is that democratic citizenship consists in civic life. We do not suppose that this image of citizenship is shared to the same extent everywhere. It is part of the self-image of Nordic democracies, though we very much doubt that it is confined to them. Citizens are active. They go to community meetings. They are concerned not only for their own welfare but the welfare of those around them. They come together to face the problems that concern them as members of a community.

It is no accident that the words *civil*, *civic*, and *community* share the same root. Our revised hypothesis then is: by taking part in the life of their community, members of immigrant-origin minority groups are showing that they share the larger society's civic values; that they are not outsiders; that they are compatriots.[23]

THE ASYLUM SEEKER SEQUENCE

To get a better view of the power of participation as a mechanism for becoming accepted as "one of us," we developed the Asylum Seeker sequence of survey experiments. The template and the three trials are laid out in table 6.1. The reasoning that led to the template is this: asylum is not automatic. Refugees must prove they have a legitimate ground. A fear of persecution for political beliefs or activities is a legitimate ground; a desire to be economically better off is not. Crucially, to determine whether refugees' claims for asylum are legitimate or not, a quasi-judicial system has been established. This system provides the full benefit of a multistage legal process. Asylum seekers have the opportunity to formally present their case and have it considered on individual merit. They also have the opportunity to formally appeal an adverse decision. Every judicial process, quasi and otherwise, is imperfect. But the assessment of claims to a legitimate reason for asylum has every appearance of a good faith effort to make decisions on a fair basis.

There is always a concern that, presented with a choice to help or not to help others, people will say not what they believe but rather what they believe they ought to say. The provision of a full and fair legal process helps mitigate a susceptibility to "faking nice." The claim to asylum has been

TABLE 6.1. THE ASYLUM SEEKER SEQUENCE

Trial # Country (Year)	1 Norway (March 2015)	European Refugee Crisis (2015–16)	2 Norway March 2016	3 Denmark 2016
Target group fill 1	Asylum seekers		Asylum seekers	Asylum seekers
Target group fill 2	Muslim asylum seekers		Muslim asylum seekers	Muslim asylum seekers
Participation fill 1	NONE		NONE	NONE
Participation fill 2	Learned the language			Learned the language
Participation fill 3	Found a job			Found a job
Participation fill 4	Actively participated in the local community		Actively participated in the local community	Actively participated in the local community

Repeatable template: Every year [COUNTRY] rejects a number of asylum applications. Applicants are entitled to file formal appeals, and some do so. Sometimes it takes several years before a final decision is made. Do you think that [TARGET GROUP FILL] who have been living in [COUNTRY] for several years [PARTICIPATION FILL] while they are waiting for a decision to be made should be granted residence, even if their appeals are rejected? Or do you think that they should not be allowed to stay?

assessed. It has failed to meet the necessary legal standards, not once but twice. Of course, even if you know that an asylum applicant does not meet the legal standards to qualify for asylum, you may sympathize with them on other grounds and believe that they, therefore, should be allowed to stay nonetheless. But it would be fantasy to suggest that a societal norm has been established pressuring majority citizens to agree that asylum seekers should be allowed to stay even if it has been determined that they do not meet the legal standard for asylum. We take full advantage of this logic in the Asylum Seeker sequence.

As the textbox below table 6.1 shows, the template employed is lengthier than in previous sequences. All respondents were told: "Every year [COUNTRY] rejects a number of asylum applications. Applicants are entitled to file formal appeals, and some do so. Sometimes it takes several years before a final decision is made." In the control condition, respondents were then asked: "Do you think that Muslim asylum seekers who have been living in [COUNTRY] for several years while they are waiting for a decision to be made should be granted residence, even if their appeals are rejected? Or do you think that they should not be allowed to stay?" In the main treatment condition, respondents were additionally told that the asylum seekers "have participated actively in their local communities" and then were asked whether they should be allowed to stay even if their appeals for residence have been rejected.

The sequence consists of three trials. Each of them also varies whether the asylum seeker in question is specified as Muslim or not. In none of the trials did the distinction influence the results. So we report only the results for the conditions that explicitly mention that asylum seekers are Muslim. After the first trial had been conducted in March 2015, exogenous events occurred that strongly impacted the asylum situation in all of Europe, not least in Scandinavia. The refugee crisis that peaked in the fall of 2015, a dramatic period for all involved, demonstrably influenced attitudes toward refugees and immigrants as well as voting patterns across many European systems.[24] For the Asylum Seeker sequence, this presented a unique opportunity to test if the results of the first trial, conducted at a time of relative tranquility and low salience of the refugee issue, would replicate at a time of stress and high tensions. Trials 2 and 3 were conducted in just such a heated context in both countries where trials were fielded, Norway and Denmark.

THE POWER OF PARTICIPATION

As a test of the Participatory Citizen hypothesis, it should suffice to observe that native citizens are significantly more likely to favor asylum applicants who are active in their communities being allowed to stay—*significantly* meaning, of course, substantively and not simply statistically. But there is much to be said for raising the bar to put the Participatory Citizen hypothesis to a tougher test. Does civic participation matter as much as other considerations that we know are substantively important? Accordingly, in a separate condition of the experiment, the asylum seekers are described as having learned Norwegian; and in a final condition, they have gotten a job. Both are accomplishments that previous research has demonstrated evoke a positive response from native citizens because both alleviate concerns about the economic and cultural costs of immigration.[25] The dependent variable is a dichotomy: either respondents affirmatively support the asylum seeker staying in Norway or they fail to do so. Whether they fail because they reject the asylum seekers staying or are merely uncertain whether they do or do not support them is neither here nor there; the point is that they have failed to support the asylum seeker staying.

Figure 6.1 presents the results of the first trial in the Asylum Seeker sequence. The first thing to note is that, in all conditions of the experiment, only a minority are in favor of allowing asylum seekers to stay. Which is reassuring from the point of view of opinion measurement. The asylum seekers have had their petitions to stay denied, after having had the benefit of going through a formal appeal process. If the general reaction was that they should nonetheless be allowed to stay, the validity of the measure would have been impeached. What is also reassuring is that the results of figure 6.1 are consistent with those of prior research. Learning the language has regularly been found to induce a positive response; so, too, has getting a job.[26] Both, obviously, are ways to demonstrate that one has become part of the larger society.

So, too, as figure 6.1 shows, is taking an active part in community affairs. Slightly more than one in three take the position that Muslim asylum seekers should be allowed to stay, even though their petition to stay has been rejected, if they have taken an active part in the life of their communities. Civic activity is as strong a recommendation as getting a job or learning

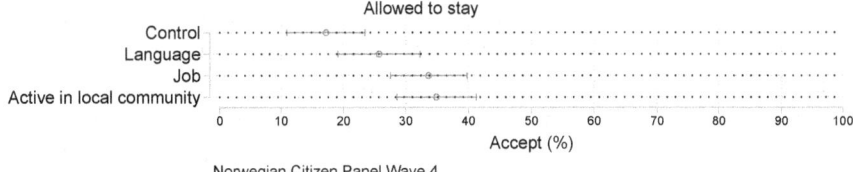

FIGURE 6.1. THE ASYLUM SEEKER SEQUENCE: THE PRE-CRISIS TRIAL. The asylum seeker has learned the language/gotten a job/been active in the local community/BLANK and should be allowed to stay. Norway, March 2015, % Accept.

the language of one's new country. Taking part in civic life is an example of citizenship, of being part, even for those who are demonstrably not citizens in a formal way.[27]

THE REFUGEE CRISIS

The results of the Asylum Seeker sequence point to the role that minorities can play in influencing their own prospects of being included. There are of course good grounds for skepticism about one-off results as a general matter. There are even stronger reasons for skepticism in this case.

Reactions to Muslim immigrants are predictably subject to unpredictable shocks. The Asylum Seeker sequence was conducted in the spring of 2015, shortly before the explosion of the European refugee crisis. In Norway, the number of refugee applications had been low and steady for years, seldom more than one thousand and more often only about half that number each month, as figure 6.2 shows. But beginning August 2015, the number jumped to two thousand, then surged to four thousand in September, skyrocketing to eight thousand in October, and nearly as many in November. Then the crisis was brought to an end, the numbers plummeting to one thousand in December and sinking to a few hundred in the months thereafter.

It deserves a moment to appreciate the shock of a crisis on this scale in a country of only a little over five million. Nothing like it had been experienced before. Nothing was in place to cope with it. There was no time for systematic planning; no time to consult; no time to prepare the public, to alleviate anxieties real people feel confronting a crisis like this. Centers to house and to feed asylum seekers, to provide medical care, to process applications for asylum had to be set up on the fly. However native citizens may have felt about refugees and asylum seekers before the refugee crisis, there is more than enough reason to believe that, in the face of a shock on this scale, their impulse to be generous will shrivel.

The Asylum Seeker experiment was accordingly repeated a year later, in March 2016, only four months after the peak surge in arrivals of people seeking refuge. This timing is as nearly immediately after the "treatment" of the influx of refugees as can be hoped for. Moreover, to better capture even relatively small responses to the refugee crisis, the design of the experiment is simplified. By eliminating the "learning Norwegian" and "getting a job" conditions, we increase the statistical power to determine whether community participation makes a substantively significant difference after the crisis as it had before.

Figure 6.3 reports the results. The key is the difference between how Norwegians felt before the crisis and how they felt after it—or rather the absence

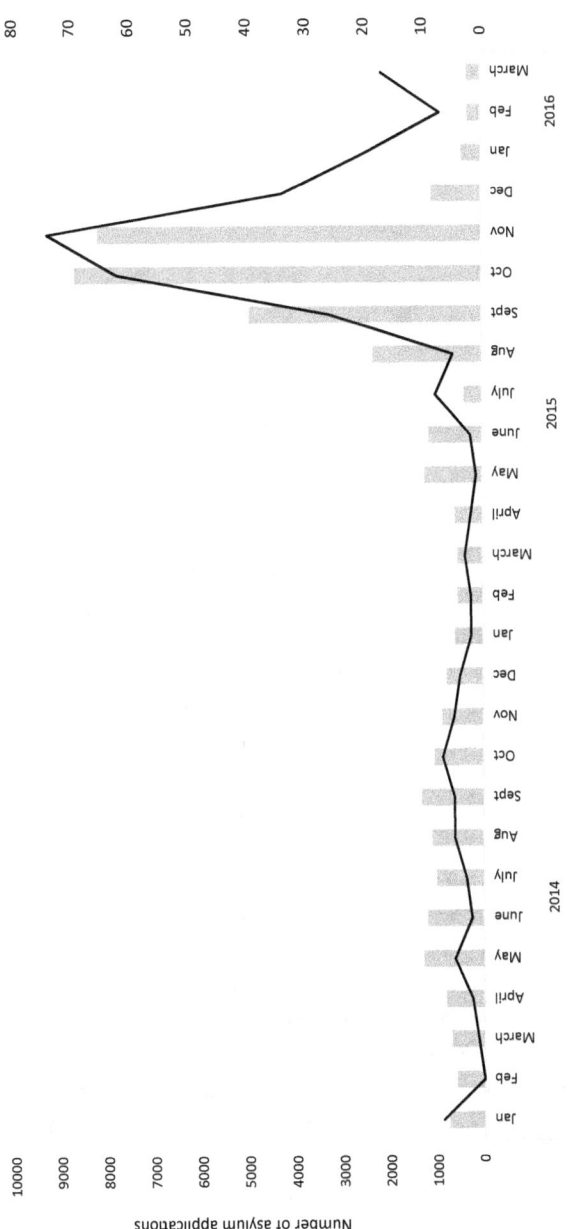

FIGURE 6.2. THE 2015 REFUGEE CRISIS IN NORWAY. Monthly numbers of refugee arrivals and establishment of new asylum centers, January 2014–March 2016. Source: The monthly number of asylum applications are freely available official statistics from the Directorate of Immigration (Utlendingsdirektoratet, UDI). The list of new asylum centers was obtained from the Directorate of Immigration specifically for this study.

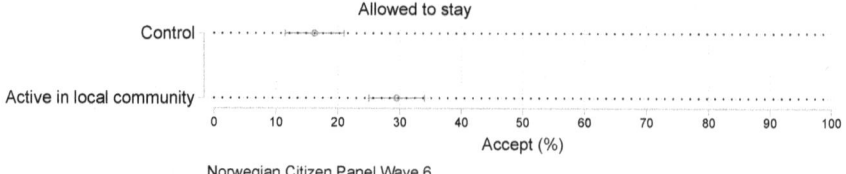

FIGURE 6.3. THE ASYLUM SEEKER SEQUENCE: THE CRISIS TRIAL. The asylum seeker has been active in the local community/BLANK and should be allowed to stay. Norway, March 2016, % Accept.

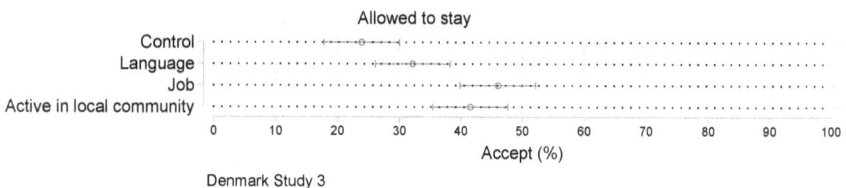

FIGURE 6.4. THE ASYLUM SEEKER SEQUENCE: THE GENERALIZABILITY TRIAL. The asylum seeker has learned the language/gotten a job/been active in the local community/BLANK and should be allowed to stay. Denmark, 2016, % Accept.

of any difference. The positive effect of having actively participated in the local community pre- and post-crisis are virtually indistinguishable. Both times, those who learn asylum seekers are active in their communities are significantly more likely to favor their being allowed to stay; where significantly means substantively significant, not merely statistically significant. Indeed figure 6.3 shows that they are on the order of twice as likely to support their being allowed to stay in the treatment condition as in the control condition.

It of course may be objected that the warmth of this response to Muslims taking part in community affairs is peculiar to Norway. Hence our decision to also repeat the Asylum Seeker template in its full version in Denmark, also in the immediate aftermath of the refugee crisis.[28] As figure 6.4 shows, the pattern of effects of the experimental treatments in the trial conducted in Denmark matches that of the trials conducted in Norway.[29] Both getting a job and learning the language boost the likelihood of a positive response, again. The effect of the former is somewhat stronger than that of the latter, again. And learning that asylum seekers are active in their communities evokes a positive response again, indeed, as favorable a response as getting a job.

THE SEAT AT THE TABLE EXPERIMENT

It would not be unfair to characterize the efficacy of a survey experiment to illuminate what is going on as nearer a candle than a searchlight. The result can be discerned, thanks to the power of randomization. But shadows always surround it. After all, a survey question is only a question in a public opinion interview, subject to all the limitations and uncertainties of any question in a public opinion interview.

So it is here. The results of the Asylum Seeker sequence show that asylum seekers strongly recommend themselves as deserving to stay by taking an active part in the life of their community. But it does not follow that civic participation more broadly practiced earns Muslim minorities plaudits for being good citizens. Taking an active part in the life of *their* communities is a good thing, in the eyes of majority citizens. But Muslims wanting to have a say in how things work out in *our* communities is another. Perhaps majority citizens believe that's a very different cup of tea. Who are *they* to have a say in what happens to *us*?

Hence the Seat at the Table experiment. Norway has three levels of government: local, national, and in between the two, regional. The regional level is the least powerful but has substantial responsibilities—among them, high schools, cultural heritage management, and public transport. The regional level is therefore a good level of governance to focus on to get a view of openness to minorities taking part in decisions that are not glamorous but bear on important aspects of everyday life. The question is, how open are majority citizens to minorities having a seat at the table at an advisory council at this level of governance?

What does it mean to be "open" to minorities taking part in making decisions, the consequences of which will affect the welfare of majorities as well as minorities? Minimally, not opposing minority participation; ideally, welcoming it. The first is necessary, the second desirable. Determining both is challenging. The Seat at the Table experiment accordingly has four conditions, two exclusionary alternatives asking directly or indirectly about a preference for a homogeneous council and two inclusionary alternatives, one asking about a preference for a diverse council and the other adding the complication of having to reach consensus.

The introductory text to the experiment reads: "Imagine that you have been asked to participate in a regional council tasked with finding solutions to challenges in developing your region." In one of the exclusionary conditions, respondents are asked to take a position on whether "it is best for the region if only people who share the same ethnic and religious backgrounds take part." This is as close to an "in-your-face" rejection of minority participation as we dared venture. In the second exclusionary condition, respondents were asked if they agreed or disagreed that "it is best for a region if only people with a long experience of living in the region take part."

Consider the requirement of having "long experience living in the region." The criterion of "experience" is systematically ambiguous. Some majority citizens, including likely a nontrivial number who are open to inclusive tolerance, will favor a participant in the regional council having experience because they believe that living in the region brings knowledge of its problems and potential. Because experience on its face can be a legitimate consideration, a requirement of "long experience in a region" can serve as a defensible proxy to screen out minorities.

In the inclusionary conditions, we first ask straightforwardly about a preference for diverse representation: whether they agree or disagree that "it is best for the region if people of different ethnic and religious backgrounds participate." In the other inclusionary condition, we introduce a complication—a requirement of reaching a consensus. Respondents are asked whether they agree or disagree that "it is best for the region if people of diverse ethnic and religious backgrounds must be in complete agreement on the final recommendations."

A requirement for a diverse council reaching consensus, the fourth condition in the experiment, also calls for comment. In crafting it, we meant to assess if those who are open to accepting minorities at the table nevertheless will have second thoughts if obtaining consensus is a requirement. This may sound ham-handed, but in a political culture like Norway's, agreement in coming to decisions is traditionally prized.[30] The wording makes the point forcefully in asking whether it is best for the region that people of different ethnic and religious backgrounds "have to" come to "complete agreement" about the council's recommendations. Our expectation was that introducing the requirement of consensus would make a considerable number of those who would otherwise favor diversity back away.

Figure 6.5 displays the main results of the experiment. Consider first those who were asked about a preference for homogeneous representation. The results are remarkable. In a country that until recently considered itself ethnically and religiously homogeneous, very few, on the order of one in five, think it is best for the region if the council is ethnically and religiously homogeneous. To be sure, considerably more, about twice as many, think it would be best for the region if the council were made up of people who had long experience living in the region. But what should take one's breath away is how many think that it is best for the region if those who are at the table have ethnically and religiously diverse backgrounds. Nearly 80 percent of those offered that alternative agreed to it. This is twice as many as agreed to the exclusionary option deliberately constructed so as not to raise any immediate red flags about minority discrimination.

The final takeaway from figure 6.5 is the difference that the complication of having to meet a requirement of reaching a consensus makes for

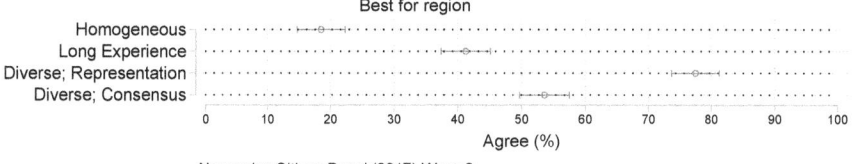

FIGURE 6.5. THE SEAT AT THE TABLE EXPERIMENT: DIVERSE VS. HOMOGENEOUS REGIONAL COUNCIL. Best for the region if people of homogenous background participate/ who have long experience living in region participate/of diverse backgrounds participate/ of diverse backgrounds have to reach consensus. Norway, % Agree.

openness to diversity in the regional council. If reaching a consensus is a premise of the council's work, then the number who think a diverse council is good for the region drops considerably. The majority is still on the side of thinking that diversity is good for the region, and this option is favored by a larger share than are the two exclusionary options. Nevertheless, approval of diversity drops considerably, suggesting that those who are open to inclusive tolerance differentiate between the best recommendations for the region, where diversity is prized by most, and consensual recommendations, where considerably fewer think diversity is a good idea.

Just as in the case of the Less Emphasis condition included in the second of Textbook experiment trial presented in chapter 5, the Seat at the Table experiment offers an opportunity to test whether those who say they are open to inclusive tolerance come down on the side of inclusion when they are offered a choice between inclusionary and exclusionary options. Figure 6.6 therefore graphs responses to all four conditions by IMCP score. The figure shows that for those who score above the midpoint on the IMCP scale (.5), inclusionary options are preferred over exclusionary ones. For those who score the lowest on the IMCP, the pattern of preferences is exactly the opposite.

Figure 6.6 also shows that the difference between the two exclusionary and the two inclusionary lines expand somewhat as we move left to right on the figure from the least motivated to control prejudice to the most. This means the distinctions we introduced, on both the exclusionary and the inclusionary sides, matter more to those who are open to inclusive tolerance than those who are not.

It is the larger takeaway of the Seat at the Table experiment that calls for attention. The largest number of majority citizens reject the opportunities put before them to restrict or to eliminate minority participation in political decisions, the consequences of which will be felt by both the majority and the minority in the region where they live. And they endorse the oppor-

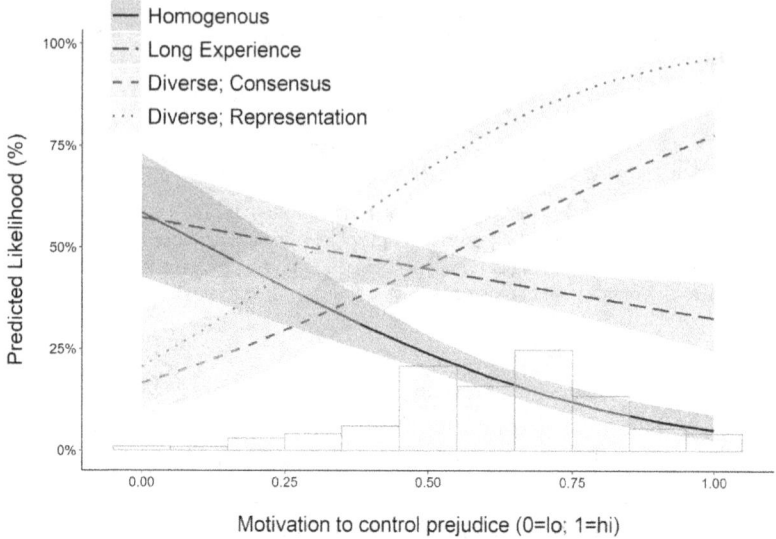

FIGURE 6.6. PREFERENCE FOR DIVERSE OR HOMOGENEOUS REGIONAL COUNCIL BY INCLUSIVE TOLERANCE. Norway, Predicted likelihood of approval (%) by IMCP.

tunities put before them to promote a more inclusive politics, with ethnic and religious minorities participating alongside majority citizens in making final decisions, the consequences of which will be felt by both. Which is to say, the results contradict the notion that majority citizens believe that it is desirable for minorities to take an active part in the life of "their" community but not in "ours." It is, instead, consistent at all points with a claim that the largest share of non-Muslims are open to the idea of Muslims taking an active part in the civic life of the larger society.

BARRIERS

Muslims are not simply dependent on the good will of a majority. The choices they make, particularly whether to take part in common local community affairs, can help shape their lives. By taking an active part in the life of their communities, majority citizens are more likely to recognize that Muslim minorities have a natural place in the larger society. This is the main result of the Asylum Seeker sequence. The results of the Seat at the Table experiment similarly go some way to showing that majority citizens are open to Muslims taking an active part in decisions made for the society as a whole. But obviously it does not follow from these studies that Muslims are welcome to participate in just the same manner as majority citizens. We now turn to consider in more depth the issue of barriers that Muslims confront when seeking to participate that members of the majority group do not.

The Election Poll Volunteer Experiment: Cross versus Hijab

For this experiment, we chose election poll volunteers as our focus. Volunteers at the polls are there to monitor voting, to ensure that it is carried out as it should be, and above all, to ensure that voters who are just about to vote face no pressures to vote for one candidate or party rather than another. This is a model setting, we suggest, to assess reactions to visible religious symbols. Accordingly, we carried out an Election Poll Volunteer experiment, where in one condition the volunteer is wearing a cross; in the other, a hijab.

The main issue we examine is propriety: what is and is not appropriate to the circumstances. Here, as in the Letter to the Editor experiment discussed in chapter 4, propriety has two dimensions. What is desirable, what ought to be done, is one dimension. What is permissible, what ought to be allowed, is the other. The two are distinct in these circumstances. You yourself might believe that people monitoring the vote ought not wear symbols of religious identification. All the same, taking into account what they believe they should wear, you may come to a judgment that they should be allowed to wear the symbol.[31]

In the Poll Volunteer experiment, a random share of respondents in the Norwegian Citizen Panel are asked whether an election day poll volunteer "should wear a [hijab/necklace with a cross] *if she usually does so.*"[32] Note the stipulation "if she usually does so." That she should customarily wear a hijab (or a cross) meets the egocentric standard of appropriateness. It is what she, the election volunteer, deems fitting day-in and day-out. It is not a matter of her choosing to wear a religious symbol in order to influence a voter. The other two-thirds of the respondents are asked the same question, also with the stipulation of customary use of course, but from a sociocentric perspective: whether the election poll volunteer should be "allowed to wear" or "should be free to wear" a hijab (or a cross).[33]

Panels A through C in Figure 6.7 display the results of the Poll Volunteer experiment. There are two quite different takeaways. The first, as panel A shows, is evenhandedness. If the volunteer usually wears a religious symbol, it makes no difference whether it is a cross or a hijab that she is wearing. Neither is warmly welcomed: possibly, because in an increasingly secular Christian-heritage society there is discomfort with a display of religious

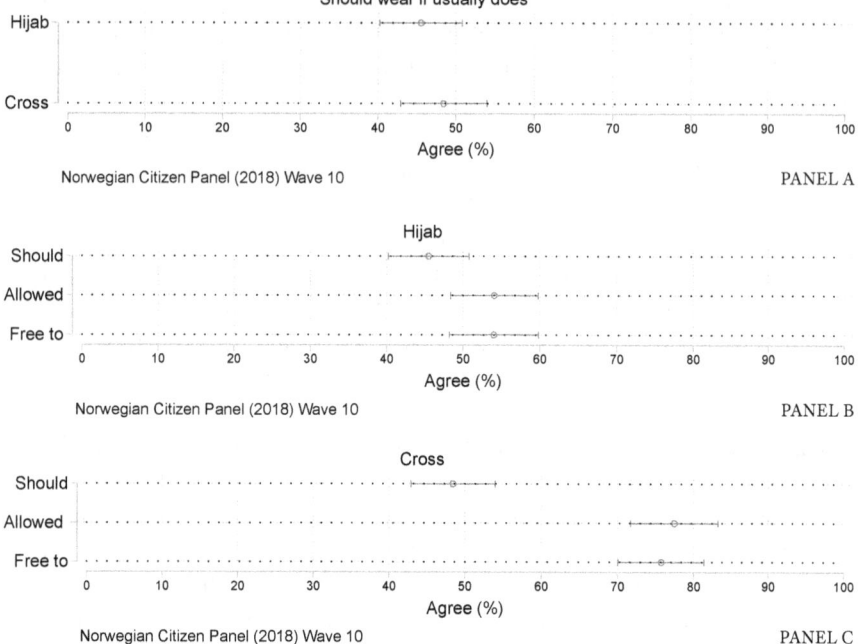

FIGURE 6.7. THE ELECTION DAY POLL VOLUNTEER EXPERIMENT. Panel A: Hijab vs. cross necklace. Should wear hijab/cross necklace if she usually does. Norway, % Agree. Panel B: Should vs. may distinction in hijab question. Should/Should be allowed/ Should be free to wear if she usually does. Norway, % Agree. Panel C: Should vs. may distinction in cross necklace question. Should/Should be allowed/ Should be free to wear if she usually does. Norway, % Agree.

commitment; more likely, because wearing a cross or hijab may send a possible political signal to citizens going into a voting booth. In any event, a half—no more—agree that the volunteer should wear a cross if she usually does; similarly, a half that she should wear a hijab if she usually does.

It is not a small thing that Muslims and Christians are held to the same standard of what is and what is not appropriate to do in a Christian-heritage society such as Norway. But when it comes to what they should be allowed to do as opposed to what they should do, there is anything but evenhandedness. The contrast between panels B and C in figure 6.7 brings this out. On the one hand, panel B shows that there is consensus—on the order of four in every five—who believe that an election poll volunteer should be allowed to wear a cross if she usually does. On the other hand, panel C displays that only a bit more than half believe she should be allowed to wear a hijab if she usually does. It is as though, if the issue is wearing a cross, native citizens recognize that what an election volunteer should do and should be allowed to do are two quite different questions. In contrast, if the issue instead is wearing a hijab, the two come to the same thing. The latitude extended to the election volunteer wearing a cross when the question is what should be allowed is not extended to her counterpart wearing a hijab.

There is a hard lesson here on the importance of the distinction between what one should do versus what one should be allowed to do. Here, in the Election Poll Volunteer experiment, as before in the Letter to the Editor experiments, over a wide range of issues and circumstances, in a democratic politics you ought to support the right of people to do what you, yourself, do not believe that it is right for them to do. But in this context, asking whether the poll watcher should be allowed to wear a cross (hijab) signals that there is an open question: perhaps yes, perhaps no. And the result: many more in the majority decide that the poll watcher should be allowed to wear a cross than be allowed to wear a hijab.

Discrimination—minorities being treated differently and worse than citizens who are members of the majority group because of ingrained intolerance—remains a deep societal issue. The results in panels B and C show discrimination in the aggregate. A considerably larger share of citizens wants to grant Christians latitude to wear symbols at the election booth. The societal tolerance for Muslims to stand out and be visible, to do and say what others disapprove of, is more limited than it is for Christians. Is this mainly a failure of those committed to inclusive tolerance to recognize the depth of the requirements of an inclusive society? Or is it mainly a problem of persistent intolerance?

The results of the analysis on display in panels A and B of figure 6.8 address these questions. Panel A first shows the variation in responses, by IMCP, in the case where we did not observe aggregate discrimination, when the issue is what the poll volunteer should wear. The figure demonstrates clearly that openness to inclusion matters decisively. There is blatant discrimination among those who are not strongly motivated to control prejudice. Among the most intolerant, nearly all, between 70 and 80 percent, believe that Christians should wear the cross as an election poll volunteer if they usually do so. Scarcely anyone among the intolerant think that Muslims should do the same. The difference in treatment is not only discriminatory, it is staggeringly so—it can hardly be bigger in a survey experiment. On the tolerant side of the figure, by contrast, the pattern is reversed. Those who score high on IMCP are not only likely to treat Muslims equally, they are more likely to believe that it is proper for a Muslim poll watcher to wear a hijab than for a Christian poll volunteer to wear a cross. The difference is not enormous, but it is telling. In the aggregate, the tendency of tolerant citizens to treat Muslims differently, and better,

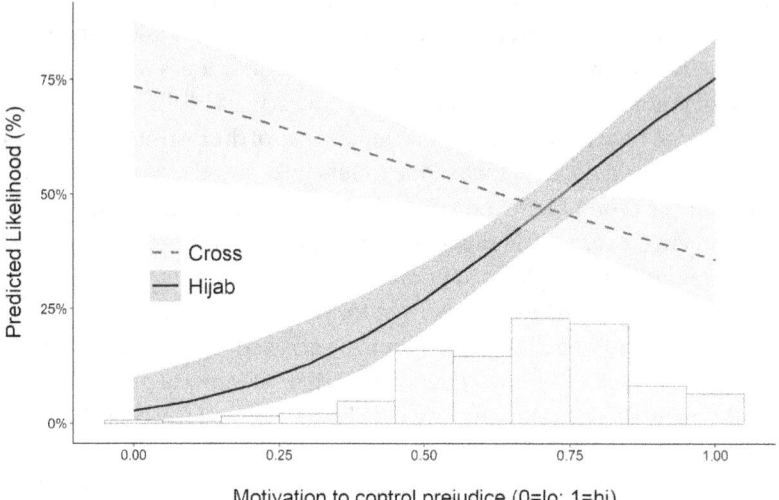

PANEL A

Data source: Norwegian Citizen Panel (2018) Wave 10

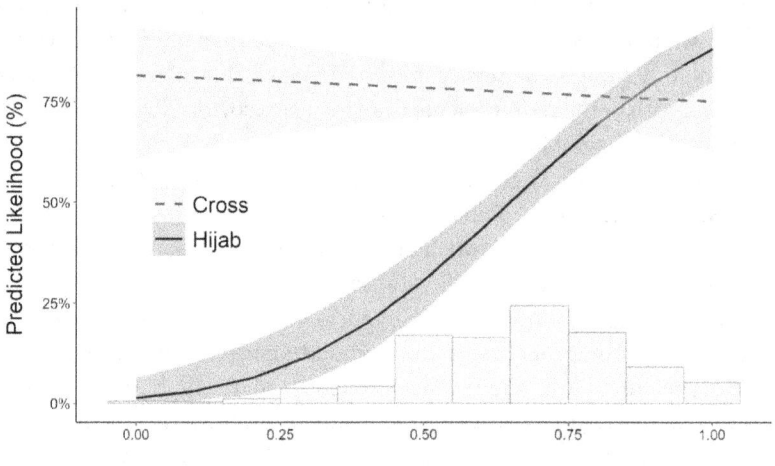

PANEL B

Data source: Norwegian Citizen Panel (2018) Wave 10

FIGURE 6.8. STANDARDS FOR PROPRIETY AND DISCRETION FOR CHRISTIANS AND MUSLIMS BY INCLUSIVE TOLERANCE. Panel A: Propriety. The election poll worker should wear hijab/cross necklace if she usually does. Norway, Predicted likelihood of approval (%) by IMCP. Panel B: Discretion. The election poll worker should be allowed to wear hijab/cross necklace if she usually does. Norway, Predicted likelihood of approval (%) by IMCP.

compensates for the tendency of the intolerant to treat them differently, and worse, in the question of what the election poll volunteer should wear.

Panel B parallels the setup of panel A, but this time the issue is what should the election poll volunteer *be allowed* to wear. Recall here that the main pattern was clear discrimination in the aggregate. It is for that reason all the more striking that the pattern in panel B is not all that different from the pattern seen in panel A. In both panels, there is at the low levels of motivation to control prejudice a pattern of stark discrimination—minorities being treated differently and worse with respect to *both* how they should behave and how they should be allowed to behave. In contrast, for those who score high on IMCP, the pattern is the opposite, or nearly so. Support for the principle that poll watchers should be allowed to wear a hijab if they usually do is just as high as for allowing them to wear a cross if they usually do—which is to say overwhelming at around 80 percent.

In summary, then, the Election Poll Volunteer experiment brings out the tenacity of intolerance and how it serves as a barrier to Muslims who wish to take part in local community affairs on a par with the majority religious group.

ENVOI

Muslims face a dilemma. The further that Muslim minorities go in sharing the beliefs and values of the larger society, the more likely they are to be accepted as members of the larger society. But the price of being accepted as members of the larger society risks a loss of their identity as Muslims. But our results suggest that this dilemma may not be quite as encompassing as many fear.

A key is the distinction between civic integration and cultural integration.[34] Following David Miller, we take civic integration to mean "people coming to share a set of principles and norms that guide their social and political life." Cultural integration, in contrast, is "when they share a common culture, which might mean having the same values and experiences, or on the other hand, having a common cultural identity."[35]

Civic and cultural integration differ on a number of dimensions, but the most relevant in this context is a difference in specificity versus vagueness. Civic integration has to do with particular behaviors. Minorities can pick them out by observing what native citizens do; native citizens can tell whether minorities share them by observing what minorities do. In contrast, it is far harder to pick out just what are the values and experiences that cultural integration consists in; and still harder, as a general principle (notable exceptions such as gender practices notwithstanding) for majorities to observe whether the views of minorities collide with theirs in societies in which cultural pluralism is itself becoming a progressively weightier value.

A final conclusion. What we believe others believe is grounded more deeply in their behavior than in their declarations of belief. This is the force of Miller's insight. The challenge for Muslim minorities in contemporary liberal democracies is to show that they "not only share a commitment to democracy as an abstract principle, but also share an understanding of what 'behaving like a democrat means.'"[36] This will not be easy, our results show intolerance remains a major obstacle, but there are openings to civic integration. Muslims who choose commitment to active citizenship and civic life are more likely to become included as fully part of liberal democratic societies.

[CHAPTER SEVEN]
LIBERAL VALUES AND MUSLIM COMMUNITIES

With time and good fortune, liberal democracies have brought to life a more expansive view of emancipative values—of liberty and equality most conspicuously, with other liberal ideals following in their wake, now including diversity.[1] Predictably unpredictable shocks (e.g., economic downturns, war, pandemic) have periodically stemmed or reversed the tide in the short run, so far. But no law of history rules out long-run democratic reversals.[2] Movements in one direction excite countermovements in another.[3] Yet, over time, the pressure of liberal values has pushed forward a larger-hearted understanding of liberal ideals, now encompassing inclusion of minorities previously marginalized from the larger society.

Our objective has been to take a further step and ask, On what terms are those who believe in liberal ideals most likely to favor a more inclusive society, on what terms least likely? That has brought to the fore the role of normative considerations and pivotal distinctions—between recognition respect and appraisal respect for one example, between what offensive speech media should or should not be allowed to transmit, for another. But always, the stronger majority citizens' belief in tolerance, the more open to inclusion they are. It is necessary now to face up to a darker side of the struggle for inclusion.

What sets the challenge of inclusion of Muslims in Western Europe apart is a conflict of values. A clash of values between non-Muslim majorities and Muslim minorities in contemporary liberal democracies is well documented, most conspicuously over the status of women, but also over child-rearing practices and, more broadly, the place of a traditional, hierarchical religious culture in a modern, cosmopolitan, democratic society.[4] From the perspective of the majority culture, the conflict is between liberal and illiberal values. What we aim to bring into view are the consequences of conflicts between liberal values themselves.

In normative theories of democratic politics, conflicts between liberal values take a well-worked shape. Having to choose between liberty and equality is the paradigmatic example. Both are liberal democratic ideals, but when a choice between them must be made, some rank liberty before equality, others equality before liberty. The conflict can be intense. But whatever the outcome, whether liberty comes out on top of equality or equality on top of liberty, the result is the advance of a liberal value. What is more, the person who values liberty also values equality, the person who values equality also values liberty. The worst outcome is that some get their second-best outcome.

What concerns us are malign conflicts between liberal values. Majority citizens who believe in tolerance are the main constituency for inclusionary proposals—they are Muslim minorities' best allies in the struggle for inclusion. One response to conflict between the values of a liberal democratic society and a traditional, religious culture is exit. Those who believe in liberal ideals can choose to stand aside in the struggle for inclusion because of their belief in liberal ideals. This is the situation we discussed at the end of chapter four regarding offensive speech. Our concern now is a more perverse outcome—when liberals make illiberal choices because they believe in liberal ideals.

THE PUBLIC RALLY EXPERIMENT

Liberals making illiberal choices because they are liberals: what can bring this about? Freedom of expression and religion are foundational values of a democratic politics. The classic studies of democratic values—Samuel Stouffer's *Communism, Conformity, and Civil Liberties*;[5] John Sullivan, James Piereson, and George Marcus's *Political Tolerance and American Democracy*[6]—fix on the willingness of citizens to support the rights of groups and ideas that they fear or intensely dislike. Deciding to reject fellow citizens' right to free speech is an archetypical example of an illiberal choice.

Some citizens are more supportive of liberal democratic ideals than others, but no one's support is absolute. There are always circumstances when a person who believes strongly in freedom of expression will decide that a group or set of ideas falls outside the pale. Rejection of Neo-Nazis and other extremists is a case in point. What sets Muslim minorities apart is that their rights as citizens are contested, not only because illiberal strains remain entrenched in contemporary democracies, but also for just the opposite reason, because core values of contemporary democracies have become progressively more liberal.

Those who favor one liberal ideal—inclusive tolerance is our focus—tend to favor a wider family of liberal ideals. Those who profess this family of liberal values do not always make liberal choices. Most often, the reason is a failure of will or sincerity. But sometimes it is because circumstances force them to choose between liberal values. This is what we aim to investigate—when those who affirm liberal values make illiberal choices just because they are committed to a liberal value.

Following the lead of political tolerance studies, we target claims to freedom of expression, religion, and assembly. The intolerant have no love for the rights of minorities. Hence our focus, again, on the tolerant. Conceptually, the strategy is to contrast reactions of those who believe in inclusive tolerance where there is no conflict between supporting the right of Muslims to freedom of religion and circumstances where the right to freedom of religion comes into conflict with another liberal value. Our strategy is to investigate the steadfastness of the support of the tolerant for foundational democratic rights as the intensity of the conflict between secular, liberal values and religious, traditional values is ratcheted up. Specifically, a right to freedom of expression and assembly is counterbalanced against Islam as an active faith, working to put across conservative views on the role of women. Operationally, the Public Rally experiment has four conditions. In the baseline condition, majority citizens were asked whether "Muslims should be allowed to hold a public event to explain Islamic values"; in a second condition, they were asked whether they should be allowed to do so "to preach" Islamic values; in a third condition, "to explain conservative ideas about women"; in a final condition, "to preach conservative ideas about women."

Figure 7.1 provides a vivid illustration of the consequences of intensifying a conflict of liberal values.[7] The principle is always the same: the right of Muslims to freedom of expression and religion. What we want to observe is how the majority public responds as the conflict between liberal values intensifies. In the absence of a conflict of liberal values, a tiny share of the non-Muslim public, around 15 percent, reject Muslims' right to free speech. Ratchet value conflict up one degree, whether substituting preaching for explaining or Islamic ideas about women for Islamic values, and opposition more than doubles to around 35 percent. Instead of a decisive majority backing the rally, a bare majority stands in support. This is a dramatic difference. But what should take one's breath away is that, if the purpose of the rally is to preach conservative ideas about women, a decisive majority, around 65 percent, opposes *allowing* Muslims to hold the rally.

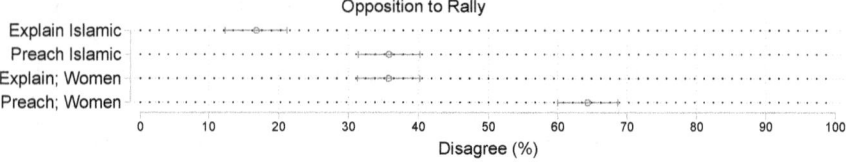

FIGURE 7.1. CONFLICT BETWEEN LIBERAL VALUES: THE PUBLIC RALLY EXPERIMENT. Explain/preach Islamic values/conservative ideas about women's position in Islam. Norway, % Oppose.

The virtually complete collapse of majority citizens' support for allowing Muslims to hold a public event cannot, purely as a matter of logic, be laid solely at the feet of those who are intolerant. Some substantial portion of the public who otherwise would be open to allowing Muslims to hold a religious rally must have defected. Having to decide whether to allow Muslims to hold a religious rally to preach conservative Islamic ideas on women puts those who believe in inclusive tolerance in a tough position. For the same reasons that they believe in inclusive tolerance, they believe in a wider set of liberal values, gender equality among them. Support Muslims holding the rally, and they have licensed propagation of restrictions on women. Oppose them holding the rally, and they have turned their backs on the right to assembly of an immigrant-origin religious minority.

Our key hypothesis is that the shift from majority acceptance to majority opposition to allowing the rally is mainly caused by the tolerant, by a change not in their beliefs but in their choices in response to a conflict between their beliefs. Figure 7.2 shows that this is the case. It displays responses to the two limiting conditions in the Public Rally experiment by IMCP score. As expected, in the absence of a conflict between liberal values, the relationship between strength of motivation to control prejudice and support for Muslims holding a religious rally is strong. What is—certainly it was to us—a surprise is that when liberal values are maximally pitted against each other, those who score highest on the IMCP scale are as opposed to allowing the rally as those who score lowest. The most liberal and the most illiberal join together in opposing the rally.[8]

Why is this worth attention? There are countless examples of the unwillingness of ordinary citizens to tolerate controversial political ideas. The first lesson here, however, is not that citizens are unwilling to tolerate what is controversial. It is, rather, how little it takes for an idea to be controversial. The wording of the Public Rally experiment is anodyne. Majority citizens are not asked to acknowledge that Muslims have a "right" to freedom of assembly and expression; only that they be "allowed" to hold a public meeting. They are not asked to allow an explicitly religious rally; only "a public event." And the objective of the event is not "to indoctrinate" or "to propagate" or even just "to advocate" Islamic ideas; it is to "preach" them, which is what believers in a faith necessarily do when they affirm their faith. As for ideas about the status of women, they are not characterized as "extreme" or even "Islamic," only "conservative." Yet, if the event is to be held to preach conservative ideas about the status of women in Islam, only a small minority, a political handful so to speak, no more than one in five, will agree that Muslims should be allowed to hold their public meeting.

The tolerant lining up right alongside the intolerant in rejecting Muslims' right to hold a public rally—to see the full force of this result, it is worth reiterating the power of randomization. The tolerant behave like the intolerant when asked to accept that Muslims may preach Islamic values about women *not* because they are any different from the tolerant in the other experimental conditions but because the choice they have to make involves a conflict of liberal values. Of course, such a conflict could have been resolved in favor of tolerating those who want to preach conservative

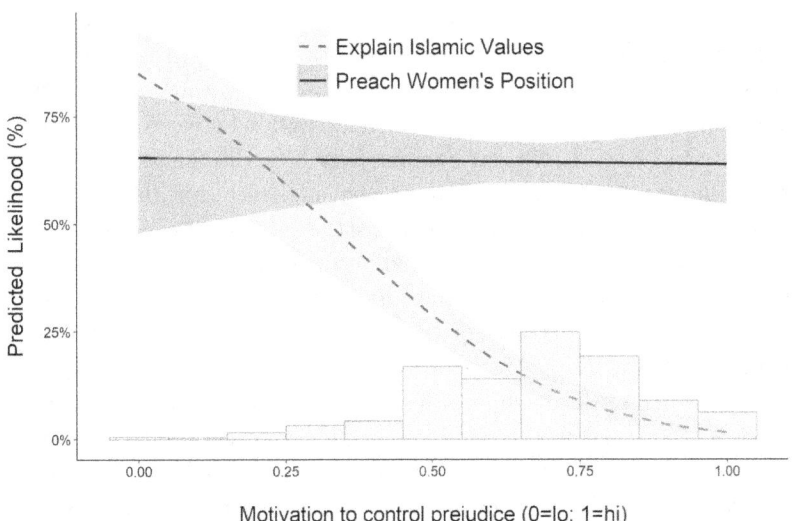

FIGURE 7.2. OPPOSITION TO PUBLIC RALLY BY INCLUSIVE TOLERANCE. Explain Islamic values/Preach conservative ideas about women's position in Islam. Norway, Predicted likelihood of opposing (%) by IMCP.

Islamic values about the position of women, but empirically that is not what we observe in this case. What we see is that under certain conditions, but not all, the tolerant and intolerant converge on a shared position. And it is not inclusionary. It is exclusionary. The tolerant, like the intolerant, deny Muslims their fundamental rights to freedom of religion, expression, and assembly.

BAD FAITH AND MUSLIM LEADERSHIP

A study conducted in the Netherlands in 1998 provided an unsettling finding about a distinctive stigma for Muslim minorities compared to other minorities of immigrant origin in the country at that time. Respondents in the Dutch sample picked out Muslims nearly twice as often as other minorities as "politically untrustworthy, in the end more loyal to their own country and government than to the Dutch society."[9] Bad faith is the charge; publicly pretending to pledge their loyalty to the ideals and institutions of the country that they have come to, but privately practicing the way of life and serving the values of the country that they have come from.[10] This is, of course, only one of the ways in which Muslims are stigmatized, but it is an especially pernicious one.

All the studies of Muslims being stigmatized are studies of attitudes toward ordinary Muslims, an example, we have become persuaded, of the urgency of a problem obscuring its depth. What we want to call out are the risks of an even deeper mistrust of the *leadership* of Muslim communities. The prospects for inclusion depend on cooperation between non-Muslim majority and Muslim minority communities. The willingness of leaders of both communities to take initiatives on behalf of inclusion hinges on their judgments of the risks of doing so, not least the risk that the commitments of leaders of one community are not credible to members of the other. Hence the importance of identifying the conditions under which non-Muslim majorities are ready to trust—or at least, not to actively distrust—the good faith of the leadership of Muslim communities.

Believe that the leadership of Muslim communities is committed to traditional Islamic customs and practices, and it is a short step to believing that they do not mean what they say when they profess to want to be part of their new country. The danger, then, is that leaders of Muslim communities labor under a double handicap in representing Muslim communities: suspect of bad faith once, by the intolerant, because they are Muslim, suspect once more, by both the intolerant and a share of the tolerant, because they are Muslim religious leaders.

A perception of Muslims as disloyal, more attached to the country and culture that they came from than the country they now live in, is a stereotype. A charge of dual loyalties is an uncommonly poisonous stereotype but not an uncommon one, at one time or another pinned on various (typically) immigrant groups, historically most often on Jews. It is, naturally, a favorite of the intolerant. And the tolerant? What sets Muslims apart is that a leadership that empowers traditional religious authorities rubs against the values of contemporary liberal democracies. The Public Rally experiment demonstrated the aversion of the tolerant simply to preaching Islamic ideas about women. Insofar as they are tolerant, they will resist stereotyping ordinary Muslims as insincere in professing commitment to their new country. But because they believe in liberal democratic ideals, tolerance among them, are they susceptible to stereotyping Muslim leaders as guilty of bad faith?

These are the considerations that stimulated the Bad Faith sequence of survey experiments. It turned out to be one of the longest sequences in the whole inquiry, totaling six trials conducted in four different countries. The template is simple. We asked, "How much do you trust or distrust Muslims when they say that they wish to be a part of our society?" The sequence, laid out in table 7.1, consists in systematically varying the characterization of Muslim leadership to determine exactly who is and who is not suspected of bad faith and why.

THE FIRST BAD FAITH IN LEADERS TRIALS

To begin, we asked a nationally representative sample of Dutch respondents, "How much do you trust or distrust . . . when they say that they want to become part of our country?," half the time asking them about Muslims, the other half about Muslim leaders.[11] The first column in table 7.2 shows that one out of every three Dutch believe that Muslims are guilty of bad faith—a minority, to be sure, but a sizable one for a stereotype as poisonous as this. It is all the more striking, then, that the Dutch are twice as likely to believe that Muslim leaders are guilty of dishonesty when they say that they want to be part of the country. Muslim leaders are doubly suspect, the first trial in the Bad Faith sequence suggests, once for being Muslims, once more for being Muslim leaders.

Because Muslim leaders are under an especially thick cloud of suspicion in the Netherlands, it does not follow that they suffer a comparable handicap throughout Western Europe. That is one question. Another no less obvious question is, Who or what are majority citizens thinking of when they are thinking of the leadership of Muslim communities? These are not

TABLE 7.1. THE BAD FAITH SEQUENCE

Trial # (Country)	1 (Denmark)	2 (Denmark)	3 (Netherlands)	4 (Norway)	5 (Norway)	6 (Great Britain)
Target group fill 1	Muslims	Muslims	Muslims	Muslims	Muslims	Muslims
Target group fill 2					Female Muslim leaders	
Target group fill 3						Muslim business leaders
Target group fill 4					Muslim local politicians	Muslim local councilors
Target group fill 5	Muslim leaders	Muslim leaders	Muslim leaders	Muslim leaders		
Target group fill 6		Muslim religious leaders		Muslim religious leaders	Muslim religious leaders	Muslim religious leaders
Target group fill 7			Muslim fundamentalists			
Target group fill 8					Muslim extremists	

Repeatable template: How much do you trust or distrust [TARGET GROUP FILL] when they say that they wish to be a part of our society?

Example: How much do you trust or distrust Muslim religious leaders when they say that they wish to be a part of our society?

challenging questions. If Muslim leaders are doubly suspect in the Netherlands, it is a good bet they are doubly suspect in Denmark. Moreover, it is a similarly safe bet that when native citizens think of Muslim leaders, it is Muslim religious leaders who come to mind. Accordingly, a series of experiments was conducted, to test the replicability and the generalizability of the initial results. Two were conducted in Denmark, and two more in Norway. Table 7.2 shows the results.

The absolute level of stigmatizing Muslim religious leaders as dishonest in their professions of commitment to their new country varies across countries. But the pattern is identical. Muslim leaders are markedly more likely than ordinary Muslims to be perceived as guilty of bad faith and percep-

TABLE 7.2. THE BAD FAITH SEQUENCE: THE FIRST FIVE TRIALS. PERCENTAGE DISTRUST IN MUSLIM LEADERS WHEN THEY SAY THEY WANT TO BECOME PART OF COUNTRY.

Trial #	Trial 1	Trial 2	Trial 3	Trial 4	Trial 5
(Country, study/wave)	Netherlands, study 2	Denmark, study 2	Denmark, study 3	Norway, wave 6	Norway, wave 8
Muslims	34.8 [29.8; 40.2] N = 322	46.1 [40.9; 51.3] N = 356	44.6 [40.1; 49.1] N = 442	23.5 [19.3; 28.4] N = 336	30.3 [25.8; 34.8] N = 393
Muslim leaders	54.8*** [48.7; 60.8] N = 261	59.6*** [54.5; 64.6] N = 364	69.1*** [64.6; 73.6] N = 443	39.0*** [33.3; 44.9] N = 272	47.6*** [42.9; 52.2] N = 370
Muslim religious leaders		63.6*** [58.5; 68.4] N = 365	66.1*** [61.6; 70.5] N = 451		51.5*** [46.8; 56.2] N = 363

Note: 95% C.I. in brackets; N = sample size; gray and *** indicate that differences from baseline condition are statistically significant at 0.01 level (ANOVA models).

tions of Muslim leaders and Muslim religious leaders are interchangeable. Speak of the leadership of Muslim communities and it is Muslim religious leaders, imams, who native citizens think of, and in thinking of them, for a substantial share of the majority public, suspicion of the sincerity of their commitment to the country comes to mind.

LIBERAL INTOLERANCE?

Imams, it is reasonable to hypothesize, epitomize for many majority citizens the illiberalism that majority citizens perceive in Islam as a faith and therefore draw fire from majority citizens who favor liberal ideals. To the extent that this is true, those who are committed to liberal ideals, inclusive tolerance among them, may join with the intolerant in stigmatizing Muslim religious leaders as being guilty of bad faith.

To test this hypothesis, figure 7.3 presents the probability of characterizing Muslim religious leaders and ordinary Muslims as dishonest in their professions of commitment to the country depending on strength of motivation to control prejudice. Both the lines for religious leaders and for ordinary Muslims descend from left to right, evidence of the decreasing likelihood of assigning bad faith to Muslim religious leaders or ordi-

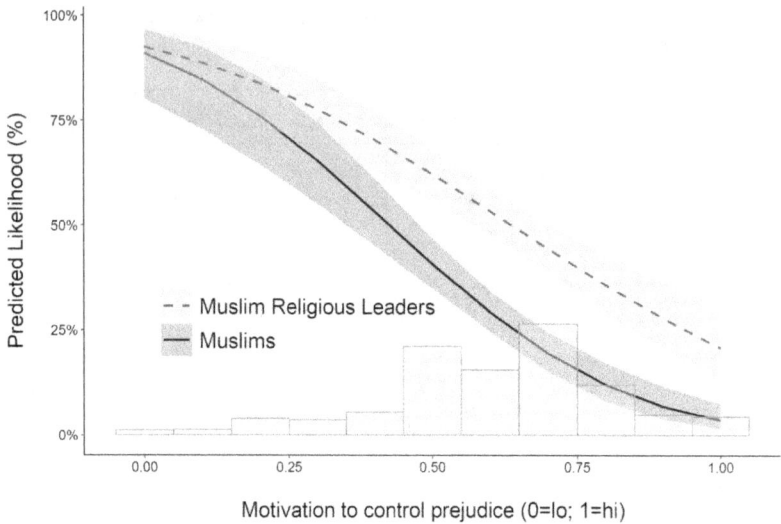

FIGURE 7.3. BAD FAITH IN MUSLIM LEADERS BY INCLUSIVE TOLERANCE. Distrust Muslim religious leaders/Muslims when they say they want to become part of society. Norway, Predicted likelihood of opposing (%) by IMCP.

nary Muslims as the motivation of majority citizens to control prejudice increases. But although both lines descend from left to right, they do not go down at the same rate. The angle of descent of the line for ordinary Muslims is steeper than the one for Muslim religious leaders. The result: the stronger the motivation of majority citizens to control prejudice, the wider the gap between the two. It is not that liberal ideals do not matter. It is that they matter much less for perceptions of Muslim religious leaders than for ordinary Muslims.

It may not be necessary, but it can do no harm, to underscore the perversity of this result. Some imams may be insincere in their commitment to the country. But what is it if not prejudice to stereotype them, as a group, as insincere in their commitment to the country? Figure 7.3 thus points to both a banal truth and a perverse truth. The banal truth is that those who are indifferent or predisposed to prejudice in general are prejudiced in their judgments of all Muslims. The perverse truth is that those who care most about fighting prejudice are responsible for Muslim religious leaders being doubly suspect, once for being Muslims, then once again for being Muslim religious leaders. As in the Public Rally experiment, a belief in tolerance, in liberal ideals, produces an intolerant, illiberal reaction.

SECULAR VERSUS RELIGIOUS TERMS OF POLITICS: DANCYGIER'S DILEMMA

Rafaela Dancygier begins her analysis of the strategic dilemma of parties of the left by reporting an incident in the 2015 UK general election. As part of its campaign to harvest Muslim votes, the Labour Party held a rally in Birmingham, a stronghold of Muslim support for the party, men separated from women. Controversy sells papers: news media featured pictures of the segregated seating. The Conservative Party charged the Labour Party with hypocrisy, campaigning on a platform for gender equality while soliciting Muslim votes by practicing gender segregation.

One more example, Dancygier contends, of the strategic dilemma of the political left. "Over the last several decades," she observes, "the Labour Party has made strong appeals to Muslim voters, and in its pursuit of votes it has chosen to empower patriarchal, traditional forces much more than it has promoted egalitarian, progressive forces."[12] The result is that parties of the left risk alienating supporters committed to equality and other liberal values by joining forces with a leadership of a minority community committed to illiberal values. Dancygier's dilemma, we would emphasize, is not a moral dilemma. The alternatives are maximizing votes by making alliances with the traditional, conservative leadership of Muslim communities and the illiberal values they epitomize or staying true to their values as a party of the left on the other. A choice between self-interest and principle is a practical, not a moral, dilemma. Practical dilemmas are integral to politics, but our concern here is with moral dilemmas, and with the choices made when liberal principles come into conflict with each other.

We have seen that, when majority citizens think of Muslim leaders, Muslim religious leaders come to mind. But it does not follow that when they think of leaders in the Muslim community, only Muslim religious leaders come to mind. The question then is whether a cloud of bad faith overhangs Muslim leadership generally. It surely will not undercut the standing of female Muslim leaders. Those who favor liberal ideals will welcome them. Beyond gender, the obvious question to ask is whether majority citizens make a distinction between religious Muslim leaders and secular Muslim leaders. And the question after that, what comes to mind when non-Muslims think of imams? Religious fundamentalists? Extremists? It is worth remarking again that, thanks to the repeatable template of the Bad Faith experiment, tests of the reaction to diverse types of Muslim leaders can be conducted while, simultaneously, exactly replicating prior tests of the reactions to Muslims, Muslim leaders, and Muslim religious leaders.

THE FINAL TRIALS IN THE BAD FAITH SEQUENCE

Figure 7.4 presents results of the fifth trial, conducted in Norway. Given the importance of demonstrating replicability of results, we first note reactions to Muslims, Muslim leaders, and Muslim religious leaders. The pattern this time is the same as before. Reactions to Muslim leaders and Muslim religious leaders are interchangeable, and levels of distrust of both are approximately twice as high as distrust of ordinary Muslims.

The first of the new questions on the agenda is whether majority citizens draw a distinction between secular and religious Muslim leaders. The easy test, of course, is whether they react differently to Muslim female leaders. Unsurprisingly, the answer is yes. Far from being doubly suspect because they are leaders in the Muslim community, they are less likely to be suspected of bad faith than ordinary Muslims. More telling are reactions to "local Muslim politicians." They, too, are not under a double handicap, suspect because they are Muslims, suspect again because they are leaders in Muslim communities. Indeed, they, too, are less likely to be suspected of bad faith than ordinary Muslims. It is worth taking a moment to enjoy the irony of a politician not being suspected of insincerity by virtue of being identified as a politician.

Why do Muslim religious leaders evoke so much suspicion? The question is harder to answer than it may seem because so many answers come immediately to mind. The one that we have focused on is a perception of dogmatism, of unreasoning commitment to extreme religious beliefs. We put this conjecture to a direct test by examining the similarity of reactions to Muslim religious leaders and Muslim extremists. Figure 7.4 shows that our conjecture was way off the mark. Reactions are nothing like the same: majority citizens are far more likely—indeed, threateningly close to twice as likely—to suspect the commitment of Muslim extremists as Muslim religious leaders.

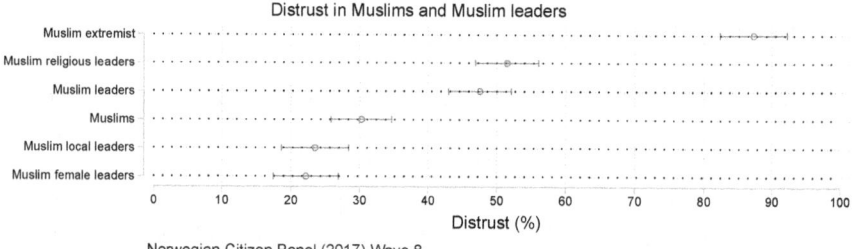

FIGURE 7.4. BAD FAITH IN MUSLIM LEADERS: FOLLOW-UP TRIAL. Distrust Muslim extremists/Muslim religious leaders/Muslim leaders/Muslims/Muslim local politicians/Muslim female leaders. Norway, % Distrust.

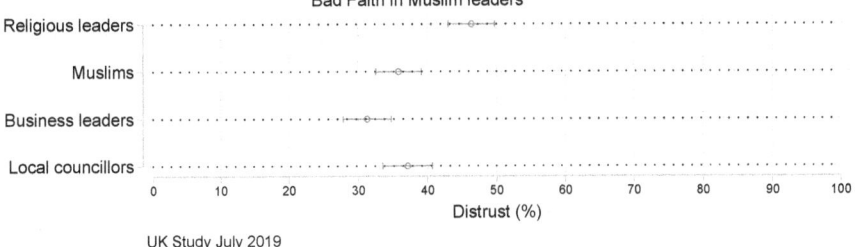

FIGURE 7.5. BAD FAITH IN MUSLIM LEADERS: FINAL EXTENSION TRIAL. Distrust Muslim religious leaders/Muslims/Muslim business leaders/Muslim local councilors. Great Britain, % Distrust.

Figure 7.5 shows the results of further tests conducted in the United Kingdom to assess the generalizability of the Norwegian results. We made one change in the design. Rather than assessing reactions to "Muslim local politicians," the British respondents were asked about "Muslim local councilors," the title of an actual official position. On all counts, the pattern of results is the same in the UK study and the Norwegian study. Native citizens are distinctly more likely to believe that Muslim religious leaders are acting in bad faith compared to ordinary Muslims and perceive Muslim local councilors the same as they do ordinary Muslims.

All the evidence to hand points to the distinction between secular and religious being pivotal. When Muslims are tied to their faith, or perhaps better, the tenets of their faith as non-Muslims understand them, they risk illiberal reactions by those who value liberal ideals. The results from both the Public Rally experiment and the Bad Faith experiment are point by point consistent with this hypothesis.

A FINAL COMMENT

One way to sum up our views is this: conflicts between liberal values take two forms. One is when you are having to settle for second best—accepting that equality will trump liberty when you would have it the other way around. Putting it this way and leaving it this way, gives an impression of domesticating conflicts between liberal values. It is as though they come down to squabbles between family members. At the end of the day, one has gotten the nod, and if your most favored child did not come out on top, at least your second most favored child did. This gets things wrong all the way down. Forced choices between, to take the paradigmatic example, liberty and equality are moral dilemmas because the cost of rejecting one is high, whichever one is rejected. Isaiah Berlin writes, "To avoid glaring inequality or widespread misery I am ready to sacrifice some, or all, of my freedom. I may do so willingly and freely: but it is freedom that I am giving up for the sake of justice or equality or the love of my fellow men. I should be guilt-stricken, and rightly so, if I were not, in some circumstances, ready to make this sacrifice. But a sacrifice is not an increase in what is being sacrificed, namely, freedom, however great the moral need or the compensation for it.... An absolute loss of liberty occurs."[13]

Yet, there is a gain of equality. What is the gain in the Bad Faith experiment? A belief in a liberal ideal, tolerance, leads to a susceptibility to intolerance—to stigmatizing imams as dishonest in professing to want to be part of the country that they live in. It is a closer call for the Public Rally experiment. When the right of Muslims to hold a public event to preach conservative ideas about women is rejected, it can be argued—indeed, has been argued when we have presented these results—that the loss is illusory, the conservative ideas of Islam about the role of women are misogynistic, and there is no right to hate speech. A gain for gender equality? Arguably, with the emphasis on arguably. And the loss? Gutting the fundamental democratic rights of Muslim minorities. Who is prepared to argue this?[14] The irony of our results, then, is that commitments to the same family of ideals that have led contemporary liberal democracies to being more open to inclusion than has been recognized can turn those who believe in these ideals against the inclusion of Muslim minorities.

APPENDIX

A Methodological Note on the Validity of the IMCP Measure

The weight of this charge of liberal intolerance rests on a presumption—namely, that the Internal Motivation to Control Prejudice index measures a commitment to tolerance. But, of course, like any measure of prosocial attitudes, it is open to a charge that respondents are saying not what they believe, but what they believe they ought to say. If so, the illiberal reactions in the Public Rally and the Bad Faith experiments are not the responses of people who believe in liberal ideals, but rather of those who want to pass themselves off as believing in liberal ideals.

It must be the case that some who say they are concerned about prejudice are saying this in order to present themselves in a socially desirable light. No measure of prosocial attitudes is wholly free of social desirability bias. The issue is how serious the bias is. Of the ways to address this question for measures of socially sensitive subjects in studies of public opinion, there is no better approach, in our judgment, than the List experiment technique.

The idea underpinning the List technique is straightforward. Assume the objective is to assess the validity of a measure of, say, racial prejudice. In the baseline condition, respondents selected at random are asked, "Please tell how many of the items on this list upset or anger you. DON'T tell me which ones, just how many." Respondents then see a list of, say, four items—the amount of money professional athletes make, government increasing taxes, and so on. In a test condition, respondents similarly selected at random, are given the same instructions, "Please tell how many of the items on this list upset or anger you. DON'T tell me which ones, just how many." The list in the test condition has the same items as the list in the baseline condition plus one more, say, "a black family moving next door to you." A respondent knows that if the amount of money professional athletes make and having a black neighbor vex him and he answers two, there is no way anyone can tell that one of the items on the list that angers him is having a black family next door. There is, however, a straightforward way to determine the percentage of respondents upset or angry at the possibility of having a black neighbor. Simply subtract the mean of the baseline condition from the mean of the test condition and multiply by one hundred.

The List technique requires careful pretesting to assess whether the number and content of the items are satisfactory. There is more than one risk, but the most exigent is the ceiling effect. It is necessary to ensure that both the mean number of items selected in the test condition is small and their variance is low. If a nontrivial number of respondents respond that, say, three or four items on a four-item list upset them, their randomized counterparts in the test will not be secure in a belief that they can pick the black neighbor next door as something that would upset them without anyone being aware that they have done so.

The IMCP assesses the strength of motivation to inhibit prejudice. There is patently a risk that a nontrivial number of respondents will give positive answers, believing that if they do so, they will present themselves in a socially desirable light. Accordingly, we conducted a List experiment to assess to what extent majority citizens give the answers they believe they ought to give in order to present themselves in a socially desirable light.

The experiment was conducted as part of a larger online interview on a nationally representative sample carried out by YouGov in Denmark. Respondents assigned to the baseline condition read:

> Please take your time and tell us how many of the following you support.
> *We do not need to know which ones, just how many.*
> Spend more money on care for the elderly

Send Danish and allied troops into Syria to help overthrow President Bashar al-Assad.
Make it easier for foreigners to come to Denmark
Allow Turkey membership in the EU

How many of these do you support?

Respondents assigned to the test condition received the same instruction and the same list of items, with one addition. The specific objective of the addition was to assess the willingness of those who score relatively high on the IMCP to give a false impression of how open they are to including Muslims and their faith. Hence the addition of a fifth item in the test condition—Prohibit Muslim women from wearing a headscarf.

The concern is to what extent majority citizens who say they want to be tolerant will show, if given the opportunity to say how they feel without anybody knowing or being able to infer what they have said, that they are not as open to inclusion as they appear to be. Table 7A.1 presents, for each quintile of the IMCP, the mean number of items endorsed in the baseline condition and the mean number of items endorsed in the test condition. The third column summarizes the difference between the first and second columns and expresses it in percentage points. The fourth column reports the number of cases.

The greater the difference between responses in the baseline and the test conditions, the larger the percentage of respondents who answered that headscarves should be made illegal, acting under the presumption that no one can tell that that is their answer. To the extent that IMCP index is measuring concern about prejudice, and not social desirability bias, the higher

TABLE 7A.1. THE LIST EXPERIMENT BY IMCP

	Baseline (mean)	Test (mean)	Difference (%)	N
Lowest	1.29	1.91	62*	120
2nd lowest	1.24	1.75	51*	331
Middle	1.27	1.70	43*	369
2nd highest	1.59	1.70	11	232
Highest	1.74	1.71	−4	183
All	1.4	1.73	33*	1220

the score on the index, the less the difference should be between baseline and test conditions; conversely, the lower the score, the greater the difference should be. Looking at the third column, we see the steady decrease in differences, indeed, elimination of a difference for high scorers on IMCP, between baseline and test conditions, notwithstanding the opportunity to say what they think believing that their anonymity is assured. This is strong evidence to suggest that respondents say what they think in questions of Muslim inclusion whether or not they believe others can hear what they say.

[CHAPTER EIGHT]

A NEW FRAMEWORK FOR THE STUDY OF INCLUSIVE POLITICS

It is a time of turmoil. Resentment, xenophobia, and ill will are in the saddle. The United Kingdom has broken away from the European Union, in no small measure because of nativist outrage at immigrants and refugees being allowed into the UK. And in one more demonstration of the ironies of a democratic politics, the UK itself may now break up thanks to the nationalist ambitions of Scotland.[1] The particularities of the UK situation are singular; the cast of its politics is not. In 2016 in the US, President Trump won enough votes for a majority in the electoral college after a campaign that echoed the slogans of nativist parties in Europe in calling for "America First." "France d'abord" had for decades been the rallying cry of the National Front in France, as it had of the Austrian Freedom Party, "Österreich zuerst."[2]

In Norway, Denmark, Switzerland, Italy, Finland, and the Netherlands, nativist right parties have been in or exercised substantial influence over government for more than a decade. Sweden and Germany appeared for a long time to be exceptions to the surge of nativist parties across Europe's oldest democracies, but recent years have seen the establishment and growth of such parties there also—Sverigedemokraterna and Die Alternative für Deutschland—although they are still at the time of writing excluded from government power.

What is more, Muslims in every country in our study have been the target of hate crimes,[3] right-wing extremist assaults,[4] discrimination in jobs and apartment rental,[5] even attacks on mosques. Yet, our results at various points suggest that there is a willingness of native citizens to acknowledge the worth of Muslims, a readiness to have them included in authorized representations of the national identity as "one of us." How can this be? How can it be true that the far right's campaign for exclusion of Muslim minorities could gain electoral ground and political power in many instances, and also true that broad majorities are open to the idea of Muslim inclusion?

THE STANDARD MODEL OF PREJUDICE AND POLITICS

At the heart of contemporary politics in the old democracies in Europe is a perverse puzzle. The far right is advancing under a nativist banner appealing for the exclusion of Muslims and Islam. Yet, on all the evidence, the psychological dispositions associated with nativism—negative out-group bias, prejudice, authoritarianism, social dominance orientation, and closed-mindedness[6]—have not become more widespread. If anything, the tide has been running in the opposite direction, in favor of the advancement of emancipatory values;[7] support for human rights;[8] motivation to control prejudice;[9] and, as our results indicate, emerging norms of respect and inclusive notions of national identity.

Why, then, has there been a surge of nativist support for the far right? Some recent work points to cultural backlash.[10] External shocks, in the form of mass migration from Muslim countries to the European continent, terror attacks, and economic strains have evoked a reaction from those supportive of traditional, conservative values—older cohorts, those who live in rural areas, men without formal qualifications, and so on.[11] In their eyes, growing religious and cultural diversity is a threat to their own identity. They respond to the threat that they perceive. In their minds they react defensively; in reality, aggressively. As they come to perceive themselves to be an embattled majority, they become an impassioned minority, mobilizing not only against the minority they seek to exclude but also against the majority within their own group that appears to them to make common cause with the Muslim minority they find threatening.[12]

The intensity of the aversion to Muslims exhibited by a minority within the majority group of citizens has given a commonsense character to the psychological paradigm accounting for the resurgence of nativism, extremism, and intolerance. Perhaps because it appears to be a matter of common sense, the logic of this paradigm tends to be taken for granted, which is all the more reason to spell it out.

The standard model of prejudice and politics has two components: long-term affective predispositions and short-term shocks. A wide array of long-term psychological factors have been brought into play: intolerance, symbolic predispositions, material interests, authoritarianism, postmaterialism (or self-expressive values), among others. They differ in significant ways. But what is of importance here is what they share—similarity and concurrence.

Similarity is the first point. Intolerance, symbolic predispositions, and values pick out different focal objects, but the objects that each is focused on—Muslims are the concern here—tend to be invested with negative emotions that establish long-term predispositions to consistently respond unfavorably to them.[13] Concurrence is the second point. The more intolerant native citizens are, the less likely they are to favor postmaterialist values; and the more likely that they are either, the more likely they are to be authoritarian.[14] Which influences which remains to be established. For our purposes, what counts is the outcome: a syndrome of psychological predispositions—authoritarianism, hostility, status anxiety, and economic insecurity among them—underpinning affective reactions to out-groups. These long-term affective predispositions are, as it were, railway tracks for prejudice and politics. For affective consistency, once established, tends to be self-reinforcing, accounting for long-running patterns in the politics of religious and cultural diversity.[15]

This syndrome of mutually buttressing affective predispositions is the core component of the standard model of prejudice and politics. But, of course, politics is a compound outcome of long-term and short-term factors. Short-term factors in the standard model take the form of external shocks. In the most general terms, external shocks are events that upset a political equilibrium, invariably in the standard model to the disadvantage of a minority group.[16] Prototypical examples are economic crises and the anxieties about material self-interest or social status they generate and the impact of immigration, and in Europe in particular Muslim immigration, and the animosity following from a clash of cultural values and identities.[17]

Many distinctions can be drawn: between beliefs and feelings is one; between opinions and attitudes is another, between both and values yet another. In practice, in public opinion research, a clean separation of cognition and affect is not possible, and distinctions between opinions and attitudes and values come down, not to a difference in kind, but rather a difference in the breadth of the class of stimulus objects to which favorable and unfavorable feelings are conditioned. This valence framework conscientiously followed favors Occam's razor. Following the lead of Donald Campbell,[18] we fix on a simplifying assumption, namely, that people are predisposed to respond favorably or unfavorably to classes of stimulus objects (e.g., Muslims, inclusion/exclusion). The stronger their feelings positive or negative, the more consistently they will respond favorably or unfavorably.

A valence framework is a foundational premise of psychological models of intergroup attitudes: in this case, negative orientations to Muslim minorities, variously expressed depending on context. The challenge is to give an account of when and why the choices that majorities make are sometimes in support of inclusion but sometimes not, without there being any change in underlying sentiments. Our proposal is to add a layer of analysis of the inclusionary options under consideration—specifically, how these may evoke widely shared normative considerations. The key point is that, *without a change in underlying sentiments*, the balance of expressed preferences on issues of inclusion can shift, pro and con, depending on the fit of particular political options with the normative premises of contemporary liberal democracies.

THE INCLUSIONARY OPTIONS FRAMEWORK

Previous work, our own included, has concentrated on the intolerant, on their anxieties and animosities. Their views are well predicted by the standard model of prejudice and politics. They are opposed to inclusion, still more so in times of crisis. By turning instead to examine those who believe in tolerance, this study aims to identify the normative considerations that underpin their judgments about when and why inclusion of Muslims is and is not acceptable.

Politics is about change at the margins. Changes in support for particular proposals for inclusion are tied to changes of fit with widely shared normative principles. Widely shared is key. For it means that the balance of opinion on issues of inclusion can shift across the political spectrum, depending on inclusionary options on offer, without any change in the balance of underlying sentiments and feelings. The challenge, then, is to identify these pivotal normative considerations.

This theoretical framework, highlighting how alternative inclusionary options engage normative premises of contemporary liberal democracy, brings new insights to the interplay between public opinion and party politics. We will highlight three. First, the framework identifies conditions under which exclusionary actors, such as the far right, are likely to gain political influence, and, this is the original contribution, when they are less likely to do so. Second, it calls attention to aspects of political strategies and policies that promote inclusion that have not received the full attention they deserve. Third, it points to polarization traps, which occur when a failure to recognize pivotal distinctions between inclusionary options leads to an overestimation of illiberal forces.

THE LIMITS OF THE FAR RIGHT

There has been much disagreement about the nature of the ideological appeal of the far right in Europe. However, in the standard text on far-right ideology, Cas Mudde argues that nativism is their core ideological feature. He defines nativism as "an ideology, which holds that states should be inhabited exclusively by members of the native group ('the nation') and that nonnative elements (persons and ideas) are fundamentally threatening to the homogenous nation-state."[19] A series of articles based on analyses of voter patterns confirms the centrality of nativism, or exclusionary ethno-nationalism, to voters of the populist radical right in Western Europe.[20]

That said, there is considerable ideological heterogeneity in what is usually considered the far-right party family in Europe.[21] Some of these parties have grown out of regional independence movements (Lega Nord in Italy; Vlaams Belang, formerly Vlaams Blok, in Belgium); others were initially tax protest movements (the Norwegian Progress Party; the Danish Progress Party, now the Danish People's Party); some were originally agrarian or rural-interest parties (the Swiss People's Party; the True Finns); yet others started out as EU-protest movements (the UK Independence Party and Alternative für Deutschland); some nativist parties historically had more direct links to extreme right milieus (the French National Front, the Austrian Freedom Party, and the Sweden Democrats); and a considerable number of them are now increasingly dedicated to preventing what they see as the existential threat of Islam (most prominently, the Dutch Freedom Party).

In Western Europe, over the course of the past thirty years or so, these far-right parties have carved out a political space to the right of the established Conservative or Christian Democratic Right by challenging the postwar consensus on what constituted illegitimate, or right-extremist, forms of nativism. They have done so by arguing, and persuading a considerable share of the electorate, often against fierce political opposition, that their nativist agenda is legitimate and democratic. This has not meant that voters who favor inclusion have started voting for the far right. Rather, voters who are unlikely to vote for the far right have become persuaded that the nativist right parties are legitimate political actors that should not be excluded from democratic politics, and that they can be accepted into governing coalitions or as supporting parties of governing coalitions.

The studies we have presented can shed light on why this occurred. To see how, we need to bring front and center the dynamics of party politics in specific institutional settings—the electoral and party systems—of the countries studied. We focus on the country where we can draw on the most studies, Norway. The Norwegian party system has more than four parties, but we have chosen to focus here on voters of the two main traditional parties of the right and left (Høyre and Arbeiderpartiet) and the two main challenger parties on the far right and far left (Fremskrittspartiet and Sosialistisk Venstreparti). We do so to maintain a parsimonious analysis and facilitate comparisons to other European multiparty systems. The analysis extends, with some adjustments, also to majoritarian contexts, such as in the US and the UK.

The far right in Norway, the Progress Party, is generally considered in the comparative literature to be less exclusionary than many of its counterparts elsewhere in Scandinavia and in continental Europe.[22] Detailed case-study analyses have argued that the Norwegian Progress Party contains several factions and that this is an important reason why the party vacillates between more and less exclusionary policies.[23] Notably, this party—unlike some other far-right parties—has activists who are mainly concerned with areas of politics other than immigration and minorities.[24] Still, minority and immigration policies are very important for the party. The Norwegian Election Studies show that voters strongly and consistently associate the Progress Party with exclusionary policies toward immigration and immigrants.[25] In that way, the Progress Party is similar to other far-right parties that have been considered electorally successful.[26]

There can be no doubt that the Progress Party has chosen a confrontational and exclusionary posture vis-à-vis Norwegian Muslims. One of the party's highly profiled controversial figures who at the time of writing has been elected party leader wrote the following on her Facebook page prior to a national government conference on integration in 2016, while she was Minister of Immigration and Integration: "I think that those who come to Norway have to adjust to our society. Here we eat pork, drink alcohol, and show our faces. One has to adapt to the values, laws, and rules of Norway when coming here. Like and share!"[27] The Progress Party was founded in 1973 and entered government for the first time in the fall of 2013, and so the party served in government for most of the data collection period reported in this volume. Until recently, the party was a minority partner in government with the Conservative Party (Høyre), the Liberal Democratic Party (Venstre), and the Christian Democratic Party (Kristelig Folkeparti). Just before the onset of COVID, the party left the governing coalition in protest over a government decision they considered too lenient in the case of a Norwegian woman who had broken Norwegian law by joining the terror organization ISIS in the war in Syria.

Against this backdrop, consider the party vote patterns in the Preach conditions of the Public Rally experiment, displayed in table 8.1. They show

TABLE 8.1. THE PUBLIC RALLY EXPERIMENT, BY PARTY VOTE IN THE NORWEGIAN PARLIAMENTARY ELECTION, 2017, PERCENTAGE OPPOSING THE RALLY

	Far Left	Left	Right	Far Right
Islamic values; preach	17.5	24.1	41.4	70.7
Women's position; preach	56.4*	67.4*	63.6*	75.0
N	(157)	(343)	(400)	(169)

Note: N = sample size; gray indicates broad-based coalitions in favor of or against inclusion.
* Difference between top and bottom rows are statistically significant at .05 level (ANOVA).

that the far right has mainly attracted the subset of voters who do not distinguish between terms of inclusion. This is in line with the findings of the literature on far-right voting that emphasize the importance of nativist and exclusionary preferences for the core far-right electorate. As table 8.1 shows, a clear majority of far-right voters, around 70 percent, do not support the right to assembly of Muslims for the purpose of preaching. This is consistent with the argument and analysis in chapter 3, which holds that those who are intolerant do not experience a value conflict and, therefore, it does not matter to them if the value of gender equality is pitted against the right to assembly of a religious minority. Most far-right voters do not favor the assembly of Muslims for preaching in any of the conditions.

The results in the top row of table 8.1 also show the ideological framework of Norwegian party politics. As a general matter, we should expect that the further to the left voters are, the less likely they are to oppose Muslims being allowed to hold a public rally. Moving from left to right, then, opposition should systematically increase. So it does, as table 8.1 shows: from one in five opposed on the far left to one in four in mainstream left parties to just under one in two for mainstream right parties.

The top row of table 8.1 displays, then, the conventional political pattern underpinned by predispositions to respond favorably or unfavorably to a class of issue objects. The bottom row of table 8.2 brings out the limitations of the dispositional framework. Now, opposition is the response of most majority citizens, above all of course on the far right but, critically, also across the political spectrum, including the far left. The balance of political preferences has swung from decisively in favor of allowing Muslims to hold a public rally to decisively opposed to their doing so—*without there being any change in the sentiments or underlying beliefs about inclusion*. The tolerant have not suddenly become intolerant, nor have they shown that they favor liberal values only superficially. The point is precisely that the tolerant do have liberal values. The critical factor is that one of the political options, Muslims preaching conservative ideas about the role of women, generates a conflict of liberal values: on the one side, freedom of speech and religion; on the other, gender equality. Because the priority of gender equality is widely agreed on across the political spectrum, the result is two entirely different outcomes, depending on the fit between the substance of the political options on the table and widely shared ideas of what is right and what is wrong.

Additional insights into how the far right has gained political power and influence follow from this analysis. Far-right parties, we observed, have been involved in two different but connected political battles. One has been the quite unusual and historically charged battle over their own legitimacy as democratic actors; the other, the usual partisan battle for votes and positions. The standard model of prejudice and politics can account well for the latter, but not the former. The results in table 8.1 make plain that, if the debate about the right of assembly of Muslim minorities brings liberal values into conflict with each other, then, opposition to even core democratic values, in this case religious freedom, is likely to resonate across the entire electorate from far left to far right. Crucially, though, the results show that this has not made the far right an appealing political option for those who are open to inclusion. But insofar as the positions of the far right have a wider resonance, it stands a better chance of being viewed as a legitimate political actor and an acceptable coalition partner. This is why, we believe, those far-right parties that have become influential actors in their political systems have tended to emphasize precisely the conflicts that pit minority inclusion against other liberal values, be they gender equality, gay rights, freedom of expression, child-rearing practices, animal rights, or secularism. The deep irony is that conflicts between liberal values can increase tolerance of the far right among those who favor inclusion of Muslim minorities.

A framework centered on substantive political options thus throws light on how far-right parties can advocate exclusionary positions, such as opposition to Muslims' right to assembly, in ways that make those committed to liberal values likely to defend the right of far-right candidates to stand for elections, and even be included in governing coalitions, in a liberal democracy. At the same time, this framework brings into view just how vital these sorts of conflicts are for the far right. Absent inclusive options generating a conflict of liberal values, the far right is on much narrower electoral ground. The exclusionary position of opposing the rally simply does not resonate among most voters of other parties, among those who are open to inclusive tolerance, unless liberal value conflict is intense.

THE STRATEGIC CONSIDERATIONS OF INCLUSIONARY ACTORS

The idea that the rise of the far right is to some extent contingent on the way other parties have responded to the political issues raised by the far right is well established. In an important analytical contribution, Bonnie Meguid distinguished three strategies that established parties (such as Labour and the Conservatives) use when competing against what she calls niche parties, which includes far-right parties.[28] According to Meguid's framework, party competition among "unequals" is not the same as party competition among equals. When unequal parties compete, established parties can dismiss the issue and insist on campaigning on something else. For example, if the far right raises concerns about Muslim inclusion, an established party that favors inclusion may decide to talk about unemployment or taxes instead. Alternatively, they may choose an adversarial strategy. In this case, if the far right argues that Muslims should be excluded, the established party may choose to argue the opposite, why Muslims should be included. Finally, they may choose an accommodative strategy. In this case, if the far right argues that Muslims should be excluded, then the established party echoes this view.

Empirical studies of how political parties, other than the far right, have approached the issue of immigration and minority inclusion have noted a trend of adopting stricter policies albeit with considerable variation and heterogeneity.[29] And there has been some empirically informed scholarly debate as to whether these policy changes have occurred in response to the far right or as part of ordinary changes in party programs in response to societal change.[30] Studies that have tried to examine the electoral consequences of these strategies differ in their conclusions.[31] An important insight from research that focuses on how programmatic political parties develop policies holds that in practice the choice for parties can often be reduced to the question of whether to hold on to a prior position or to adopt changes.[32] A problem in the empirical analyses of this question, noted by, among others, Tjitske Akkerman, is that existing datasets on party policies tend to favor comprehensiveness and often lack "sufficient granularity to capture the diverse positions in a particular area, such as immigration and integration policy."[33] The new analytical framework for inclusive politics that we propose provides a theoretical rationale to suggest that substantive granularity is a necessary condition for analyses of the consequences of the strategic decisions of inclusionary actors.

Viewed from a standard valence framework, parties and policies are either pro- or anti-immigrant; pro- or anti-Muslim, some more so than others, and if they choose to compete on issues of inclusion/exclusion, they have to choose a side and thereby adopt either an accommodative or an adversarial strategy, again some strategies more accommodative or more adversarial than others. In contrast, the framework we propose highlights additional strategic considerations. First of all, we have seen that terms of inclusion matter to voters across the electorate. In some cases, such as that shown in table 8.1, we have even seen that the terms are particularly important to voters of parties other than the far right. This is a reason why a dismissive political strategy is likely to be electorally unwise, particularly if coupled with a valence approach. The inclusionary options framework we propose brings out that, if all parties other than the far right decide that they are broadly "pro-minority" but would rather talk about something else, then the far right can take charge of the political debate about inclusion and focus on the conflicts of liberal values that provide them maximal opportunities to mobilize allies across the whole spectrum. They may not succeed, as not all far-right parties make prudent strategic choices, but the party competitive context will be propitious. A key implication from the framework we propose is that inclusionary actors who would like to assemble a broad coalition in favor of inclusion should *not* ignore or dismiss the politics of religious and cultural diversity but instead develop policies and strategies that are mindful of pivotal distinctions between inclusionary options.

The framework we propose does *not* imply that it is possible at this juncture for inclusive actors to eliminate the far right by opportunistically "framing" the issue of inclusion. The premise of "framing" studies is that preferences between alternatives can be radically altered by opposing presentations of the alternatives, even when the alternatives on offer are either substantively similar or, at the limit, logically interchangeable. The framework we propose instead draws attention not to the framing but to the *substance* of inclusionary options and the normative principles—the political ideas and values—that underpin them. It follows that the strategic choice facing actors who favor inclusion is not whether they should stand up to or copy the far right. The evidence we have presented throughout this volume suggests that inclusionary actors need *not* adopt exclusionary policies in order to minimize the resonance of the far right in the electorate. The new framework instead calls for attention to the substance of the inclusionary options on the table and in particular to the normative considerations underpinning them.

The most revealing evidence in support of this argument that adopting an exclusionary agenda is not necessary to compete effectively against the far right resulted from the National Identity Construction sequence of experiments presented in chapter 5. Recall that in the course of that sequence we came to question the idea that inclusive national identities were broadly accepted. Ambivalence was a possibility that we had not taken into account. So the counter-experiment, in addition to asking whether respondents agreed that textbooks should reflect the importance of the new diversity of Norway, also asked one random subset whether textbooks should place less emphasis on the new diversity of Norway and another random subset whether textbooks should place more emphasis on it.

The first row of table 8.2 shows the percentage of Norwegians agreeing that school textbooks should be written to reflect the new diversity of Norway by party vote. The decisive majorities in agreement across the political spectrum, with the exception only of the far-right Progress Party, are striking. The second row shows the percentage believing that diversity should be de-emphasized. There is no support for de-emphasizing diversity on the left and, this is politically telling, only minimal support on the mainstream right. Only among voters of the far right is there a majority in favor of textbooks that put less emphasis on current diversity. In all other parties, the majority favors textbooks written to reflect current ethnic and religious diversity. This set of results is weighty evidence, we believe, that actors who favor inclusion need not adopt exclusionary ideals in order to isolate and contain the far right.

The inclusive options framework adds, then, to the analysis of the strategic considerations of inclusive actors. It draws attention in particular to the need for knowing and taking into account the normative considerations

TABLE 8.2. THE COUNTERFACTUAL TEXTBOOK EXPERIMENT BY PARTY VOTE IN THE NORWEGIAN PARLIAMENTARY ELECTION, 2017, PERCENTAGE AGREE

	Far Left	Left	Right	Far Right
Reflect Diversity	82.4	69.6	52.8	29.3
Less Emphasis on Diversity	12.9*	24.5*	33.3*	59.1*
N	(65)	(210)	(208)	(85)

Note: N= sample size; gray indicates broad-based coalitions in favor of inclusion.

* Difference between top and bottom rows are statistically significant at .05 level (ANOVA).

that matter to those who are open to inclusive tolerance, not those who are intolerant and favor exclusion. We now turn to discuss the highest risk in the politics of inclusion—polarization traps.

POLARIZATION TRAPS

In contemporary democracies, there is growing concern about polarization and populism. Populism emanates from a supposed schism between a virtuous and unified people and a distanced elite. In populist reasoning "elites" can be many different sorts of actors—politicians, experts, established media, judges and courts, businesspeople/the rich, international organizations. A key point in populist reasoning is that the elites are out of touch and have strayed away from "the will of the people," and that a populist leader or a populist party is needed to reassert virtuous democratic government.

Populism is then, among other things, a suspicion on the part of those who are being governed that those who govern cannot be trusted to act in their best interest. Many scholars of the far right in Europe have noted the tendency of the far right to employ populist rhetoric—so much so that some have argued that contemporary thinking about populism is too colored by the empirical examples of the populist radical right in Europe.[34] Still, it is instructive to ask what it is about the issues that concern nativists that lends them so well to populism. One aspect is, of course, exclusionary nationalism, where those who "rightfully" belong to the nation (the natives) are juxtaposed to immigrants (foreigners). The emphasis put on this distinction makes less salient other differences among natives. A lack of attention to pluralism works to unify both nativist and populist reasoning.[35]

Here we want to draw attention to another important aspect that brings together right-wing populism and nativism, namely the assumption of a popular majority in favor of exclusion of minorities, whether of immigrant origin or not. The results of our studies, all in all, show that this assumption is mistaken. However, the finding that the terms of inclusion matter to those who are open to inclusion means that when we interpret public opinion through an affect or valence framework, we are likely to encounter many situations where a plurality, even sometimes a majority, of native citizens risk being labeled as "anti-Muslim," not because they are prejudiced against Muslims but instead because they take exception to a claim that they have an obligation to support particular proposals made in the name of inclusion.

Consider the finding, reported in chapter 6, that majorities in Norway *disagree* that Muslim culture and tradition should be *protected*. Many, viewing this finding through the lens of an affect or valence model, would conclude that anti-Muslim sentiment and intolerance is rampant. However, the analysis we presented shows that, if the question was instead whether Muslim culture and tradition should be respected, the vast majority, on the order of 70 percent, were on board. Many of the tolerant drew a line at appraisal respect—the idea that they themselves ought to believe that Muslim values and practices are praiseworthy. They were all the same ready to agree that the larger society has a responsibility to publicly acknowledge that Muslim traditions and culture should be treated with respect. The key point is that the balance of opinion, across the mainstream political spectrum, turns on the strategic choice of inclusionary options, in the case at hand on the choice between recognition respect and appraisal respect. To choose to campaign for inclusion on the grounds that the larger society has a responsibility to show appraisal respect for the culture of Muslims risks creating a polarization trap. Here is how.

Imagine a group of non-Muslims who hold differentiated views about Muslims and are supportive of inclusive tolerance. They are committed to showing recognition respect to Muslim values and traditions, but not appraisal respect. They are themselves Christians, and showing recognition respect is as far as they are willing to go in holding other religions in esteem. Now, suppose that legal activists, working to promote minority rights, believe that the larger society's responsibility goes further than acknowledging that Muslim culture should be treated with respect; indeed, that a society that values pluralism has a duty to help sustain the culture of minorities. From their perspective, the Christian group is not fully, truly supportive of inclusion; and insofar as they interpret the beliefs of others about inclusion from a psychological perspective, the Christian group's unwillingness to stand behind a genuinely pluralistic society is from their point of view, at best, evidence that their commitment to tolerance is superficial or, considering the facility with which people are able to conceal unsavory motives, an indication that they are intolerant and anti-Muslim. The key point is that concentrating on dispositions and motivational explanations establishes incentives for each group to perceive the other as opposed to, or at the least insufficiently committed to, liberal democratic values, even though they both in fact are so.

Chapter 3 demonstrated that recognition respect has widespread support, appraisal respect does not. Table 8.3 shows the political implications of concentrating on psychological dispositions and neglecting inclusionary options and the normative considerations that underpin them. The top row shows the political landscape if the option on offer is that Muslims have a right to have their culture and traditions treated with respect; the

TABLE 8.3. RECOGNITION VS. APPRAISAL RESPECT OF MUSLIM CULTURE, BY PARTY VOTE IN THE NORWEGIAN PARLIAMENTARY ELECTION 2017, PERCENTAGE AGREE

	Far Left	Left	Right	Far Right
Respect	88.2	72.6	61.0	35.4
Protect	70.6	35.9*	29.6*	14.3*
N	(68)	(300)	(282)	(121)

Note: N = sample size; gray indicates broad-based coalitions in favor of or against inclusion.
* Difference between top and bottom rows are statistically significant at .05 level (ANOVA).

bottom row, the political landscape if the option on offer is that Muslims have a right to have their culture and traditions protected. A right to be treated with respect commands decisive support across the political spectrum, very much including the mainstream right. The exclusionary right stands alone in opposition. But when the option on offer is Muslims having a right to have their culture and traditions protected, the political landscape is turned upside down. Now, support has cratered across the political spectrum. Whereas 73 percent of partisans on the left support recognition respect, only 36 percent support appraisal respect. Similarly, whereas fully 61 percent of the main right support recognition respect, only 30 percent support appraisal respect. The far left stands alone, with 70 percent in support of appraisal respect.

The crucial feature of a polarization trap, then, is that a failure to recognize pivotal distinctions between inclusionary options can lead to an overestimation of public support for exclusionary agendas both among those who are open too inclusion and those who fight for exclusion.

BEYOND PARTY POLITICS

The potential of the new framework for the study of inclusive politics to inform those actors who want to work for inclusion extends beyond ordinary party politics. Above all, the question of inclusionary options is vital to Muslims themselves. A big question raised by the proposed framework is, therefore, Are the paths to inclusion which are acceptable to large shares of the non-Muslim population acceptable to Muslims themselves?

Opinion on this question among Muslims naturally varies. But we cannot doubt that learning about potential openings for inclusion will better enable members of Muslim communities to come to grips with the struggle they are in. It is understandable that members of the Muslim minority community, viewing non-Muslim majority opinion through a valence framework, believe that majorities are anti-Muslim or at the least unsympathetic to Muslims. A poignant example, discussed at some length in chapter 4, is offensive speech.

The issue is characteristically posed in free-speech terms. To take an example, in the Letter to the Editor experiment, Norwegians were asked if a newspaper should be allowed to publish letters that are offensive to Muslims. The response of non-Muslim majority citizens is, overwhelmingly, yes.[36] So ingrained is the habit of inferring feelings about a minority from the positions that majorities take on policies regarding minorities that it would be odd if many Muslims did not take this support for allowing letters that are offensive to Muslims to be published as evidence that non-Muslim majority citizens believe that they are "fair game" for insults. It is all the same wrong. As chapter 4 also showed, non-Muslim majority citizens are at least as likely to take exactly the same position for letters that are offensive to Christians. Still more important, though they believe that editors have a free speech right to publish letters that are offensive to Muslims, most non-Muslims also believe that they should *not* publish them. This distinction between "may" and "should" speaks to the friction inherent in liberal democratic ideals. If your fellow citizens may say only what you yourself believe that they should say, the right to free speech vanishes.

The valence model at the core of the standard framework for the study of prejudice and politics puts the focus on feelings—how positively or negatively non-Muslim majority citizens feel about Muslims, how favorably or unfavorably they feel about inclusion or exclusion. Often, the choices in politics are between more versus less: between more government spending for the poor versus less, between increasing health care benefits or keeping them the same, between more restrictive or less restrictive immigration politics. And at the end of the day choices between more versus less can come down to how positively or negatively one group feels about another. But, to speak plainly, in politics ideas matter, too. Hence the significance of conflicts between liberal ideals, such as between recognition respect versus appraisal respect, and between what should be said versus what should be allowed to be said. These are not reducible to more or less. The distinctions between the alternatives on offer matter because they represent different ideas about what should and should not be done. The point of the new framework for the study of inclusive politics that we propose is to bring ideas to the center of theories of inclusive politics, and to do so *not* instead of the well-established focus on affect, but in addition to it.

[CHAPTER NINE]
INVITATIONS

We said at the outset that this book is a beginning, not the end of a research program on inclusive politics. It is time to spell out what we mean.

EXPANDING THE SCOPE OF INQUIRY

Intolerance has been the focus of previous research. It should remain a focus of ongoing research so long as calls for exclusion of Muslim minorities are a driving force in mass politics in established democracies. But a focus solely on exclusion is a negative research agenda. At best, it brings out how particular factors and specific circumstances strengthen intolerance and, by inference, how intolerance may be weakened, albeit only indirectly as a rule and in any case only over the long run.[1]

Expanding the scope of inquiry by turning the spotlight from intolerance to tolerance, from exclusion to inclusion—both conceptually and empirically—is our appeal. Many things follow in turn.

RETHINKING TOLERANCE

One is an invitation to rethink tolerance itself. Standardly, tolerance has been conceived of as a willingness to put up with, to tolerate, ideas or groups you disagree with or dislike. But once inclusion of Muslim minorities is the focus, it is clear that a mere willingness to tolerate, though necessary for inclusion, is not sufficient. A more affirmative conception of tolerance is needed—inclusive tolerance we have called it.

More than one marker of openness to inclusive tolerance would serve. We have chosen a measure of concern about prejudice and internal motivation to control it (IMCP). Our prediction is that other related measures would return much the same results. But we do not expect that the final word has been said in that discussion.

THE INCLUSIONARY OPTIONS FRAMEWORK

We started with a hunch that what inclusion asks of those who are open to it will matter. Finding in initial trials that this indeed is so led to a realization that the standard model of prejudice and politics is silent on what the pivotal distinctions might be. From this insight followed the need for a new analytical framework for the study of inclusive politics, one that focuses on the inclusionary political options on the table, and specifically on the normative premises that underpin them and, more precisely still, whether they matter to the largest share of citizens—those who are open to inclusive tolerance.

This book is in some ways an essay on the requirement of respect in contemporary liberal democracies. Fair opportunities for education, employment, housing, and social protection are necessary conditions of inclusion. But Muslim minorities in Western Europe live their lives among non-Muslim majorities, even though they do not live next to them. The character of their lives follows from recognition—or denial—of their dignity, of respect for who they are and what they value. Respect, dignity, we have been told, are merely symbolic goods: desirable but of secondary importance. To which we would reply, it has been our experience that a taken-for-granted recognition of one's worth is of secondary importance primarily to those assured of it.

What is called for if contemporary liberal democracies are to respect Muslims and their faith? Tolerance in the sense of agreeing to accept the rights of others to follow an outlook on life that you strongly disagree with is not enough. But to go further and ask citizens to find merit in an outlook on life that is, in their eyes, illiberal is to ask them to be hypocrites. Hence the importance of distinguishing between recognition respect and appraisal respect.

To our knowledge, the importance of this distinction has not been appreciated in previous studies. Yet, it is vital. To borrow Jeremy Waldron's words, "a guarantee of dignity is what enables a person to walk down the street without fear of insult or humiliation, to find the shops and exchanges open to him, and to proceed with an implicit assurance of being able to interact with others without being treated as a pariah."[2] For Muslims, a guarantee of dignity calls for a readiness to respect their worth as Muslims.

Non-Muslim majority citizens, multiple sequences of our experiments have shown, accept that the larger society has a responsibility to acknowledge the worth of Muslims and their culture, and to do so publicly. A quite different thing is appraisal respect: a readiness to evaluate Muslim beliefs and practices as praiseworthy, even, possibly, deserving of emulation. Majority citizens accept that the larger society has a responsibility to respect Muslim traditions and practices. They do not accept that it has a duty to admire or sustain them.

A second distinction, between what may and what should be said, goes to the heart of speech as a mirror of dignity. For many Muslims, as for many Christians, a willingness to tolerate speech that is offensive, that mocks and insults their faith, is evidence of a desire to hurt, to deny them and their faith the respect that they deserve. Majority citizens disagree, the Letter to the Editor experiments show. Hate speech should be prohibited, but offensive speech, even speech that is deliberately, intensely critical and offensive to Muslims, should be allowed.

One response is to take this as evidence of ordinary citizens' understanding of what the principle of freedom of expression requires. Still, a decent respect for hypocrisy is always in order. It is perfectly obvious that some native citizens will declare that their hands are tied by their commitment to freedom of speech, though in truth they don't mind at all Muslims being knocked about in the public sphere. All the more reason for us to underline that the Letters to the Editor experiment sequence showed repeatedly that on the issue of what speech is allowable, respondents applied the same standards to Christians as to Muslims.

It is understandable that evidence of impartiality may not be entirely satisfying to a Muslim, not least because in Christian-heritage societies, Christianity and Christians quite obviously are nowhere near as likely to be a target of offensive speech as Islam and Muslims. Hence the importance of the distinction between what citizens believe that others *should be allowed* to say and what they *should* say. If you believe that others should be allowed to say only what you believe that they should say, you've quashed their right to disagree with you. Commitment to freedom of expression requires accepting that others may say offensive things. What you believe that they should and should not say is another matter and goes to your understanding of what common decency calls for. The key point is that non-Muslim majority citizens believe that mocking, insulting, or expressing contempt for Muslims is wrong.

These distinctions, and others we have discussed, are pivotal in the sense that they can turn majorities in favor of or against inclusion. While there can be no doubt that the areas of life we have covered in this volume are central in the struggle for inclusion, we do not suppose that our account of pivotal distinctions is complete.

CONFLICT BETWEEN LIBERAL VALUES

Most of the pivotal distinctions we have highlighted take a familiar form of juxtaposing one inclusionary principle against another. Even more telling, in several instances where we directly contrasted approval of inclusionary and exclusionary options (the Less Emphasis experiment in chapter 5 and the Seat at the Table experiment in chapter 6), we observed that the inclusionary option was vastly more popular than the exclusionary one. By contrast, in chapter 7, we brought forward examples of when the liberal value of inclusionary tolerance comes into conflict with other liberal values, and the outcome is not inclusionary, but illiberal—massive support for the exclusion of Muslim minorities from fundamental democratic rights.

And what follows from this? The need to take account of conflicts between liberal democratic values—conflicts that can lead those who support liberal values to make illiberal choices, not because they are insufficiently liberal but just because they truly support liberal ideals.

This is a new challenge for liberal democracies. In the past, the risk was that ordinary citizens would undercut liberal democratic institutions by a failure to support the rights of groups or of ideas that they fear or strongly disagree with. That threat remains. But now there is an additional hazard. Those who believe in liberal democratic values are at risk of making illiberal choices because, in their eyes, some Muslim tenets or practices are illiberal.

Liberal values promoting illiberal choices, does it really come to this? The results of the Public Rally experiment show that those who are most supportive of inclusive tolerance, although backing the right of Muslims to hold public rallies under most circumstances, are as likely as those who are the most intolerant to oppose Muslims being allowed to hold a religious rally to preach conservative ideas regarding women. One can respond that Muslim ideas about women are a form of hate speech, demeaning women and denying them equality with men. This has in fact been an argument made in response to presentations of the results of the Public Rally experiment. It is not out of bounds to argue that the views of others are misogynistic. But denying them the right to gather together to advocate their ideas and faith is a denial of a foundational democratic right. If preaching conservative ideas about women as a profession of faith is illegal, it is not obvious that a right to freedom of religion remains; still less, that a right to hold views that are merely controversial remains.

How far does this argument extend? How deep are these conflicts? This study is incomplete, as all studies are, and what is more, incomplete in particularly obvious ways, not least a need to enlarge its scope to include a wider range of contemporary liberal democracies at a minimum; still more obviously, a need to take into account the beliefs, concerns, and convictions of Muslims as well as non-Muslims. But when we say here that our study is incomplete, we have something stronger in mind. The question to face is, If the results we have obtained are reliable, what are now the pressing questions that need answers?

The Bad Faith experiment has been conducted six times: twice in Denmark, once in the Netherlands, twice in Norway, once in the UK. The issue is not whether to have confidence in the empirical results. Without exception, majority citizens are more likely to distrust Muslim religious leaders than ordinary Muslims "when they say that they want to become part of our country." The challenge is to understand more fully what the empirical results signify. It is safe to say that the loyalty of Muslim religious leaders is suspect because they personify Islam as non-Muslim majority citizens fear it is. Safe to say, yes, but also, unacceptably vague. Are imams suspect because, in the mind's eye of majority citizens, they are the personification of an illiberal creed? Or, more simply, of a foreign creed? Or, yet again, of a religious creed deformed by extremism?

Then again, vagueness may be the point. It beggars belief to suppose that majority citizens have anything like a definite idea of what Islam entails. So far as they have an impression of it, it is a blurry impression of a religion that is foreign, illiberal, belligerent at finding itself in societies that by its lights are godless and immoral. This surely describes the mental territory of the intolerant.

Our call is to explore a new territory—the beliefs, the concerns, the convictions of majority citizens who are open to a more inclusive society. Doing so points in a different direction, not to a diffuse image of Islam but to more particularized aspects. The tolerant value the larger family of liberal ideals for the same reasons that they value tolerance. Our own results, above all, from the Public Rally experiment, demonstrate the power of gender inequality to ignite a counterreaction, the tolerant lining up right alongside the intolerant in denying Muslims the right to hold a religious rally to preach Islam's conservative ideas regarding women. But the issue of gender roles cannot be the sole Muslim tenet or practice that the tolerant react against.

Here is a thought experiment. Suppose that Islamic ideas about the status of women matched those of the majority culture. Would the concerns that those who hold liberal values about Muslim culture evaporate? It is nearer the mark to suggest that, for those who favor liberal ideals, Islam stands for illiberal values, plural—among them, rigid and punitive child-rearing practices, self-isolation from the larger society, commitment to a religious rather than secular outlook.

It will be a challenge to establish what, in the minds of non-Muslim citizens, is central and what is peripheral. An obvious example is the purported divide between those who favor a secular culture and those who favor religious values. If this is right, it is not obvious in what sense it is right. Some no doubt are opposed to religion, but the largest number of non-Muslim citizens are not committed to seeing that theirs is a Godless culture. Christianity remains a religion that is practiced, albeit increasingly limited to ceremonial occasions (e.g., baptisms or confirmations), and through occasional church attendance. For that matter, it would be extravagant to characterize citizens at large as committed root-and-branch to science. More interestingly, and more instructively, the ties between Christianity and a secular, liberal society are more complex than current conversations acknowledge. It has been well argued that "Christian conscience was the force which began to make Europe 'secular'; that is, to allow many religions or no religion in a state, and repudiate any kind of pressure upon the man who rejected the accepted and inherited axioms of society."[3] It cannot be said that the insights of traditional scholarship have been fully exploited.

TAKING PART

The Election Poll Volunteer experiment points to another possible way to go forward. The experiment brings into play a double contrast, between wearing a cross or wearing a hijab, and between what one should do and what one should be allowed to do. Majority citizens subscribe in equal numbers to the propositions that the poll volunteer should wear a hijab if she usually does and that she should wear a cross if she usually does. The counterweight finding is that far more declare that the poll volunteer *should be allowed* to wear a cross than support her Muslim counterpart wearing a hijab. What could explain this pattern of responses? On one side, an equal amount of tolerance of Muslims and Christians if the question turns on accepting that they wear a religious symbol that they usually wear. Yet clearly not extending the same leeway to the Muslim poll worker as to the Christian one, when the question is what she should be allowed to wear.

Experiments on proposed constructions of mosques, investigating reactions depending on the architectural style and size of the mosque, suggest that mere visibility is a source of opposition.[4] The suggestion is that prominence of Islamic religious/cultural symbols in public spaces carry implicit claims to cultural ascendency.[5] This is a suggestion that manifestly deserves to be followed up on, but it leaves obscure what Islamic religious/ cultural symbols may signify to citizens who favor liberal ideals. Perhaps, it is no more than an image of imams as dogmatic, domineering, repressive figures; perhaps, no more than the image of a way of life that is foreign, adversarial, outmoded; or, perhaps (...)

The risk in this line of reasoning, from our point of view, is focusing single-mindedly on the psychology of politics at the expense of politics itself. The lines along which Muslim communities are politically organized matter. Coalitions between political parties on the left and traditional Muslim leadership offer gains in trade for both: for the political parties, efficiency in mobilizing voters, for traditional Muslim leaders, buttressing control over Muslim communities. Insofar as the influence of patriarchal, traditional authorities is reinforced, majority citizens' identification of the leadership of Muslim communities with Muslim religious leaders is based in reality. In turn, the willingness of leaders of both majority and minority communities to take initiatives for cooperative ventures is sapped, the former because majority citizens most likely to support them suspect the bad faith of Muslim religious leaders and therefore are likely to suspect proposals that they back; the latter because separation from the larger liberal society secures the sway of traditional hierarchical values and their own leadership positions in Muslim communities.

Assimilation is not the goal; inclusion is. The results of the Asylum Seeker experiment, as we have turned them over in our minds, point to a possibility that deserves more extensive consideration. The experiment focuses on whether refugees, who have been living in Norway for several years, should be allowed to stay even though their claim to asylum has been rejected after formal legal proceedings. When told that the refugees "have participated actively in their local communities," majority citizens were markedly more likely to want the refugees to be allowed to stay. This speaks, we have argued, to the importance that majority citizens attach to civic participation.

Civic participation is an aspect of cultural integration,[6] worth carving out because it is concretely grounded in public life. For Muslims, civic participation speaks to a sharing not only of "a commitment to democracy as an abstract principle, but also [sharing] an understanding of what 'behaving like a democrat' means."[7] "Behaving like a democrat" captures the vital point. Standardly, we explain why people behave as they do because they have the beliefs that they do. The logic of the Declaration of Loyalty and Asylum Seeker experiments points to the obverse: we infer the beliefs of people from their behavior. When do majority citizens believe that Muslims mean what they say when they say that they want to be part of the country? Not when they declare it; not even, as the Declaration of Loyalty experiment showed, when they collectively and publicly declare their loyalty. What counts more, the Asylum Seeker experiment teaches, is what Muslim minorities do. Civic participation is a value in the countries we study. Civic participation does not call for Muslims to value being Muslim any less. Civic participation should receive more attention as a, perhaps even the, path to civic integration.

POLARIZATION TRAPS

Throughout the account given in this volume, it is as though there are two lines drawn: one identifying what should be done if a society aims to be inclusive, the other identifying the point beyond which support for inclusion collapses. To take an example, excepting the far right, there is agreement across the political spectrum that national identities are and should be constructed rather than assigned. But if the continuity of the process of reconstructing a national identity is disrupted, agreement sinks across the political spectrum. The intolerant throw their weight against inclusion on any terms. The tolerant are open to more inclusive conceptions of the national identity provided there is continuity in the process of its construction. The distinction between continuous and interrupted processes of national identity construction is pivotal. It can turn majorities in favor of or against inclusion.

In this lies the risk of polarization traps. The standard model of prejudice and politics de-emphasizes the granularities of inclusionary political options, and the breadth of support for the normative premises that underpin them. One illustration of this is the tendency, both in academic literature and in public debate, to categorize policies and actors in terms of valence, for example as pro- or anti-Muslim, or pro- or anti-immigrant.

The analyses we have presented in this volume demonstrate why such conceptions miss critical aspects of the pattern of public opinion on cultural and religious diversity. Polarization traps capture the political risks of operating on incomplete theories of public openness to inclusive politics, particularly for actors who favor and fight for inclusion. The risk is overestimation of the breadth of the appeal of the exclusionary agenda in ways that turn into self-fulfilling prophesies. Approaching the struggle for inclusion with attention to pivotal distinctions between inclusionary options will likely minimize the risk of falling into polarization traps. But that is easier said than done. For this reason, furthering the conceptual and empirical analysis of polarization traps is urgent.

THE ETHOS AND ARCHITECTURE OF SURVEY EXPERIMENTS

In describing our approach, we have felt most comfortable characterizing it as learning as you go; most comfortable because, far from starting with a theory then deducing hypotheses, textbook style, we often had to grope our way forward, and we sometimes had to double back because we missed a step in reasoning. This is what we believe to be the true experimentalist ethos, to conduct an experiment not because you know the answer but because you recognize that the answer you anticipate may well be wrong. Hence our methodological credo: You can't win if you can't lose.

But there is a deeper methodological lesson about the architecture of survey experimental research. This volume has profited from unique access to the Norwegian Citizen Panel that made the repeated fielding of sequences of survey experiments possible. This has made possible an iterative approach, learning from the results of each step the next step to take. We wish we had it in our power to see that many more scientists have similar platforms to learn as they go.

LIBERAL IDEALS AND DEMOCRATIC STRAINS

Surmounting challenges of intolerance and irrationality in the past is no guarantee of surmounting them now or in the future. Democratic politics is an innately risky undertaking. But the premise of this book is that it is a potentially progressive enterprise. This study accordingly is committed to a simple claim. It is time to turn from a narrow concentration on those within the majority public who are bent on exclusion to the much larger number who are open to inclusion. How far are they willing to go? Where do they draw the line? And why do they draw it there and not elsewhere? The expansion of liberal democratic ideals simultaneously opens up and sets limits in the struggle for inclusion and both the opportunities and the limits are bound up with the moral authority and the moral limits of liberal democratic ideals.

Acknowledgments

This study has been in the works for nearly a decade. Over the years, we have benefited in ways too many to count from the generosity of colleagues around us. Conceding the inevitability of failure, we shall do our best to acknowledge them.

We first want to thank those who helped us collect data, Stefan Dahlberg for the study in Sweden reported in chapter 6; Annelies Blom in Germany and Sveinung Arnesen in Norway, who made the European Internet Panel Study reported in chapter 2 possible; Robert Ford and Maria Sobolewska for the studies in Great Britain; Yphtach Lelkes for studies in the Netherlands; the Runes (Stubager and Slothuus) and Michael Bang Petersen in Aarhus for the studies in Denmark; and Ted Carmines for the studies in the US. Without their help, the studies in this book could not have been carried out.

We are deeply indebted to our colleagues who have made the Norwegian Citizen Panel a reality. Without this unique infrastructure, we would not have hit on the method of sequential factorials. The thrill of the opportunity to conduct an experimental trial, to learn from it, then to conduct another and realize that an unanticipated question demands an answer, and then to carry out yet another trial to attempt to answer it—few have had this opportunity. We hope that the use we have made of this research infrastructure will make those at the University of Bergen and the Trond Mohn Foundation who funded the NCP proud. Our sincere gratitude extends to the highly professional Norwegian Citizen Panel core crew, Erla Løvseth, Hiwa Målen, Ingrid Ovidia Moe Telle, Lise Bjånesøy, Mikael Johanesson, Sveinung Arnesen, Stefan Dahlberg, Marta R. Eidheim, Runa F. Langaas, Erik Knudsen and the company ideas2evidence, and especially Øivind

Skjervheim and Asle Høgestøl, who prepared, piloted, fielded, and documented each and every study to the highest scientific standards. Their hard work and dedication gave us the opportunity to do this study.

Initial support from the National Science Foundation and the University of Bergen got us off the ground. Large grants from the Trond Mohn Foundation (DIGSSCORE) and the Research Council of Norway (TERMS) allowed us to expand and complete the project. A grant from the Europe Center at the Freeman Spogli Institute for International Studies supported the last round of studies. And, yet again, our largest debt at Stanford is to the Institute for Research in Social Science under the direction of our colleagues Karen Cook and Chris Thomsen, which provided funding, release time for writing, and an abundance of encouragement.

For opportunities to present drafts and early versions of chapters, we are grateful for the seminar series and symposiums of the Department of Comparative Politics at the University of Bergen and the Political Science Department at the University of Gothenburg; Ashley Jardina on behalf of the Duke Behavior and Identities Workshop; Joost van Spanje and Wouter van der Brug at the University of Amsterdam; Petra Schleiter at the University of Oxford; Marc Hetherington on behalf of the American Politics Research Group at the University of North Carolina, Chapel Hill; the Gothenburg-Barcelona-Bergen Workshop on Experimental Political Science; V-Dem and Anna Lührman, who organized the excellent conference on democracy with the Max Planck Institute in Berlin; and to the Hertie School for their invitation to present at their workshop on hate speech. The feedback received at all these meetings and events helped mature and sharpen the ideas presented in this volume.

In this series of events, one deserves special mention. The municipal program in Bergen, Norway, organized by Elisabeth Harnes at RVTS-Vest, where we have had numerous occasions to present research findings to leaders of Muslim communities, including imams, and mentors who work to fight extremism and facilitate inclusion. These meetings brought into sharp focus what is at stake in the struggle for inclusion.

We are almost embarrassed at the great number of colleagues who, in the course of this decade, have taken the time to engage with the ideas presented in this volume. Most especially, we have benefited immensely from colleagues who read and sent us comments and feedback on the (many) earlier drafts of this book either in part or in their entirety: Paul Beck, Scott Blinder, Eamonn Callan, Katherine Clayton, Raphaela Dancygier, Peter Esaiasson, Morris P. Fiorina, Paul Goren, Stephen Haber, Robert Huckfeldt, Hanspeter Kriesi, David Miller, Jordi Munoz, Lise Rakner, Nicholas Sambanis, Byron Shafer, Mike Tomz, and Endre M. Tvinnereim.

Sniderman owes a singular debt to Jackie Sargent and Eliana Vasquez for help on all administrative fronts, still more for friendship. In the final stages, Ingrid K. Faleide provided critical research assistance and helped produce several of the most telling figures included in the volume. Last but not least, Chuck Myers, editor and partner, was indispensable in helping us cross the finish line.

[APPENDIX]

Documentation of Survey Experiments by Figure

FIGURE 2.4. The Differentiation Experiment

Source: The 2017 European Internet Panel Study.[1] The data were collected in France, Norway, Iceland, Germany, the Netherlands, and Sweden between May 1, 2017, and January 10, 2018.
Variable name: eips2017i
Total N: 17,964
Wording:

> Imagine that [a populist right-wing party/a non-populist right-wing party/a Christian congregation/a Muslim congregation/an anti-Islamic group/a neo-Nazi group/a Muslim fundamentalist group] has asked to rent a local community house in order to hold a meeting for its members and sympathizers. To what extent do you agree that the [same group as above] should be allowed to rent the local community house for this purpose?

Scale: 10/11-point Agree–Disagree

PANEL A. FRANCE

Source: The ELIPSS panel (Longitudinal Internet Studies for Social Sciences)[2]
Field period: July 12–September 28, 2017
N: 2,507

PANEL B. GERMANY

Source: The German Internet Panel (GIP), Wave 29[3]
Variable name: ZH29062
Field period: May 1–31, 2017
N: 2,706

PANEL C. NETHERLANDS

> Source: The LISS panel (Longitudinal Internet Studies for the Social Sciences)
> Field period: May 15–June 14, 2017
> *N*: 5,622

PANEL D. NORWAY

> Source: Norwegian Citizen Panel, Wave 9[4]
> Field period: May 11–June 6, 2017
> *N*: 2,706

PANEL E. SWEDEN

> Source: The Citizen Panel, Wave 28[5]
> Field period: December 12, 2017–January 10, 2018
> *N*: 2,507

FIGURE 3.1. Affirmation of Diversity

PANEL A. NORWAY

> Source: Norwegian Citizen Panel, Wave 2, March 2014[6]
> Variable name: w02_dv210a, b
> *N*: 844
> Wording:
>
>> To what extent do you agree or disagree with the following statement?
>> It is important to [recognize/celebrate] the new diversity in Norway.
>
> Scale: 7-point Agree–Disagree

PANEL B. UNITED STATES (WHITES ONLY)

> Source: Cooperative Congressional Election Study, 2013[7]
> Variable name: IUB466-8
> *N*: 989
> Wording (English):
>
>> How strongly do you agree with the following statement?
>> It is important to [acknowledge/respect/celebrate] the new diversity of America.
>
> Scale: 4-point Agree–Disagree

FIGURE 3.2. Public Affirmation of Diversity

> Source: Muslim Inclusion Study 2, Great Britain, November 2015[8]
> Variable name: manc13; text_1
> *N*: 1,692

Wording (English):

> How strongly do you agree with the following statement?
> It is important to [acknowledge/respect/celebrate] the new diversity of America.

Scale: 4-point Agree–Disagree

FIGURE 3.3. Respect for Muslim Culture: First Trial

Source: Norwegian Citizen Panel, Wave 1, November 2013[9]
Variable name: w01_dv25, w01_dv26
N: 1,175
Wording:

> How much do you agree or disagree with the following statement:
> [Muslim/Immigrant] culture should be [respected/protected].

Scale: 7-point Agree–Disagree

FIGURE 3.4. Respect for Muslim Culture: Follow-up Trials

PANEL A. UNITED STATES (WHITES ONLY)

Source: Muslim Inclusion Study 1, United States, September 2012–May 2013[10]
Variable name: w3_q56a-b
N: 692
Wording (English):

> Muslims have right to have their traditions and culture [respected/protected].

Scale: 4-point Agree–Disagree

PANEL B. GREAT BRITAIN

Source: Muslim Inclusion Study 2, Great Britain, November 2015
Variable name: manc14
N: 866
Wording (English):

> To what extent do you agree or disagree with the following statement:
> Muslim immigrants have a right to have their traditions and culture [respected/protected].

Scale: 4-point Agree–Disagree

FIGURE 3.5. Recognition Respect vs. Appraisal Respect

PANEL A. NORWAY

> Source: Norwegian Citizen Panel, Wave 15, May/June 2019[11]
> Variable name: r15meme7_a
> N: 885
> Wording:
>
>> Muslims in Norway have the right to have their cultures and traditions [respected/supported/preserved].
>
> Scale: 7-point Agree–Disagree

PANEL B. GREAT BRITAIN

> Source: Muslim Inclusion Study 5, Great Britain, July 2019[12]
> Variable name: respect1
> N: 2,372
> Wording:
>
>> Muslims in Britain have the right to have their cultures and traditions [respected/supported/helped to keep going].
>
> Scale: 5-point Agree–Disagree

FIGURE 3.6. Respect Principles by Inclusive Tolerance

PANEL A. AFFIRMATION OF DIVERSITY. NORWAY

> Source: Norwegian Citizen Panel, Wave 2, March 2014
> Variable name: w02_dv210a, b
> N: 820
> Wording:
>
>> To what extent do you agree or disagree with the following statement?
>> It is important to [recognize/celebrate] the new diversity in Norway.
>
> Scale: 7-point Agree–Disagree

PANEL B. RECOGNITION RESPECT VS. APPRAISAL RESPECT. NORWAY

> Source: Norwegian Citizen Panel, Wave 1, November 2013
> Variable name: w01_dv25, w01_dv26
> N: 1,153

Wording:

> Muslims in Norway are entitled to [respect for/protection of] their traditions and culture.

Scale: 7-point Agree–Disagree

Elements of Internal Motivation to Control Prejudice (IMCP)

Source: Norwegian Citizen Panel, Wave 1, November 2013[13]
Variable name: w01_dv38_1, 2, 3, 4
Wording:

> How well or poorly would you say that the following description fits you:
> __ 1: It is important to me personally to be unprejudiced toward immigrants.
> __ 2: I would not like to be perceived as racist, not even unto myself.
> __ 3: I feel guilty if I have negative feelings toward immigrants.
> __ 4: I try to be unprejudiced toward immigrants due to my own conviction.

Scale: 7-point Well–Poorly

FIGURE 4.1. Hate Speech vs. Offensive Speech: First Trial. Norway

Source: Norwegian Citizen Panel, Wave 5, October/November 2015[14]
Variable name: r5dv10a, b, c, d
N: 1,384
Wording:

> Newspaper editors sometimes receive letters from readers that [threaten/express hatred toward/express prejudice toward/express a negative view toward] immigrants in Norway. To what extent do you agree or disagree that newspaper editors should publish such readers' letters?

Scale: 7-point Agree–Disagree

FIGURE 4.2. Hate Speech vs. Offensive Speech: Evenhandedness

PANEL A. LETTERS ABOUT MUSLIMS THAT ARE OFFENSIVE / EXPRESS HATRED. NORWAY

Source: Norwegian Citizen Panel, Wave 8, March 2017[15]
Variable name: r8mi3_i, 1
N: 291
Wording:

> Should Norwegian newspapers publish letters that [are offensive to/express hatred against] Muslims?
> Yes/No

PANEL B. LETTERS ABOUT MUSLIMS/CHRISTIANS THAT ARE OFFENSIVE. NORWAY

    Source: Norwegian Citizen Panel, Wave 8, March 2017
    Variable name: r8mi3_g, i
    N: 268
    Wording:

        Should Norwegian newspapers publish letters that are offensive to [Christians/Muslims]?
        Yes/No

PANEL C. LETTERS ABOUT MUSLIMS/CHRISTIANS THAT EXPRESS HATRED. NORWAY

    Source: Norwegian Citizen Panel, Wave 8, March 2017
    Variable name: r8mi3_j, 1
    N: 292
    Wording:

        Should Norwegian newspapers publish letters expressing hatred against [Christians/Muslims]?
        Yes/No

FIGURE 4.3. The May/Should Distinction: The Unreasonable Letters Trial

PANEL A. LETTERS ABOUT IMMIGRANTS THAT ARE CRITICAL/UNREASONABLE/INACCURATE. NORWAY

    Source: Norwegian Citizen Panel, Wave 5, October/November 2015
    Variable name: r5dv14d, e, f
    N: 652
    Wording:

        Should newspapers in Norway publish letters that are intensely critical of immigrants [NONE/on inaccurate grounds/on unreasonable grounds]?
        Should publish/Should not publish

PANEL B. MAY/SHOULD PUBLISH CRITICAL LETTERS. NORWAY

    Source: Norwegian Citizen Panel, Wave 5, October/November 2015
    Variable name: r5dv14a, d
    N: 438
    Wording:

        Should newspapers in Norway [NONE/be allowed to] publish letters that are intensely critical of immigrants?

DOCUMENTATION OF SURVEY EXPERIMENTS BY FIGURE › 163

a. Should be allowed to publish/Should not be allowed to publish

d. Should publish/Should not publish

PANEL C. MAY/SHOULD PUBLISH UNREASONABLE LETTERS. NORWAY

Source: Norwegian Citizen Panel, Wave 5, October/November 2015
Variable name: r5dv14b, e
N: 445
Wording:

Should newspapers in Norway [NONE/be allowed to] publish letters that are intensely critical of immigrants?

b. Should be allowed to publish/Should not be allowed to publish

e. Should publish/Should not publish

PANEL D. MAY/SHOULD PUBLISH INACCURATE LETTERS. NORWAY

Source: Norwegian Citizen Panel, Wave 5, October/November 2015
Variable name: r5dv14c, f
N: 481
Wording:

Should newspapers in Norway [NONE/be allowed to] publish letters that are intensely critical of immigrants?

c. Should be allowed to publish/Should not be allowed to publish

f. Should publish/Should not publish

FIGURE 4.4. The May/Should Distinction: The Contemptuous Speech Trial

Source: Norwegian Citizen Panel, Wave 18, June 2020[16]
Variable name: r18memeletters
Wording:

To what extent do you agree or disagree that Norwegian newspapers should [NONE/be allowed to] publish posts that [criticize/mock/show contempt for/express hatred toward] [Muslims/Christians] and their religious values?

Scale: 7-point Agree–Disagree

PANEL A. MAY PUBLISH LETTERS ABOUT MUSLIMS THAT ARE CRITICAL/MOCK/SHOW CONTEMPT/EXPRESS HATRED. NORWAY

N: 653

PANEL B. MAY/SHOULD PUBLISH CRITICAL LETTERS ABOUT MUSLIMS. NORWAY

N: 328

PANEL C. MAY/SHOULD PUBLISH LETTERS ABOUT MUSLIMS THAT MOCK/SHOW CONTEMPT/EXPRESS HATRED. NORWAY

N: 330

PANEL D. MAY/SHOULD PUBLISH LETTERS CRITICAL OF MUSLIMS/CHRISTIANS. NORWAY

N: 667

PANEL E. MAY/SHOULD PUBLISH LETTERS THAT SHOW CONTEMPT FOR MUSLIMS/CHRISTIANS. NORWAY

N: 654

FIGURE 4.5. The May vs. Should Distinction by Inclusive Tolerance. Norway

N: 273

FIGURE 5.1. The Textbook Experiment: The First Two-Letter Trial

Source: Cooperative Congressional Election Study, United States, 2013
Variable name: IUB458-462
N: 757
Wording:

> How strongly do you agree with the following statement:
> Textbooks should be [written/rewritten] to reflect the [cultural/ethnic/cultural and ethnic] diversity of America.

Scale: 4-point Agree–Disagree

PANEL A. PROCESS OF CONSTRUCTION. TEXTBOOKS SHOULD BE WRITTEN/REWRITTEN TO REFLECT DIVERSITY. UNITED STATES

N: 757

PANEL B. TYPE OF DIVERSITY. TEXTBOOKS SHOULD REFLECT CULTURAL/ETHNIC/CULTURAL AND ETHNIC DIVERSITY. UNITED STATES

N: 348

FIGURE 5.2. The Textbook Experiment: The Second Two-Letter Trial. Norway

Source: Norwegian Citizen Panel, Wave 2, March 2014
Variable name: w02_dv29a, b
N: 848

Wording:

> To what extent do you agree or disagree with the following statement? School books should be [written/rewritten] such that they reflect the new diversity in Norway.

Scale: 7-point Agree–Disagree

FIGURE 5.3. The Counterfactual Textbook Experiment

PANEL A. FIRST TRIAL. NORWAY

Source: Norwegian Citizen Panel, Wave 7, November 2016[17]
Variable name: r7mi5_1
N: 601
Wording:

> Textbooks for primary and lower secondary school should be written [with more emphasis on the new /to reflect the new/less emphasis on new ideas about] cultural diversity in Norway.

Scale: 7-point Agree–Disagree

PANEL B. REPLICATION TRIAL. NORWAY

Source: Norwegian Citizen Panel, Wave 12, June 2018[18]
Variable name: r12dv15
N: 1,488
Wording:

> Primary and lower secondary school textbooks should be written so that they [put more emphasis on/put less emphasis on/reflect] the new cultural diversity in Norway.

FIGURE 5.4. Continuity vs. Interruption in the Process of National Identity Construction

PANEL A. DENMARK

Source: Muslim Inclusion Study 3, Denmark, 2016[19]
Variable name: q20a-d
N: 1,828
Wording:

> To what extent do you agree or disagree with the following statement? School books should be [developed/revised/rewritten/redone] such that they reflect the new diversity in Denmark.

Scale: 4-point Agree–Disagree

PANEL B. GREAT BRITAIN

Source: Muslim Inclusion Study 5, Great Britain, July 2019
Variable name: textbook1
N: 3,107
Wording:

> To what extent do you agree or disagree with the following statement? [Additional textbooks should be written/School textbooks should be expanded/School textbooks should be updated/School textbooks should be redone] to reflect the cultural and religious diversity of Britain.

Scale: 5-point Agree–Disagree

PANEL C. NORWAY

Source: Norwegian Citizen Panel, Wave 15, May/June 2019
Variable name: r15meme7_b
N: 1,328
Wording:

> To what extent do you agree or disagree that schoolbooks should be [added/expanded/updated/redone/written] to reflect the cultural and religious diversity of Norway.

Scale: 7-point Agree–Disagree

PANEL D. NETHERLANDS

Source: Muslim Inclusion Study 4, Netherlands, 2019[20]
Variable name: writenewbooks, booksupdated, expandbooks, booksredone
N: 1,579
Wording:

> To what extent do you agree or disagree with the following statement?
> School books should be [added/expanded/updated/redone] to reflect the cultural and religious diversity of the Netherlands.

Scale: 5-point Agree–Disagree

FIGURE 5.5. The Principle of Continuous Construction: Additional Test. Great Britain

Source: Muslim Inclusion Study 2, Great Britain, November 2015
Variable name: q14a-b
N: 2,762
Wording:

> To what extent do you agree or disagree with the following statement?

Truly respecting the cultural and ethnic diversity of our country calls for [fresh thinking/opening a new chapter] in what our country stands for.

Scale: 5-point Agree–Disagree

FIGURE 5.6. The Continuity Principle by Inclusive Tolerance

PANEL A. ASSIGNED VS. CONSTRUCTED NATIONAL IDENTITY. NORWAY

Source: Norwegian Citizen Panel, Wave 12, June 2018
Variable name: r12dv15
N: 985
Wording:

Primary and lower secondary school textbooks should be written so that they [put less emphasis on/reflect] the new cultural diversity in Norway.

Scale: 7-point Agree–Disagree

PANEL B. CONTINUITY VS. INTERRUPTION IN THE PROCESS OF NATIONAL IDENTITY CONSTRUCTION. NORWAY

Source: Norwegian Citizen Panel, Wave 2, March 2014
Variable name: w02_dv29a, b
N: 824
Wording:

To what extent do you agree or disagree with the following statement?
School books should be [written/rewritten] such that they reflect the new diversity in Norway.

Scale: 7-point Agree–Disagree

FIGURE 6.1. The Asylum Seeker Sequence: The Pre-Crisis Trial. Norway. March 2015

Source: Norwegian Citizen Panel, Wave 4, March 2015[21]
Variable name: r4dv51a, b, c, d
N: 761
Wording:

Do you think that asylum seekers who have been living in Norway for several years [NONE/and have learned Norwegian/and have found a job/and have participated actively in their local communities] while they are waiting for a decision to be made should be granted residence, even if their appeals are rejected? Or do you think that they should not be allowed to stay?
Should be allowed to stay/Should not be allowed to stay

FIGURE 6.3. The Asylum Seeker Sequence: The Crisis Trial. Norway. March 2016

Source: Norwegian Citizen Panel, Wave 6, March 2016[22]
Variable name: r6dv52a, b, c, d
N: 625
Wording:

> Do you think that [NONE/Muslim] asylum seekers who have been living in Norway for several years [NONE/and have participated actively in their local communities] while they are waiting for a decision to be made should be granted residence, even if their appeals are rejected? Or do you think that they should not be allowed to stay?
> Should be allowed to stay/Should not be allowed to stay

FIGURE 6.4. The Asylum Seeker Sequence: The Generalizability Trial. Denmark. 2016

Source: Muslim Inclusion Study 3, Denmark, 2016
Variable name: q17a1, q17c1, q17e1, q17g1
N: 919
Wording:

> Do you think that [NONE/Muslim] asylum seekers who have been living in Denmark for several years [NONE/and have learned Danish/and have found a job/ and have participated actively in their local communities] while they are waiting for a decision to be made should be granted residence, even if their appeals are rejected? Or do you think that they should not be allowed to stay?
> Should be allowed to stay/Should not be allowed to stay

FIGURE 6.5. The Seat at the Table Experiment, Diverse vs. Homogeneous Regional Council. Norway

Source: Norwegian Citizen Panel, Wave 8, March 2017
Variable name: r8mi2_a, b
Wording:

> Imagine that you have been selected to participate in a regional committee that will find solutions to challenges related to the development of your region. To what extent do you agree or disagree that it is best for the region that only people [who share the same ethnic and religious backgrounds/ with a long experience of living in the region] participate in the committee?

Scale: 7-point Agree–Disagree
Variable name: r8mi2_c, d
Wording:

> Imagine that you have been selected to participate in a regional committee that will find solutions to challenges related to the development of your region. To

what extent do you agree or disagree that it is best for the region that people with different ethnic and religious backgrounds [participate in/must be in complete agreement about the proposals to] the committee?

Scale: 7-point Agree–Disagree

FIGURE 6.6. Preference for Diverse or Homogeneous Regional Council by Inclusive Tolerance. Norway

Diverse vs. homogeneous council best for region by IMCP
Variable name: r8mi2_a-d
N: 2,108

FIGURE 6.7. The Election Day Poll Volunteer Experiment

Source: Norwegian Citizen Panel, Wave 10, October/November 2017
Variable name: r10mi9_1
Wording:

To what extent do you agree or disagree that volunteers who are present at polling stations during parliamentary elections should [wear a hijab/wear a visible cross/be allowed to wear a hijab/be allowed to wear a visible cross/be free to wear a hijab/be free to wear a visible cross] if that is something they usually do?

Scale: 7-point Agree–Disagree

PANEL A. HIJAB VS. CROSS NECKLACE. NORWAY

N: 599

PANEL B. SHOULD VS. MAY DISTINCTION IN HIJAB QUESTION. NORWAY

N: 843

PANEL C. SHOULD VS. MAY DISTINCTION IN CROSS NECKLACE QUESTION. NORWAY

N: 821

FIGURE 6.8. Standards for Propriety and Discretion for Christians and Muslims by Inclusive Tolerance

PANEL A. PROPRIETY. NORWAY

N: 592

PANEL B. DISCRETION. NORWAY

N: 525

FIGURE 7.1. Conflict between Liberal Values. Norway

Source: Norwegian Citizen Panel, Wave 10, October/November 2017
Variable name: r10mi9_3
N: 1,645
Wording:
Some Norwegian Muslims have asked for permission to hold a public event to [explain/preach] [Islamic values/conservative notions about the position of women in Islam]. To what extent do you agree or disagree that they should be allowed to hold such an event?

FIGURE 7.2. Opposition to Public Rally by Inclusive Tolerance. Norway

N: 828

FIGURE 7.3. Bad Faith in Muslim Leaders by Inclusive Tolerance. Norway

Source: Norwegian Citizen Panel, Wave 8, March 2017
Variable name: r8mi4_b, f
N: 734
Wording:
How much do you trust or distrust [Muslim religious leaders/Muslims] when they say that they wish to be part of our society?

FIGURE 7.4. Bad Faith in Muslim Leaders: Follow-up Trial. Norway

Norwegian Citizen Panel, Wave 8, March 2017
Variable name: r8mi4_a-f
N: 2,098
Wording:
How much do you trust or distrust [Muslim extremists/ Muslim religious leaders/ Muslim leaders/ Muslim local politicians/female Muslim leaders/Muslims] when they say that they wish to be part of our society?

FIGURE 7.5. Bad Faith in Muslim Leaders: Final Extension Trial. Great Britain

Source: Muslim Inclusion Study, Great Britain, July 2019
Variable name: leader1
N: 3,073
Wording:

How much do you trust or distrust [Muslim religious leaders/ Muslim local councilors/female Muslim leaders/Muslims] when they say that they wish to be part of our society?

Scale: 5-point Trust–Distrust

Notes

CHAPTER ONE

1. To avoid repetitive and stilted styling, "non-Muslim majority citizens" and "majority citizens" are used interchangeably.

2. Our focus is contemporary liberal democracies. Both words, liberal and democratic, do work. So sometimes we shall use one, sometimes the other. But to avoid misunderstanding, to be unmistakably clear, *liberal* in this context is not liberal as opposed to conservative, or left as opposed to right. It is liberal in the sense employed by Berlin, among many, who in *Four Essays on Liberty* speaks of conflicts between liberal values; that is, values on which there is broad agreement, such as for example the autonomy of the individual and the equality of rights.

3. We are building on the work of many. For one of the first and arguably the most ambitious research program on values broadly conceived, see Goren, *On Voter Competence*; Goren et al., "A Unified Theory,"; Goren, "Core Principles." See also Federico and Malka, "The Contingent, Contextual Nature."

4. For companion arguments on humanitarianism, see Feldman and Steenbergen, "The Humanitarian Foundation"; Hartman et al., "Easing the Heavy Hand." For an original line of research on racial sympathy, see Chudy, "Racial Sympathy." For new research on tolerance as a positive disposition, see Hjerm et al., "A New Approach"; Feldman et al., "The Interplay of Empathy."

5. Schleifer, *Tocqueville's Democracy*, 352.

6. E.g., Hainmueller and Hangartner, "Who Gets a Swiss Passport?"; Sides and Citrin, "European Opinion about Immigration."

7. Storm, Sobolewska, and Ford, "Is Ethnic Prejudice Declining in Britain?"; Statham, "How Ordinary People View Muslim Group Rights"; Helbling, *Islamophobia in the West*; Wright et al., "Multiculturalism and Muslim Accommodation."

8. Sniderman and Hagendoorn, *When Ways of Life Collide*.

9. E.g., Inglehart and Norris, "Trump and the Populist"; Ivarsflaten, "What Unites Right-Wing Populists"; Mudde, *Populist Radical Right Parties in Europe*.

10. Interview with CBN in May 2012 and on Twitter, December 2016.

11. Berntzen 2019, *Liberal Roots of Far Right Activism*; Bail, *Terrified*.

12. Kepel, with Jardin, *Terror in France*.

13. Eatwell, "Community Cohesion," 205.

14. In our own presentations of results at community meetings, this is the result that most impressed Muslim participants.

15. Stenner, *Authoritarian Dynamic*.

16. Sidanius and Pratto, *Social Dominance*.

17. Jost et al., "Political Conservatism."

18. E.g., Inglehart and Welzel, *Modernization*; Dalton *Citizen Politics*; Welzel, *Freedom Rising*.

19. Dalton, *Citizen Politics*, 138.

20. Blinder, Ford, and Ivarsflaten, "Discrimination, Anti-prejudice" and "Better Angels"; Ivarsflaten, Blinder, and Ford, "Anti-Racism Norm."

21. Modood, *Multicultural Politics*, 5. For the most extended analysis of speech as a mirror of dignity, see Waldron, *Harm in Hate Speech*.

22. Research on national identity is burgeoning. It can be divided, roughly, into two clusters: studies of long-established orientations (e.g., patriotism, nationalism, chauvinism) and studies inspired by social identity theory. See Huddy, "Unifying National Identity," and Kalin and Sambanis, "How to Think about Social Identity," for especially useful overviews of both. Our objective is to add to this literature by examining a new dependent variable: attitudes toward authorized changes in the definition of national identities. For an innovative study of opposition to the expressive rights of Muslims as a function of the interplay between degree of national identification and diverse representations of a nation's history, see Smeekes, Verkuyten, and Pope, "Mobilizing Opposition towards Muslim Immigrants."

23. E.g., Sniderman and Hagendoorn, *When Ways of Life Collide*.

24. For an illuminating parallel, see Chadwick's analysis of the dilemma of the Catholic church, committed by its conception of religion as a development in history, faced with reconciling the opposing claims of truth in history and dogma: Chadwick, *Acton and History*, 32–34.

25. We are thankful to David Miller for emphasizing this and several other important points in a careful reading of an early version of the manuscript.

26. For the concept of a permissive consensus, see V. O. Key, *Public Opinion and American Democracy*.

27. Framing effects refer to contrasting preferences in choosing between alternatives that are substantively equivalent or, at the limit, logically interchangeable. A favorite example: choices whether to have surgery or not vary radically depending on whether the patient is said to have a nine out of ten chance of surviving or, alternatively, a one of ten chance of dying. The classic work is Kahneman and Tversky, *Judgement under Uncertainty*.

28. Smith, *Did Darwin Get It Right?*, 6.

29. We are indebted to our colleagues Avidit Acharya and Justin Grimmer for discussions and encouragement to work through the development of sequential factorials.

30. This brings benefits, though time will tell whether the benefits outweigh the costs: there is something to wonder about a premise that regulation is required because investigators, consciously or otherwise, too often take advantage of loopholes in data analysis; what reason is there to suppose that they will not, again consciously or otherwise, take advantage of loopholes in regulation?

CHAPTER TWO

1. Bleich, *The Freedom to Be Racist?*; Helbling and Traunmüller, "What Is Islamophobia?"
2. Alon and Omer, *The Psychology of Demonization*, 1.
3. Bail, *Terrified*.
4. Caiani, della Porta, and Wagemann, *Mobilizing on the Extreme Right*.
5. Berntzen, *Liberal Roots of Far Right Activism*.
6. Ivarsflaten, Blinder, and Bjånesøy, "Populist Radical Right Persuades Citizens."
7. Sniderman et al., *Paradoxes of Liberal Democracy*.
8. Berntzen and Weisskircher, "Anti-Islamic PEGIDA Beyond Germany."
9. Several research articles address the European refugee crisis, e.g., Bansak, Hainmueller, and Hangartner, "Economic, Humanitarian, and Religious Concerns"; Bansak, Hainmueller, and Hangartner, "Europeans Support a Proportional Allocation,"; Hangartner et al., "Exposure to the Refugee Crisis."
10. Nordø and Ivarsflaten, "The Scope of Exclusionary Public Response to the European Refugee Crisis"; Bye, Bygnes, and Ivarsflaten, "Imagining vs. Experiencing"; Bjånesøy, "Effects of the Refugee Crisis on Perceptions."
11. Solheim, *Terrorism and Attitudes toward Out-groups*.
12. Sniderman et al., "Reactions to Terror Attacks,"; Blinder, Ford, and Ivarsflaten, "Discrimination, Antiprejudice Norms"; Solheim, *Terrorism and Attitudes Toward Out-groups*.
13. Gibson and Gouws, *Overcoming Intolerance*.
14. The reference is to Hege Storhaug, one of the best known anti-Islamic activists in Norway. The book being referred to is, very likely, Storhaug Hege (2015), *Islam: Den 11. Landeplage*. [Islam: The 11th plague]. Oslo: Kolofon.
15. Griffin, *The Nature of Fascism*; Griffin, *Fascism*.
16. Stouffer, *Communism, Conformity, and Civil Liberties*; Sullivan, Piereson, and Marcus, *Political Tolerance and American Democracy*.
17. All studies and their sources are listed at the end of the book. An appendix contains the needed background information for each figure: documentation of survey question wording (English translation), variable names, sample sizes, and statistical model used.

18. Sniderman et al., *Paradoxes of Liberal Democracy*.

19. For pedagogical reasons and in the interest of consistency across studies, we have dichotomized all response scales. In the cases where response scales had a middle category, we have consistently across all studies coded those choosing the middle-category on the exclusionary side. This makes our estimates of openness to inclusion appropriately conservative.

20. See, e.g., Adida, Laitin, and Valfort, *Why Muslim Integration Fails*; Wright et al., "Multiculturalism and Muslim Accommodation."

21. Sniderman et al., *Paradoxes of Liberal Democracy*.

22. This is consistent with previous research, e.g., Helbling and Trainmüller, "What Is Islamophobia?" Interestingly, a similar pattern of nondiscrimination in Sweden was also found for this country only in another comparative survey experimental study, Blinder, Ford, and Ivarsflaten, "Discrimination, Antiprejudice Norms."

23. See Helbling and Traunmüller, "State Support of Religion," for a study that relates this difference to different policies toward regulating Christian organizations, and Blinder, Ford, and Ivarsflaten, "Discrimination, Antiprejudice Norms," for a study that relates such differences to multicultural policies more broadly.

CHAPTER THREE

1. Mill, *On Liberty*, 63.
2. Darwall, "Two Kinds of Respect," 38.
3. Darwall, "Two Kinds of Respect," 38.
4. Darwall, "Two Kinds of Respect," 38.
5. See Crowder, *Theories of Multiculturalism*, particularly chapters 5 and 9.
6. Our colleague Eamonn Callan, reading a preliminary account of the initial results, directed us to Darwall's analysis of respect. It is a pleasure to acknowledge our debt to Eamonn.
7. Confidence intervals of 95 percent are indicated in the figure and not repeated in the text to ease reading. Only in extremely small samples would a difference of this magnitude not be statistically significant. Our experiments typically have a sample size of 1,000 or larger (see appendix for documentation of each study), so a difference of this order is always going to be statistically significant.
8. To expect the *same* results is to fall victim to a standard of specious precision: comparisons across countries are an invitation to guesswork, given issues in translation, differences in response format, and "house" effects, not to mention the imprecision of measures of attitudes, beliefs, and opinions. On the other hand, *similarity* of results is an inherently vague standard.
9. Instructively, considering the incentives for normative theorists each to carve out a distinctive take, on the necessity for public acknowledgment of worth, all agree. See Crowder, *Theories of Multiculturalism*.
10. We are thankful to David Miller for making this suggestion after reading a very early version of this chapter.

11. We are thankful to participants at the Norwegian Political Science Association's meeting in Bergen in January 2018 for forcefully making this point.

12. See Darwall, "Two Kinds of Respect," 126, for a full exposition of the grounds to distinguish between a norm of respect and a duty of care.

13. A careful reader will at this point notice that this is an instance where we did not stay true to our own ideal of always also trying a new idea.

14. Plant and Devine, "Motivation to Respond without Prejudice"; Dunton and Fazio, "Measure of Motivation to Control Prejudice."

15. We follow the work of Ivarsflaten, Blinder, and Ford, "The Anti-Racism Norm"; Blinder, Ford, and Ivarsflaten, "The Better Angels" and "Discrimination, Anti-prejudice Norms."

16. It also turns out (as demonstrated in the appendix to chapter 7, "A Methodological Note on the Validity of the IMCP") that this measure demonstrably is not strongly contaminated by social desirability bias. Respondents who are not committed to inclusive tolerance feel free to report their sincere beliefs at least in anonymous online surveys.

17. Devine," Stereotypes and Prejudice."

18. The items read: I attempt to act in non-prejudiced ways towards Muslims because it is personally important to me; I get angry with myself when I have a prejudiced thought; I try to be unprejudiced towards Muslims due to my own convictions; I do not want to appear racist, even to myself.

CHAPTER FOUR

1. This is par for the course, it should be said, for forms of prejudice generally—anti-Semitism, to cite one example, racial prejudice, to cite another.

2. Bleich, "What Is Islamophobia?," 1582, emphasis in original.

3. Bleich, *The Freedom to Be Racist?*

4. Austenå, *Arven etter Staniske vers*; Vogt, *Islam på norsk*.

5. Engelstad, "Sataniske vers."

6. Austenå, *Arven etter Staniske vers*.

7. Insungset, *Hvem skjøt William Nygaard?*, back cover.

8. Modood, *Multicultural Politics*, 120. See the general discussion, subsection "Muslim Honor and Liberal Legislation," 118–24.

9. Modood, *Multicultural Politics*, 5.

10. Post, "Hate Speech," 127. For a previous solid analysis of boundaries drawn about speech in the Norwegian context, see Midtbøen, Steen-Johnsen, and Thorbjørnsrud, *Boundary Struggles*.

11. Post, "Hate Speech," 123.

12. *Erbakan v. Turkey* judgment of July 6, 2006, § 56, "Hate Speech."

13. We of course are not claiming that the political substance of the issues around speech raised by Muslims are not fundamentally different from those raised about immigrants. We are in fact claiming exactly the opposite. What we mean here is that

it appears that Norwegians at this point in time appear to answer these questions similarly regardless of whether they are asked about immigrants or Muslims.

14. To our way of thinking, this is a limitation of the first generations of survey experiments assessing responses to "primes" and cues. The step to take is to learn how respondents react when, as in life, there is more than one normative standard in play.

15. The results we report were replicated when asked about Muslims specifically in the third and fourth trials.

16. Orange, "Riots Rock Malmö."

CHAPTER FIVE

1. The now standard work is Abdelal et al., *Measuring Identity*.
2. See Huddy and Khatib, "American Patriotism."
3. See, for example, Citrin, Wong, and Duff, "Meaning of American National Identity,"; Theiss-Morse, *Who Counts as an American?*
4. The closest work, to our knowledge, is Citrin and Sears, *American Identity*, a searching analysis of the interplay of national identity and multiculturalism in the United States.
5. Anderson, *Imagined Communities*.
6. For a classic exposition of the logic, see Bertrand Russell's "The Bald Man's Fallacy."
7. Patten, "Rethinking Culture."
8. Italics for emphasis in text only.
9. Hence the brouhahas that predictably break out in America. Should textbooks include "creationism"? How about an "Afrocentric" focus? See Podair, *The Strike That Changed New York*, for analysis of the historic clash over community control of Ocean Hill-Brownsville schools.
10. Quoted by Krech, "Does Behavior Really Need a Brain?," 9.
11. James, *Principles of Psychology*, 139. The quote continues: "Similarity makes us unite what discontinuity might hold apart."
12. Cf. David Hume's analysis of personal identity. Hume's proposal: "We may trace the succession of time by a like succession of ideas, and conceiving first one moment, along with the object then existent, imagine after a change in the time without any . . . interruption in the object; in which case it gives us the idea of unity."
13. Ibid.
14. Italics for emphasis in the text: the wording was not italicized in the online questionnaires.

CHAPTER SIX

1. It should not be necessary to enumerate the studies that have demonstrated the minimal engagement of mass publics with politics. There is value, however,

NOTES TO CHAPTER 6 › 177

in calling attention to recent research qualifying this familiar portrait. See Lupia, *Uninformed*. Also, Gilens, "Political Ignorance," and Barabas et al., "Question(s) of Political Knowledge."

2. For a comprehensive and critically balanced review and evaluation of systematic research on participatory democracy, see Colombo and Kriesi, "Beyond Elections." For a contrary judgment, see Myers et al., "Does Group Deliberation Mobilize?"

3. This account does double duty: first, to make plain that so far as our initial hypothesis was derived from theory, it was the wrong theory; second, to scotch in advance a competing account of the results of the Asylum Seeker experiment sequence.

4. Colombo and Kriesi, "Beyond Elections."

5. "We" in the text refers to Sniderman, but we both are indebted to Lelkes and Dahlberg for permission to draw directly on their work. For a full report, see Lelkes, Dahlberg, and Sniderman, "Muslims as Strategic Actors."

6. Notwithstanding that Sweden now has some serious challenges of minority inclusion to contend with, see, e.g., Esaiasson, *Förorten*.

7. Sniderman et al., *Paradoxes of Liberal Democracy*, 14, table 2.1, European Social Survey.

8. The survey experiment was included in the Citizen Panel III, hosted by LORe (Laboratory of Opinion Research), which is an undertaking by the MOD (Multidisciplinary Opinion and Democracy) research group at University of Gothenburg (http://www.mod.gu.se/) in Sweden.) The first two waves of the Citizen Panel were launched in late 2011 and early 2012. During two weeks in October 2011, from October 17 to 31, the third Citizen Panel was launched. Altogether, the Citizen Panel III was sent to 9,995 persons and achieved a response rate of 73 percent. Three reminders were sent out to the respondents on October 19, 21, and 24, 2011. Due to its length, the survey was divided into two parts. Both parts began with an identical block of standing block questions, followed by different survey experiments from different scholars. Part 1 consisted of six experiments and 3,684 out of 5,025 respondents answered the survey (73.3%). Part 2, in which this particular experiment was included, consisted of five experiments and was sent to 4,970 respondents, where 3,619 persons answered the survey (72.8%).

9. It is a great pleasure to acknowledge our debt to Robert Klemmensen and Asbjørn Sonne Nørgaard of the University of Southern Denmark, who advanced and argued for this counterhypothesis before—it should be underscored—analysis of the data had begun.

10. Scores run from 1, strongly disagree, to 4, strongly agree.

11. Not too much should be made of the difference between the second and third conditions. Substantively, the difference between the two conditions is modest, amounting to less than 2 percent movement on the 4-point scale).

12. Both mechanisms are notoriously imperfect. See Gilens, *Affluence and Influence*; Achen and Bartels, *Democracy for Realists*.

13. See Pateman, *Participation and Democratic Theory*. We have benefited from

Pateman's analysis, in many projects, for many years. See also Davis, "Cost of Realism," for a sharp contrast of descriptive and prescriptive versions of democratic theory. Mansbridge, *Beyond Adversary Democracy*, provides a notably clear-eyed account of participatory democracy in her study of New England town hall meetings.

14. See Lupia, *Uninformed*, for the most comprehensive conceptual and empirical challenge to the minimal knowledge claim.

15. Lately, this point has been made most forcefully in Achen and Bartels, *Democracy for Realists*.

16. Quoted by Krouse, "Two Concepts of Democratic Representation," 528–29.

17. Mill, quoted in Pateman, *Participation and Democratic Theory*, 31.

18. Mill, quoted in Pateman, *Participation and Democratic Theory*, 30.

19. Mill, *Collected Works*, 186.

20. Davis, "Cost of Realism."

21. This point has been made in many different ways by, e.g., Putnam, *Bowling Alone*; Rothstein and Stolle, "Social Capital in Scandinavia"; and Sønderskov and Dinesen, "Danish Exceptionalism."

22. Again, we want to repeat that it was not the magnitude of the differences between conditions that struck us. It was the force of the result turning out just as our colleagues at the University of South Denmark had predicted.

23. This is consistent with the striking finding of Sobolewska and her colleagues. They show that, in the Netherlands, the act of voting counts as much in favor as evidence of integration as having Dutch friends. Sobolewska, Galandini, and Lessard-Phillips, "Public View of Immigrant Integration," 68, fig. 1. It should be noted that meeting the responsibility to vote is in the context of immigrants exhibiting a train of indicators of integration—full-time employment, obeying the law, and for long-time residents, having immigrated as children (64).

24. E.g., Bansak, Hainmueller, and Hangartner, "Economic, Humanitarian, and Religious Concerns"; Bansak, Hainmueller, and Hangartner, "Europeans Support a Proportional Allocation"; Hangartner, et al., "Exposure to the Refugee Crisis"; Nordø and Ivarsflaten, "The Scope of Exclusionary Public Response to the European Refugee Crisis"; Bye, Bygnes, and Ivarsflaten, "Imagining vs. Experiencing"; Bjånesøy, "Effects of the Refugee Crisis on Perceptions."

25. Hainmueller and Hopkins, "Public Attitudes"; Sniderman and Hagendorn, "When Ways of Life Collide"; Sniderman, Hagendorn, and Prior, "Predispositional Factors and Situational Triggers."

26. Hainmueller and Hopkins, "Public Attitudes."

27. What is being tested is the impact on native citizens of Muslims' participation in civil society. The impact on Muslims themselves is a different matter—and a complex one. For insight into complexities of estimating the impact of civic participation and, most notably, the issue of self-selection, see Aggeborn, Lajevardi, and Nyman, "Disentangling the Impact."

28. The experimental design is the same; the wording—judged by back translation—is interchangeable; however, the formatting of the response, though similar, is not identical. The Norwegian studies offered, in addition to allowing refugees to

stay or not allowing to stay, a third "Not sure" option; the Danish study offered only the first two.

29. The pattern is the same, but not the levels, given the crudity of measures.

30. Lijphart, *Patterns of Democracy*.

31. A cross and hijab are not necessarily equally visible. For our purposes, it suffices if both are readily visible. The logic of the question imposes a condition of ready visibility. It would make no sense to ask whether a person should or should not wear a necklace with a cross unless the necklace was readily visible.

32. "If she usually does" is not italicized in the questionnaire.

33. The purpose of comparing reactions to two different wordings—"should be allowed to do X" and "should be free to do X" is to address a possible ambiguity. Responding that people "should be allowed to do X" may be the same as saying that you are willing to tolerate or to put up with their doing it—that is, you are willing to allow it but grudgingly. Alternatively, to say that people "should be free to do X" may be the same as saying, "Well, if that's what you want to do, go right ahead and do it." If the first meaning is right, respondents will react to the two differently; if the second is right, they will react similarly. Analysis shows that respondents reacted similarly.

34. For an innovative study on the efficacy of cultural integration, see Choi, Poertner, and Sambanis's "Parochialism, Social Norms" field experiment leveraging a shared norm of anti-littering in Germany.

35. Miller, *Strangers in Our Midst*, 133.

36. Miller, *Strangers in Our Midst*, 133.

CHAPTER SEVEN

1. This line of reasoning is most prominently associated with Inglehart and his colleagues.

2. As the politics of Eastern Europe, to take only the example that comes quickest to mind, makes plain.

3. Whig theories of democratic development have no more plausibility than the Whig interpretation of history overall. Researchers, Dalton shrewdly observes, risk ignoring "Newton's third law: for every action, there is an equal and opposite reaction," Dalton, *Political Realignment*, 27. See also Evans and Menon, *Brexit and British Politics*.

4. E.g., Sniderman and Hagendoorn, *When Ways of Life Collide*; Norris and Inglehart, *Sacred and Secular*.

5. Stouffer, *Communism, Conformity, and Civil Liberties*.

6. Sullivan, Pierson, and Marcus, *Political Tolerance and American Democracy*.

7. For a broad-gauged normative analysis, see Klosko, *Democratic Procedures and Liberal Consensus*.

8. Notice also that the most socially intolerant (IMCP score <0.4) oppose the rally regardless of terms.

9. Sniderman and Hagendoorn, *When Ways of Life Collide*.

10. Studies of Muslim beliefs and attitudes are as necessary as they are challeng-

ing. The hazards in the interpretation and estimates of representativeness are formidable. For a pioneering study of dual loyalties, see Breidahl, "Dual or Divided Loyalties."

11. Italicized for emphasis here. The response format was a 5-point scale anchored at one pole by "fully trust" and at the other by "fully distrust." This experiment, like some others, had a third condition, assessing reactions to "moderate Muslims." In this experiment, as in all the others, responses to Muslims and to moderate Muslims are remarkably similar. We do not report them because, as we realized well after the fact, they are systematically ambiguous. Does the similarity indicate that majority citizens tend to perceive Muslims as moderate or, alternatively, that even Muslims characterized as moderate do not even get the benefit of a doubt and are, instead, perceived as likely to be insincere in their commitment to the country as any other Muslim?

12. Dancygier, *Dilemmas of Inclusion*, 1.

13. Berlin, *Four Essays on Liberty*, 125.

14. It is important to call out the seminal counterarguments of MacKinnon, *Only Words*.

CHAPTER EIGHT

1. Hobolt, "The Brexit Vote"; Vasilopoulou, "Campaign Frames."

2. Mudde, *Populist Radical Right Parties in Europe*.

3. For one example, record levels of hate crimes have been recorded in the United Kingdom, Tell MAMA, "Normalising Hatred."

4. Europol, "Terrorism Situation and Trend Report 2019."

5. E.g., Adida, Laitin, and Valfort, *Why Muslim Integration Fails*.

6. E.g., Hetheringtonand Weiler, *Authoritarianism and Polarization in American Politics*.

7. Inglehart and Welzel, Modernization, *Cultural Change, and Democracy*.

8. Simmons, *Mobilizing for Human Rights*.

9. Blinder, Ford, and Ivarsflaten, "Better Angels."

10. Norris and Inglehart, *Cultural Backlash*.

11. E.g. Dancygier and Donnelly, "Attitudes toward Immigration in Good Times and Bad"; Kriesi, "Political Consequences of the Economic Crisis."

12. We want to thank Hanspeter Kriesi for calling this point to our attention, pointing to religious minorities in the Netherlands who became more radical when society secularized and churches emptied. For in-depth studies of similar processes in the US, see Hochschild, *Strangers in Their Own Land*; Cramer, *Politics of Resentment*.

13. We are following the lead of Campbell in his classic article, "Social Attitudes and Other Acquired Behavioral Dispositions."

14. Which influences which, and whether there is a still "deeper" factor that all are influenced by, remains to be established.

15. This framework can accommodate short-term reactions, for example, by incorporating economic shocks, though precisely how this works remains to be settled. In any case, the reaction takes the form of affective consistency.

16. In principle, positive shocks are conceivable—for example, humanitarian crises which evoke a sympathetic response—but as a practical matter, since they are so infrequent and their impact tends to be so brief, positive shocks are not an important component of the standard model of prejudice and politics.

17. Ivarsflaten, "What Unites Right-Wing Populists."

18. The argument for conceptual spareness is made by Campbell, "Social Attitudes," in unmatched detail and depth.

19. Mudde, *Populist Radical Right Parties in Europe*, 19.

20. Van der Brug, Fennema, and Tillie, "Anti-immigrant parties in Europe,"; Carter, *The Extreme Right in Western Europe*; De Lange, "A New Winning Formula?"; Ivarsflaten, "What Unites Right-Wing Populists."

21. Ivarsflaten, Blinder, and Bjånesøy, "Populist Radical Right Persuades Citizens."

22. Mudde, *Populist Radical Right Parties in Europe*.

23. Jupskås, "The Norwegian Progress Party." The Progress Party received 15.2 percent of the vote in the most recent parliamentary election (2017). This made the Progress Party the third largest party in the Norwegian Parliament after the Labor Party (27.4 %) and the Conservative Party (25 %). The Socialist Left Party received only 6 percent of the votes in the 2017 election.

24. Art, *Inside the Radical Right*.

25. Aardal, *Velgere og valgkamp*.

26. See, e.g., Ivarsflaten, "What Unites Right-Wing Populists," for an analysis of voter patterns which shows that in this respect the Norwegian case was early on similar to that of other prominent European far-right parties in, for example, France, the Netherlands, Denmark, Belgium, and Switzerland.

27. Aftenposten October 28th, 2016: Listhaug: "Her i Norge spiser vi svin, drikker alkohol og viser ansiktet vårt." (Tjernshaugen, Karen) This minister, Listhaug, was later promoted to Minster of Justice, but was forced to step down from government after parliament threatened a vote of no-confidence over another controversial Facebook post, which insinuated the common right-extremist trope of a conspiracy between the Labor Party and Muslim terrorists.

28. Meguid, *Party Competition between Unequals*.

29. E.g., Adams and Somer-Topcu, "Policy Adjustment by Parties."

30. E.g., Abou-Chadi and Krause, "The Causal Effect of Radical Right Success."

31. For a discussion of divergent findings, see van Spanje and de Graaf, "How Established Parties Reduce Other Parties."

32. Bale et al., "If You Can't Beat Them, Join Them?"

33. Akkerman, "Immigration policy and electoral competition," 56.

34. Mudde and Kaltwasser, *Populism in Europe and the Americas*; Bonikowski, "Three Lessons."

35. Müller, *What Is Populism?*

36. Eighty-three percent believe that newspapers should be allowed to print them.

CHAPTER NINE

1. The paradigmatic example is the long-running trend driven by economic modernization to more liberal, more tolerant liberal democracies. This is of course the thesis of Inglehart and his colleagues.

2. To be clear, Waldron, *Harm in Hate Speech* (220), does not distinguish between recognition and appraisal respect. But his words call to life what recognition respect requires and why.

3. Chadwick, *Secularization of the European Mind in the Nineteenth Century*, 23.

4. Results not presented since experimental sequence ongoing.

5. See Miller, "Majorities and Minarets," for analysis of normative considerations of implicit claims to dominance of architecture in public space.

6. For an ingenious study of the partial influence of shared cultural norms (in this instance, not littering) to inhibit discrimination on responses to Muslim immigrants, see Choi, Poertner, and Sambanis, "Parochialism, Social Norms."

7. Miller, *Strangers in Our Midst*, 133.

APPENDIX

1. Arnesen, *A Guide to The 2017 European Internet Panel Study (EIPS)*.
2. Arnesen et al., *Few Questions on Europe*.
3. Blom et al., German Internet Panel.
4. Ivarsflaten et al., Norwegian Citizen Panel, Wave 9.
5. Martinsson et al., Citizen Panel 28.
6. Ivarsflaten et al., Norwegian Citizen Panel, Wave 2.
7. Ansolabehere and Schaffner, 2013 CCES Common Content.
8. YouGov for Ivarsflaten and Sniderman, Muslim Inclusion Study 2.
9. Ivarsflaten et al., Norwegian Citizen Panel, Wave, 1.
10. Types of Racism Study for Sniderman, Muslim Inclusion Study 1.
11. Ivarsflaten et al., Norwegian Citizen Panel Wave, 15.
12. YouGov for Ivarsflaten and Sniderman, Muslim Inclusion Study 5.
13. These are the four IMCP items that have been fielded repeatedly, but in some versions we ask explicitly about Muslims, in others about immigrants. In the Norwegian context, where we have had the most opportunities to examine the measure, it appears not to matter whether the items ask about immigrants or Muslims. This is also consistent with findings on other questions which we report in the book.
14. Ivarsflaten et al., Norwegian Citizen Panel, Wave 5.
15. Ivarsflaten et al., Norwegian Citizen Panel, Wave 8.
16. Ivarsflaten et al., Norwegian Citizen Panel, Wave 18.
17. Ivarsflaten et al., Norwegian Citizen Panel, Wave 7.

18. Ivarsflaten et al., Norwegian Citizen Panel, Wave 12.
19. YouGov for Ivarsflaten and Sniderman, Muslim Inclusion Study 3.
20. Lucid Software for Elisabeth Ivarsflaten and Paul Sniderman, Muslim Inclusion Study 4.
21. Ivarsflaten et al., Norwegian Citizen Panel, Wave 4.
22. Ivarsflaten et al., Norwegian Citizen Panel, Wave 6.

Bibliography

Aardal, Bernt, and Johannes Bergh, eds. *Velgere og valgkamp En studie av stortingsvalget i 2017.* Oslo: Cappelen Damm, 2019.

Abdelal, Rawi, Yoshiko Herrera, Alastair Ian Johnston, and Rose McDermott. *Measuring Identity: A Guide for Social Scientists.* New York: Cambridge University Press, 2019.

Abou-Chadi, Tariq, and Werner Krause. "The Causal Effect of Radical Right Success on Mainstream Parties' Policy Positions: A Regression Discontinuity Design." *British Journal of Political Science* 50, no. 3 (July 2018). https://doi.org/10.1017/S0007123418000029.

Achen, Christopher H., and Larry M. Bartels. *Democracy for Realists: Why Elections Do Not Produce Responsive Government.* Princeton: Princeton University Press, 2016.

Adams, James, and Zeynep Somer-Topcu. "Policy Adjustment by Parties in Response to Rival Parties' Policy Shifts: Spatial Theory and the Dynamics of Party Competition in Twenty-Five Postwar Democracies." *British Journal of Political Science* 39, no. 4 (October 2009): 825–46.

Adida, Claire L., David Laitin, and Marie-Anne Valfort. *Why Muslim Integration Fails in Christian-Heritage Societies.* Cambridge, MA: Harvard University Press, 2016.

Aggeborn, Linuz, Nazital Lajevardi, and Par Nyman. "Disentangling the Impact of Civic Association Membership on Political Participation." *British Journal of Political Science* (June 2020). https://doi.org/10.1017/S0007123419000772.

Akkerman, Tjitske. "Immigration Policy and Electoral Competition in Western Europe: A Fine-Grained Analysis of Party Positions over the Past Two Decades." *Party Politics* 21, no. 1 (2015): 54–67. https://doi.org/10.1177/1354068812462928.

Alon, Nahi, and Haim Omer. *The Psychology of Demonization.* New York: Routledge, 2005.

Anderson, Benedict. *Imagined Communities: Reflections on the Origin and Spread of Nationalism.* 2nd ed. 1983. London: Verso, 1991.

Art, David. *Inside the Radical Right*. Cambridge: Cambridge University Press, 2011.
Austenå, Ann Margit. *Arven etter Sataniske vers*. Oslo: Cappelen Damm, 2011.
Bail, Christopher A. *Terrified: How Anti-Muslim Fringe Organizations Became Mainstream*. Princeton, NJ: Princeton University Press, 2014.
Bale, Tim, Christoffer Green-Pedersen, André Krouwel, Kurth Richard Luther, and Nick Sitter. "If You Can't Beat Them, Join Them? Explaining Social Democratic Responses to the Challenge from the Populist Radical Right in Western Europe." *Political Studies* 58, no. 3 (2010): 410–26. https://doi.org/10.1111/j.1467-9248.2009.00783.x.
Bansak, Kirk, Jens Hainmueller, and Dominik Hangartner. "How Economic, Humanitarian, and Religious Concerns Shape European Attitudes towards Asylum Seekers." *Science* 354, no. 6309 (2016): 217–22. https://doi.org/10.1126/science.aag2147.
Bansak, Kirk, Jens Hainmueller, and Dominik Hangartner. "Europeans Support a Proportional Allocation of Asylum Seekers." *Nature Human Behavior* 1, no. 7 (June 2017): 1–6. https://doi.org/10.1038/s41562-017-013.
Barabas, Jason, Jennifer Jerit, William Pollock, and Carlisle Rainey. "The Question(s) of Political Knowledge." *American Political Science Review* 108 (November 2014): 840–54. https://doi.org/10.1017/S0003055414000392.
Berlin, Isaiah. *Four Essays on Liberty*. New York: Oxford University Press, 1969.
Berntzen, Lars Erik. *Liberal Roots of Far Right Activism: The Anti-Islamic Movement in the 21st Century*. Routledge, 2019.
Berntzen, Lars Erik, and Manes Weisskircher. "Anti-Islamic PEGIDA beyond Germany: Explaining Differences in Mobilisation." *Journal of Intercultural Studies*, 37, no. 6 (2016): 556–73. https://doi.org/10.1080/07256868.2016.1235021.
Bjånesøy, Lise. "Effects of the Refugee Crisis on Perceptions of Asylum Seekers in Recipient Populations." *Journal of Refugee Studies* 32 (2019): 219–37. https://doi.org/10.1093/jrs/fey070.
Bleich, Erik. *The Freedom to Be Racist? How the United States and Europe Struggle to Preserve Freedom and Combat Racism*. New York: Oxford University Press, 2011.
Bleich, Erik. "What Is Islamophobia and How Much Is There? Theorizing and Measuring an Emerging Comparative Concept." *American Behavioral Scientist* 55 (September 2011): 1581–600. https://doi.org/10.1177/0002764211409387.
Blinder, Scott, Robert Ford, and Elisabeth Ivarsflaten. "Discrimination, Antiprejudice Norms, and Public Support for Multicultural Policies in Europe: The Case of Religious Schools." *Comparative Political Studies* 52, no. 8 (February 2019): 1232–55. https://doi.org/10.1177/0010414019830728.
Blinder, Scott, Robert Ford, and Elisabeth Ivarsflaten. "The Better Angels of Our Nature: How the Anti-prejudice Norm Affects Policy and Party Preferences in Great Britain and Germany." *American Journal of Political Science* 57, no. 4 (April 2013): 841–57. https://doi.org/10.1111/ajps.12030.
Bonikowski, Bart. "Three Lessons of Contemporary Populism in Europe and the United States." *Brown Journal of World Affairs* 23, no. 1. (Fall/Winter 2016): 9–24.

Breidahl, Karen N. "Dual or Divided Loyalties." In *Liberal Nationalism and Its Critics*, edited by Gina Gustavsson and David Miller, 227–48. Oxford: Oxford University Press, 2020.

Bye, Hege H., Susanne Bygnes, and Elisabeth Ivarsflaten, "The Local-National Gap in Intergroup Attitudes and Far-Right Underperformance in Local Elections." *Frontiers in Political Science*, 3:660088, 2021.

Caiani, Mauela, Dontella della Porta, and Claudius Wagemann. *Mobilizing on the Extreme Right: Germany, Italy, and the United States*. Oxford: Oxford University Press, 2012.

Campbell, Donald T. "Social Attitudes and Other Acquired Behavioral Dispositions." In *Methodology and Epistemology for Social Science*, edited by Samuel Overman. Chicago: University of Chicago Press, 1988.

Carter, Elisabeth. *The Extreme Right in Western Europe: Success or Failure?* Manchester: Manchester University Press, 2005.

Chadwick, Owen. *Lord Acton*, 1902.

Chadwick, Owen. *The Secularization of the European Mind in the Nineteenth Century*. New York: Cambridge University Press, 1975.

Choi, Donghuyun Dann, Matthias Pertner, and Nicholas Sambanis. "Parochialism, Social Norms, and Discrimination toward Immigrants. *Proceedings of the National Academy of Science* 116 (August 2019): 16274–79. https://doi.org/10.1073/pnas.1820146116.

Citrin, Jack, Carolyn Wong, and B. Duff. "The Meaning of American National Identity." In *Social Identity, Intergroup Conflict, and Conflict Resolution*, edited by Richard D. Ashmore, Lee Jussim, and David Wilder, 71–100. New York: Oxford University Press, 2001.

Citrin, Jack, and David Sears. *American Identity and the Politics of Multiculturalism*. New York: Cambridge University Press, 2004.

Chudy, Jennifer, "Racial Sympathy and Its Political Consequences, *Journal of Politics* 83, no. 1 (September 2020). https://doi.org/10.1086/708953.

Colombo, Celine, and Hanspeter Kriesi, "Beyond Elections as Instruments of Representative Democracy." In *Oxford Handbook on Political Representation in Liberal Democracy*, edited by Robert Rohrschnieder and Jacques Thomassen. Oxford: Oxford University Press, 2020.

Cramer, Katherine J. J. *The Politics of Resentment: Rural Consciousness in Wisconsin and the Rise of Scott Walker*. Chicago: University of Chicago Press, 2016.

Crowder, George. *Theories of Multiculturalism: An Introduction*. Malden, MA: Polity, 2013.

Dalton, Russell J. *Political Realignment: Economics, Culture, and Economic Change*. Oxford: Oxford University Press, 2018.

Dalton, Russell J. *Citizen Politics: Public Opinion and Political Parties in Advanced Industrialized Democracies*. Thousand Oaks, CA: Sage, 2002.

Dancygier, Rafaela. *Dilemmas of Inclusion*. Princeton: Princeton University Press, 2017.

Dancygier, Rafaela, and Michael Donnelly. "Attitudes toward Immigration in Good

Times and Bad." In *Mass Politics in Tough Times*, edited by Nancy Bermeo and Larry M. Bartels, 148–85. New York: Oxford University Press, 2014.

Darwall, Stephen L. "Two Kinds of Respect." *Ethics* 88 (October 1977): 36–49. https://doi.org/10.1086/292054.

Davis, Lane. "The Cost of Realism: Contemporary Restatements of Democracy." *Western Political Quarterly* 17 (1974): 37–46.

De Lange, Sarah. "A New Winning Formula? The Programmatic Appeal of the Radical Right." *Party Politics* 13, no. 4 (July 2007): 411–35. https://doi.org/10.1177/1354068807075943.

Devine, Patricia G. "Stereotypes and Prejudice: Their Automatic and Controlled Components." *Journal of Personality and Social Psychology* 56, no. 1 (1989): 5–18. https://doi.org/10.1037/0022-3514.56.1.5.

Directorate of Immigration (Norway), UDI (Utlendingsdirektoratet). "Statistics on Immigration." https://www.udi.no/en/statistics-and-analysis/statistics/.

Dunton, Bridget C., and Russel H. Fazio. "An Individual Difference Measure of Motivation to Control Prejudiced Reactions." *Personality and Social Psychology Bulletin* 23, no. 3 (March 1997): 316–26. https://doi.org/10.1177/0146167297233009.

Eatwell, Roger. "Community Cohesion and Cumulative Extremism in Contemporary Britain." *Political Quarterly* 77, no. 2 (2006): 204–16. https://doi.org/10.1111/j.1467-923X.2006.00763.x.

Engelstad; Marianne. "Sataniske vers og Muhammed-karikaturer: En analyse av de muslimske miljøenes og myndighetenes reaksjoner på og håndtering av Rushdie-saken og karikaturstriden i Norge og Danmark." MA thesis. University of Oslo: Department of Archeology, Conservation, and History, 2013.

Erbakan v. Turkey. Judgment of 6 July 2006 § 56, "Hate Speech." European Court of Human Rights, 2019. https://www.echr.coe.int/Documents/FS_Hate_speech_ENG.pdf.

Esaiasson, Peter. *Förorten: Ett samhällsvetenskapligt reportage*. Stockholm: Timbro, 2020.

Europol. "European Union Terrorism Situation and Trend Report 2019 (TE-SAT)." European Agency for Law Enforcement Cooperation, 2019. https://www.europol.europa.eu/activities-services/main-reports/terrorism-situation-and-trend-report-2019-te-sat.

Evans, Geoffrey, and Anand Menon. *Brexit and British Politics*. Cambridge: Polity, 2017.

Federico, Christopher M., and Ariel Malka. "The Contingent, Contextual Nature of the Relationship between Needs for Security and Certainty and Political Preferences." *Advances in Political Psychology* 39 (February 2018): 3–48. https://doi.org/10.1111/pops.12477.

Feldman, Stanley, Leonie Huddy, Julie Wronski, and Partick Lown. "The Interplay of Empathy and Individualism in Support for Social Welfare Policies." *Political Psychology* 41, no. 2 (September 2019): 343–62. https://doi.org/10.1111/pops.12620.

Feldman, Stanley, and Marco Steenbergen, "The Humanitarian Foundation of Public

Support for Social Welfare." *American Journal of Political Science* 45 (July 2001): 658–77. https://doi.org/10.2307/2669244.

Gibson, Jim, and Amanda Gouws. *Overcoming Intolerance in South Africa: Experiments in Democratic Persuasion.* Cambridge Studies in Public Opinion and Political Psychology. Cambridge: Cambridge University Press, 2002. https://doi.org/10.1017/CBO9780511550331.

Gilens, Martin. *Affluence and Influence.* Princeton: Princeton University Press, 2012.

Gilens, Martin. "Political Ignorance and Collective Policy Preferences." *American Political Science Review* 95 (June 2001): 379–96.

Goren, Paul. "Core Principles and Policy Reasoning in Mass Publics, *British Journal of Political Science* 31 (January 2001): 159–77. https://doi.org/10.1017/S0007123401000072.

Goren, Paul. *On Voter Competence.* New York: Oxford University Press, 2013.

Goren, Paul, Harald Schoen, Jason Riefler, Thomas Scotto, and William Chittick. "A Unified Theory of Value-Based Reasoning and US Public Opinion." *Political Behavior* 38 (May 2016): 977–97. https://doi.org/10.1007/s11109-016-9344-x.

Griffin, Roger, ed. *Fascism.* Oxford: Oxford University Press, 2009.

Griffin, Roger. *The Nature of Fascism.* London: Routledge, 1993.

Hangartner, Dominik, Elias Dinas, Moritz Marbach, Konstantinos Matakos, and Dimitrios Xefteris. "Does Exposure to the Refugee Crisis Make Natives More Hostile?" *American Political Science Review* 113, no. 2 (May 2019): 442–55. https://doi.org/10.1017/S0003055418000813.

Hainmueller, Jens, and Daniel J. Hopkins. "Public Attitudes toward Immigration" *Annual Review of Political Science* 17 (2014): 369–84. https://doi.org/10.1146/annurev-polisci-102512-194818.

Hainmueller, Jens, and Dominik Hangartner. "Who Gets a Swiss Passport? A Natural Experiment in Immigrant Discrimination." *American Political Science Review* 107, no. 1 (February 2013): 159–87. https://doi.org/10.1017/S0003055412000494.

Hartman, Todd K., Benjamin J. Newman, Patrick L. Lown, and Stanley Feldman. "Easing the Heavy Hand: Humanitarian Concern, Empathy, and Opinion on Immigration" *British Journal of Political Science* 45 (November 2013): 583–607. https://doi.org/10.1017/S0007123413000410.

Helbling, Marc, and Richard Traunmüller. "What Is Islamophobia? Disentangling Citizens' Feelings toward Ethnicity, Religion and Religiosity Using a Survey Experiment." *British Journal of Political Science* 50, no. 3 (2018): 811–828. https://doi.org/10.1017/S0007123418000054.

Helbling, Marc, and Richard Traunmüller. "How State Support of Religion Shapes Attitudes toward Muslim Immigrants: New Evidence from a Sub-National Comparison." *Comparative Political Studies* 49, no. 3 (2016): 391–424. https://doi.org/10.1177/0010414015612388.

Helbling, Mark. *Islamophobia in the West: Measuring and Explaining Individual Level Attitudes.* New York: Routledge, 2012.

Hetherington, Marc J., and Jonathan D. Weiler. *Authoritarianism and Polarization in American Politics.* Cambridge: Cambridge University Press, 2009.

Hjerm, Mikael, Maureen A. Eger, Andrea Bohman, and Filip Fors Connolly. "A New Approach to the Study of Tolerance: Conceptualizing and Measuring Acceptance, Respect, and Appreciation of Difference. *Social Indicators Research* 147 (September 2019): 897–919. https://doi.org/10.1007/s11205-019-02176-y.

Hobolt, Sara B. "The Brexit Vote: A Divided Nation, a Divided Continent." *Journal of European Public Policy* 23, no. 9 (2016): 1259–77. https://doi.org/10.1080/13501763.2016.1225785.

Hochschild, Arlie Russell. *Strangers in Their Own Land*. New York: New Press, 2016.

Huddy, Leonie. "Unifying National Identity Research: Interdisciplinary Perspectives." In *Dynamics of National Identity*, edited by Jürgen Grimm, Leonie Huddy, Peter Schmidt, and Josef Seehalter. New York: Routledge, 2016.

Huddy, Leonie, and Nadia Khatib. "American Patriotism, National Identity, and Political Involvement." *American Journal of Political Science* 51 (2007): 63–77. https://doi.org/10.1111/j.1540-5907.2007.00237.x.

Hume, David. *A Treatise of Human Nature*. Oxford: Clarendon University Press, 1978.

Inglehart, Ronald, and Pippa Norris. "Trump and the Populist Authoritarian Parties: The Silent Revolution in Reverse." *Perspectives on Politics* 15, no. 2 (2017): 443–54. https://doi.org/10.1017/S1537592717000111.

Inglehart, Ronald D., and Christian Welzel. *Modernization, Cultural Change, and Democracy*. New York: Cambridge University Press, 2005.

Isungset, Odd. *Hvem skjøt William Nygaard?* Oslo: Tiden, 2010.

Ivarsflaten, Elisabeth, Scott Blinder, and Lise Bjånesøy. "How and Why the Populist Radical Right Persuades Citizens." In *The Oxford Handbook of Electoral Persuasion*, edited by Elizabeth Suhay and Alex Trechsel. Oxford: Oxford University Press, 2019.

Ivarsflaten, Elisabeth, Scott Blinder, and Robert Ford. "The Anti-racism Norm in Western European Immigration Politics: Why Consider It and How to Measure It." *Journal of Elections Public Opinion and Parties* 20, no. 4 (October 2010): 421–45. https://doi.org/10.1080/17457289.2010.511805.

Ivarsflaten, Elisabeth. "What Unites Right-Wing Populists in Western Europe? Re-Examining Grievance Mobilization Models in Seven Successful Cases." *Comparative Political Studies* 41, no. 1 (2008): 3–23. https://doi.org/10.1177/0010414006294168.

James, William. *Principles of Psychology*. Vols. 1 and 2. Pantianos Classics, 1890.

Jost, John T., Jack Glaser, Arie W. Kruglanski, and Frank J. Sulloway. "Political Conservatism as Motivated Social Cognition." *Psychological Review* 129, no. 3 (2003): 330–75. https://doi.org/10.1037/0033-2909.129.3,339.

Jupskås, Anders R. "The Norwegian Progress Party: Between a Business Firm and a Mass Party." In *Understanding Populist Party Organisation: The Radical Right in Western Europe*, edited by Reinhard Heinisch and Oscar Mazzoleni. London: Palgrave Macmillan, 2016.

Kahneman Daniel, and Amos Tversky. *Judgement under Uncertainty: Heuristics and Biases*. New York: Cambridge University Press, 1982.

Kalin, Michael, and Nicholas Sambanis. "How to Think about Social Identity."

Annual Review of Political Science 21 (May 2018): 239–57. https://doi.org/10.1146/annurev-polisci-042016-024408.

Kepel, Gilles, with Antoine Jardin. *Terror in France: The Rise of Jihad in the West*. Princeton, NJ: Princeton University Press, 2017.

Key, V. O. *Public Opinion and American Democracy*. New York: Knopf, 1961.

Klosko, George. *Democratic Procedures and Liberal Consensus*. Oxford: Oxford University Press, 2000.

Krech, David. "Does Behavior Really Need a Brain?" In *William James: Unfinished Business*, edited by Robert B. MacLeod, 1–12. Washington, DC: American Psychological Association, 1969.

Kriesi, Hanspeter. "The Political Consequences of the Economic Crisis in Europe: Electoral Punishment and Popular Protest." In *Mass Politics in Tough Times*, edited by Nancy Bermeo and Larry M. Bartels, 197–333. New York: Oxford University Press, 2014.

Krouse, Richard W. "Two Concepts of Democratic Representation: James and John Stuart Mill. *Journal of Politics* 44 (2019): 509–37. https://doi.org/10.2307/2130598.

Lelkes, Yphtach, Stefan Dahlberg, and Paul M. Sniderman. "Muslims as Strategic Actors in the Politics of Inclusion: The Political Logic of Civic Agency." Paper prepared for the Annual Meeting of the Midwest Political Science Association, 2012.

Lijphart, Arend. *Patterns of Democracy*. New Haven, CT: Yale University Press, 2012.

Lupia, Arthur. *Uninformed*. New York: Oxford University Press, 2016.

MacKinnon, Catharine A. *Only Words*. Cambridge, MA: Harvard University Press, 1993.

Mansbridge, Jane. *Beyond Adversary Democracy*. Chicago: University of Chicago Press, 1983.

Meguid, Bonnie. *Party Competition between Unequals: Strategies and Electoral Fortunes in Western Europe*. New York: Cambridge University Press, 2009.

Midtbøen, Arnfinn, Kari Steen-Johnsen, and Kjersti Thorbjørnsrud, eds. *Boundary Struggles: Contestations of Free Speech in the Public Sphere*. Oslo: Cappelen Damm Akademisk, 2017.

Mill, John Stuart. *Collected Works*. Toronto: University of Toronto Press, 1963.

Mill, John Stuart. *On Liberty*. London: Penguin Classics, 1985.

Miller, David. *Strangers in Our Midst*. Cambridge, MA: Harvard University Press, 2016.

Miller, David. "Majorities and Minarets: Religious Freedom and Public Space." *British Journal of Political Science* 46 (2014): 437–56. https://doi.org/10.1017/S0007123414000131.

Modood, Tariq. *Multicultural Politics: Racism, Ethnicity and Muslims in Britain*. Minneapolis: University of Minnesota Press, 2005.

Mudde, Cas. *Populist Radical Right Parties in Europe*. Cambridge: Cambridge University Press, 2007.

Mudde, Cas, and Cristóbal Rovira Kaltwasser, eds. *Populism in Europe and the Ameri-*

cas: *Threat or Corrective for Democracy*. Cambridge: Cambridge University Press, 2012.
Müller, Jan-Werner. *What Is Populism?* Philadelphia: University of Pennsylvania Press, 2016.
Myers, Daniel C, Hunter G. Gordon, Hyungjin Myra Kim, Zachary Rowe, and Susan Door Goold, "Does Group Deliberation Mobilize? The Effect of Public Deliberation on Willingness to Participate in Politics." *Political Behavior* 42 (2020): 557–80. https://doi.org/10.1007/s11109-018-9507-z.
Nordø, Åsta Dyrnes, and Elisabeth Ivarsflaten. "The Scope of Exclusionary Public Response to the European Refugee Crisis." *European Journal of Political Research*, Early View, 2021.
Norris, Pippa, and Ronald Inglehart. *Cultural Backlash: Trump, Brexit, and Authoritarian Populism*. Cambridge: Cambridge University Press, 2019.
Norris, Pippa, and Ronald Inglehart. *Sacred and Secular: Religion and Politics Worldwide*. New York: Cambridge University Press, 2011.
Orange, Richard. "Riots Rock Malmö after Far-Right Swedish Activists Burn Qur'an." *Guardian*, August 29, 2020. https://www.theguardian.com/world/2020/aug/29/riots-rock-malmo-after-far-right-swedish-activists-burn-quran.
Pateman, Carole. *Participation and Democratic Theory*. New York: Cambridge University, 1970.
Patten, Alan. "Rethinking Culture: The Social Lineage Account." *American Political Science Review* 105, no. 4 (November 2011): 735–49.
Plant, E. Ashby, and Patricia G. Devine. "Internal and External Motivation to Respond without Prejudice." *Journal of Personality and Social Psychology* 75, no. 3 (September 1998): 811–32. https://doi.org/10.1037/0022-3514.75.3.811
Podair, Jeral E. *The Strike That Changed New York*. New Haven, CT: Yale University Press, 2002.
Post, Robert. "Hate Speech." In *Extreme Speech and Democracy*, edited by Ivan Hare and James Weinstein, 123–38. New York: Oxford University Press, 2009.
Putnam, Robert D. *Bowling Alone: The Collapse and Revival of American Community*. New York: Simon & Schuster, 2001.
Rothstein, Bo, and Dietlind Stolle. "Introduction: Social Capital in Scandinavia." *Scandinavian Political Studies* 26, no. 1 (March 2003): 1–26. https://doi.org/10.1111/1467-9477.t01-1-00077.
Schleifer, James T. *The Making of Tocqueville's Democracy in America*. 2nd ed. Indianapolis: Liberty Fund, 1980.
Sidanius, Jim, and Felicia Pratto. *Social Dominance*. New York: Cambridge University Press, 1999.
Sides, John, and Jack Citrin. 2007. "European Opinion about Immigration: The Role of Identities, Interests and Information." *British Journal of Political Science* 37, no. 3 (July 2007): 477–504. https://doi.org/10.1017/S000712340700025.
Simmons, Beth A. *Mobilizing for Human Rights: International Law in Domestic Politics*. New York: Cambridge University Press, 2009.
Smeekes, Anouk, Maykel Verkuyten, and Edwin Poppe. "Mobilizing Opposition

towards Muslim Immigrants: Nation Identification and the Representation of National History." *British Journal of Social Psychology* 5 (2011): 265–80. https://doi.org/10.1348/014466610X516235.

Smith, John Maynard. *Did Darwin Get It Right?* New York: Penguin, 1998.

Sniderman, Paul M., Michael Bang Petersen, Rune Slothuus, Rune Stubager, and Philip Petrov. "Reactions to Terror Attacks: A Heuristic Model." *Political Psychology* 40, no. S1 (March 2019): 245–58. https://doi.org/10.1111/pops.12575.

Sniderman, Paul M., Michael Bang Petersen, Rune Slothuus, Rune Stubager, and Philip Petrov. *Paradoxes of Liberal Democracy: Islam, Western Europe, and the Danish Cartoon Crisis.* Princeton, NJ: Princeton University Press, 2014.

Sniderman, Paul M., and Louk Hagendoorn, *When Ways of Life Collide*. Princeton, NJ: Princeton University Press, 2007.

Sniderman, Paul M., Louk Hagendoorn, and Markus Prior. "Predispositional Factors and Situational Triggers: Exclusionary Reactions to Immigrant Minorities." *American Political Science Review* 98 (February 2004): 35–50.

Sobolewska, Maria, Silvia Galandini, and Laurence Lessard-Phillips. "The Public View of Immigrant Integration: Multidimensional and Consensual. Evidence from Survey Experiments in the UK and the Netherlands." *Journal of Ethnic and Migration Studies* 42 (2016): 58–79. https://doi.org/10.1080/1369183X.2016.1248377.

Solheim, Øyvind Bugge. "Terrorism and Attitudes toward Out-groups: A Political Perspective." PhD dissertation. University of Oslo: Department of Political Science, 2019.

Sønderskov, Kim Mannemar, and Peter Thisted Dinesen. "Danish Exceptionalism: Explaining the Unique Increase in Social Trust over the Past 30 Years." *European Sociological Review* 30, no. 6 (2014): 782–95. https://doi.org/10.1093/esr/jcu073.

Statham, Paul. "How Ordinary People View Muslim Group Rights in Britain, the Netherlands, France and Germany: Significant 'Gaps' between Majorities and Muslims?" *Journal of Ethnic and Migration Studies* 42, no. 2 (July 2015): 217–36. https://doi.org/10.1080/1369183X.2015.1082288.

Stenner, Karen. *The Authoritarian Dynamic.* New York: Cambridge University Press, 2005.

Storm, Ingrid, Maria Sobolewska, and Robert Ford. "Is Ethnic Prejudice Declining in Britain? Change in Social Distance Attitudes among Ethnic Majority and Minority Britons." *British Journal of Sociology* 68 (April 2017): 410–34. https://doi.org/10.1111/1468-4446.12250.

Stouffer, Samuel A. *Communism, Conformity, and Civil Liberties: A Cross-Section of the Nation Speaks Its Mind.* New York: Doubleday, 1955.

Sullivan, John L., James Piereson, and George E. Marcus. *Political Tolerance and American Democracy.* Chicago: University of Chicago Press, 1993.

Tell MAMA. "Normalising Hatred: Tell MAMA Annual Report 2018." London: Faith Matters, 2019. https://tellmamauk.org/wp-content/uploads/2019/09/Tell%20MAMA%20Annual%20Report%202018%20_%20Normalising%20Hate.pdf.

Theiss-Morse, Elisabeth. *Who Counts as an American?* New York: Cambridge University Press, 2009.
Tjernshaugen, Karen. "Listhaug: 'Her i Norge spiser vi svin, drikker alkohol og viser ansiktet vårt.'" *Aftenposten*, October 18, 2016. https://www.aftenposten.no/norge/politikk/i/0Aj02/listhaug-her-i-norge-spiser-vi-svin-drikker-alkohol-og-viser-ansiktet-vaart.
van der Brug, Wouter, Meindert Fennema, and Jean Tillie. "Anti-immigrant Parties in Europe: Ideological or Protest Vote?" *European Journal of Political Research* 37 (January 2000): 77–102.
van Spanje, Joost, and Nan Dirk de Graaf. "How Established Parties Reduce Other Parties' Electoral Support: The Strategy of Parroting the Pariah. *West European Politics* 41, no.1 (2018): 1–27. https://doi.org/10.1080/01402382.2017.1332328.
Vasilopoulou, Sofia. "Campaign Frames in the Voters' Minds." In *EU Referendum Analysis 2016: Media, Voters and the Campaign*, edited by Daniel Jackson, Einar Thorsen, and Dominic Wring. Bournemouth: Bournemouth University, The Centre for the Study of Journalism, Culture and Community, 2016.
Vogt, Kari. *Islam på norsk: Moskeer og islamske organisasjoner i Norge.* Oslo: Cappelen Damm, 2008.
Waldron, Jeremy. *The Harm in Hate Speech.* Cambridge, MA: Harvard University Press, 2012.
Welzel, Christian. *Freedom Rising.* New York: Cambridge University Press, 2013.
Wright, Mathew, Richard Johnston, Jack Citrin, and Stuart Soroka. "Multiculturalism and Muslim Accommodation: Policy and Predisposition across Three Political Contexts." *Comparative Political Studies*, 50, no. 1 (January 2017), 102–32. https://doi.org/10.1177/0010414015626448.

Data Sources

Ansolabehere, Stephen, and Brian Schaffner. "2013 CCES Common Content." Harvard Dataverse, V1, 2019. https://doi.org/10.7910/DVN/KPP85M.

Arnesen, Sveinung. *A Guide to the 2017 European Internet Panel Study (EIPS)*. NORCE Norwegian Research Centre and University of Bergen, Bergen, Norway, 2018. https://bookdown.org/sveinungarnesen78/eips2017-guide/.

Arnesen, Sveinung, Laurent Lesnard, Anne Cornilleau, Anne-Sophie Cousteaux, ELIPSS Team. *Few Questions on Europe, Fondation Nationale des Sciences Politiques (FNSP)*, Data Archive: Centre de Données Socio-Politiques (CDSP), Version 0, 2017.

Blom, Annelies G., Barbara Felderer, Franziska Gebhard, Jessica Herzing, Ulrich Krieger. *German Internet Panel, Wave 29 (May 2017)*. SFB 884 Political Economy of Reforms, Universität Mannheim, GESIS Data Archive, Cologne, 2018. ZA6903 Data file Version 2.0.0, https://doi.org/10.4232/1.12976.

Das, Marcel, Joris Mulder, Anne Cornilleau, Anne-Sophie Cousteaux, Laurent Lesnard, Annelies Blom, Sveinung Arnesen, Gudbjorg A. Jónsdottir: *European Internet Panel Study (EIPS) wave 4*, CentERdata, Tilburg, 2017.

Martinsson, Johan, Andreasson, Maria, Markstedt, Elias, Lindgren, Elina. Technical report *Citizen Panel 28—2017*, Gothenburg: University of Gothenburg, LORE, 2018.

Norwegian Citizen Panel, Wave 18, 2020. Data collected by ideas2evidence for the Norwegian Citizen Panel, University of Bergen. 1st NSD ed.

Norwegian Citizen Panel, Wave 15, 2019. Data collected by ideas2evidence for the Norwegian Citizen Panel, University of Bergen. 1st NSD ed. https://doi.org/10.18712/NSD-NSD2743-V1.

Norwegian Citizen Panel, Wave 12, 2018. Data collected by ideas2evidence for Elisabeth Ivarsflaten, University of Bergen. 1st NSD ed. https://doi.org/10.18712/NSD-NSD2605-V1.

Norwegian Citizen Panel, Wave 10, 2017. Data collected by ideas2evidence for Elisabeth Ivarsflaten, University of Bergen. 2nd NSD ed. https://doi.org/10.18712/NSD-NSD2546-V2.

Norwegian Citizen Panel, Wave 9, 2017. Data collected by ideas2evidence for Elisabeth Ivarsflaten, University of Bergen. 3rd NSD ed. https://doi.org/10.18712/NSD-NSD2479-V3.

Norwegian Citizen Panel, Wave 8, 2017. Data collected by ideas2evidence for Elisabeth Ivarsflaten, University of Bergen. 3rd NSD ed. https://doi.org/10.18712/NSD-NSD2478-V3.

Norwegian Citizen Panel, Wave 7, 2016. Data collected by ideas2evidence for the Norwegian Citizen Panel, University of Bergen. 4th NSD ed.

Norwegian Citizen Panel, Wave 6, 2016. Data collected by ideas2evidence for Elisabeth Ivarsflaten, University of Bergen. 5th NSD ed. https://doi.org/10.18712/NSD-NSD2344-V5.

Norwegian Citizen Panel, Wave 5, 2015. Data collected by ideas2evidence for Elisabeth Ivarsflaten, University of Bergen. 5th NSD ed. https://doi.org/10.18712/NSD-NSD2343-V5.

Norwegian Citizen Panel, Wave 4, 2015. Data collected by ideas2evidence for the Norwegian Citizen Panel, University of Bergen. 6th NSD ed. https://doi.org/10.18712/NSD-NSD2342-V6.

Norwegian Citizen Panel, Wave 2, 2014. Data collected by ideas2evidence for Elisabeth Ivarsflaten, University of Bergen. 4th NSD ed. https://doi.org/10.18712/NSD-NSD2112-V4.

Norwegian Citizen Panel, Wave 1, 2013. Data collected by ideas2evidence for Elisabeth Ivarsflaten, University of Bergen. 4th NSD ed. https://doi.org/10.18712/NSD-NSD2065-V4.

Muslim Inclusion Study 5, Great Britain. July 2019. Data collected by YouGov for Elisabeth Ivarsflaten and Paul Sniderman, in collaboration with Robert Ford and Maria Sobolewska.

Muslim Inclusion Study 4, the Netherlands, 2019. Data collected by Lucid Software for Elisabeth Ivarsflaten and Paul Sniderman, in collaboration with Yphtalk Lelkes.

Muslim Inclusion Study 3, Denmark, 2016. Data collected by YouGov for Elisabeth Ivarsflaten and Paul Sniderman, in collaboration with Rune Slothuus, Rune Stubager, and Michael Bang-Pedersen.

Muslim Inclusion Study 2, Great Britain. November 2015. Data collected by YouGov for Elisabeth Ivarsflaten and Paul Sniderman, in collaboration with Robert Ford and Maria Sobolewska.

Muslim Inclusion Study 1, United States, 2013. Data collected as part of multiwave panel in the United States, September 2012–May 2013, by Types of Racism Study for Paul Sniderman, in collaboration with Edward G. Carmines.

Index

accusation condition, 90
acquiescence bias, 76
affective consistency, 181n15
Afghanistan, 19, 21
Africa, 21
Akkerman, Tjitske, 136
alternative right movement, 17
"America First," 128
American exceptionalism, 75
Anderson, Benedict, 70–71
anti-Islamic views, 17, 21, 28–30; lack of attempt to distinguish among Muslims, 18–19
anti-Semitism, 175n1
appraisal respect, 5, 140–41, 145; diversity, 41; duty of care, 44; recognition respect, distinction between, 11–12, 15, 35–38, 46–50, 52, 69, 111, 142, 144, 182n2
Asia, 21
assimilation, 4, 7, 149
Asylum Seeker sequence, 95–98, 100–101, 104, 149–50
Atlas Shrugs (blog), 17
Austria, 128
authoritarianism, 4, 129–30

bad faith, 116–19, 121
Bad Faith sequence, 14, 117, 121, 123–24, 147
Belgium, 132, 181n26
Berlin, Isaiah, 123–24, 171n2
Birmingham (England), 121
Bleich, Erik, 173n1, 175n2, 175n3
Blinder, Scott, 174n22, 174n23, 175n15

Callan, Eamonn, 174n6
Campbell, Donald, 130
Christianity, 55, 145; secular society, 148
citizenship, 88, 110; civic life, 98; democratic citizenship, 92–94
Citizen Panel III, 177n8
civic integration, 110; cultural integration, distinction between, 109
civic life, 89, 104; citizenship, as example of, 98, 110; democratic citizenship, 94; taking part in, 8
civic participation, 94, 97, 101, 149; cultural integration, aspect of, 149–50
Civil War, 70
Conservative Party, 121, 136
Conservative Party (Norway), 181n23
continuity: of consciousness, 79; continuity principle, 80, 82; of narrative, 79; of national identity, 87, 150; of process, 8, 71, 79, 82–84; similarity, overlapping of, 79, 83; of substance, 7–8. *See also* discontinuity
control conditions, 90–92
counter-Jihadi community, 17
COVID, 133
cumulative extremism, 3

Dalton, Russell J., 179n3
Dancygier, Rafaela, 121
Danish People's Party, 132. *See also* Danish Progress Party
Danish Progress Party, 132. *See also* Danish People's Party

Darwall, Stephen L., 44, 174n6
Declaration of Loyalty experiment, 89–92, 149–50
democratic politics, 151
demonization, 3, 17, 19, 21–22, 24, 30, 34; *daemon*, root of, 16; generalization, 16; hostile beliefs, 16; threat perception, 16
Denmark, 12, 14–15, 79, 80, 96, 100, 118, 125, 128, 147, 181n26
Die Alternative für Deutschland, 128
differentiation, 3, 19, 25–30, 33–34
dignity, 37, 55, 57, 61, 144; what may be said and what should be said, 145
direct democracy, 88
discontinuity, 80–83, 176n11. *See also* continuity
discrimination, 22, 67; minority, 102, 107, 109; of Muslims, 31–33, 90–91, 107, 128
diversity, 25, 40, 50, 103; acknowledge v. celebrate, 41–42; acknowledge v. respect, 42; acknowledge worth of, 43; affirmation of, 38; appraisal respect, 41; celebration of, 44; fresh thinking, 83; and liberal democracies, 111; national identity, 8, 80, 82, 85; opening a new chapter, 83; private v. public, 42–43; recognition, 41; recognition of worthiness of, 41–42; recognition respect principle, 43; school textbooks, 74–82, 84, 138; tolerance, 84; valuing of, 90
duty of care: appraisal respect, 44

Election Poll Volunteer experiment, 106–7, 109, 148; appropriateness, 105; even-handedness, 105; propriety, 105
Esaiasson, Peter, 177n6
Europe, 1, 3, 6, 9, 21, 31–33, 49, 54, 57, 67–68, 71, 74–76, 90, 117, 130, 133, 139, 144, 148; anti-Islamic activism in, 17–18, 29; far right, 132; Muslims, and conflict of values, 111; nativist parties, rise of, 128–29; refugee crisis in, 19, 96
European Court of Human Rights, 58
European Internet Panel Study (EIPS), 29, 31
European Union (EU), 128, 132
exclusion, 3–4, 31, 33–34, 116, 135–37, 141–43, 146, 151
experimentalist ethos, 151

"faking nice," 95
far right, 2–3, 10, 19, 33, 131–34, 137, 139, 181n26; accommodative strategy, 136; democratic actors, legitimacy of, 135;
Facebook, as primary channel of, 17; nativist support for, 129; prejudice and politics model, 135
field experiments, 15
Finland, 128
Ford, Robert, 174n22, 174n23, 175n15
Fortuyn, Pim, 17
framing, 11; framing effects, 172n27; framing studies, 137
France, 15, 18, 29, 31, 128, 181n26
freedom of assembly, 113, 116, 135
freedom of expression, 10, 112–13, 136, 145
freedom of religion, 9–10, 112–13, 116, 135, 146
freedom of speech, 6, 54–55, 135, 142, 145; inclusive tolerance, 68; and prejudice, 67; rejection of, as illiberal choice, 112
Freedom Party (PVV), 3, 128, 132
Fresh Thinking, 83–84

Gates of Vienna (blog), 17
gay rights, 135
gender equality, 5, 114, 121, 124, 135; v. religious freedom, 9; right to assembly, 134
generic fascism, 28–29
Germany, 15, 18, 29, 31, 74, 128; refugee crisis, 19
Griffin, Roger, 28

hate crimes, 6, 128
hate speech, 9–10, 55, 145–46
Helbling, Marc, 174n22, 174n23
Hume, David, 176n12
hypocrisy, 145

identity: and continuity, 7, 80, 83; as conundrum, 71; cultural diversity, as threat to, 129; and similarity, 83; Sir John Cutler's stockings analogy, 71, 79; as socially constructed, 7, 71, 82. *See also* national identity
identity movement, 17
Immersion (Serrano). *See Piss Christ* (Serrano)
immigration, 137; minority inclusion, 136; and prejudice, 2
inclusion, 8, 12, 29, 49, 71, 83, 85, 87–88, 107, 131–32, 134–37, 141–42, 144, 151; acceptance, 4, 35; acknowledgment of worth, 5; appraisal respect and recognition respect, 5; broad support of, 10; as call for action, 7; comparatively tolerant, as key to, 34; as goal, 149; intolerance, 4, 150; liberal democracies, 1–2, 4, 7; moral limits on, 2;

pivotal distinctions, 145–46; polarization trap, 1, 11; and respect, 4; and tolerance, 2, 111–12, 150
inclusionary options, 4, 10, 12, 35, 39, 43, 131, 141, 146; normative premises, pivotal distinctions between, 11; substance of, 137–38; tolerance, 49
inclusive politics, 15, 136, 137, 141–44, 150
inclusive tolerance, 2, 4–6, 10, 49–50, 55, 66–67, 85, 102–3, 113–14, 135–36, 143, 146; freedom of expression and religion, 9; freedom of speech, 68
in-group, 30, 33
Internal Motivation to Control Prejudice (IMCP), 49–50, 66–68, 84–85, 103, 107, 109, 114, 124–27, 143–44
intolerance, 1–2, 33, 35, 53, 107, 109–10, 114, 117, 129–31, 134–35, 143, 147, 151; and diversity, 84; exclusion, 34; and inclusion, 4, 150; intolerance of, 58; may and should, 67; tolerance, converging of, 115–16, 119–20, 124
Ireland, 74
ISIS, 133
Islam 3, 10, 21, 28, 53, 113, 115, 119, 132, 145, 147–48
Islamic Defense Council, 54
Islamization, 17–18, 22
Islamophobia, 3, 16, 22, 24, 33, 53, 67
Isungset, Odd, 54
Italy, 74, 128, 132

James, William, 79, 83
Jews, 117

Khomeini, Ayatollah, 54

Laboratory Opinion Research (LORe), 177n8
Labor Party (Norway), 181n23
Labour Party, 121, 136
Lega Nord, 132
Less Emphasis condition, 103, 146
letters to the editor, 55–56, 58–64, 66–68
Letter to the Editor experiment, 105, 107, 142, 145
libel, 55
liberal democracies, 5, 8, 12, 24, 33, 53, 110, 131, 146, 151, 171n2; diversity, 111; free speech, 54; illiberal strains in, 2–3, 10; inclusion, 1–2, 4, 7; out-groups, 63; pluralism, valuing of, 35–36; and respect, 144
liberal values, 114, 119, 142; conflict of, 9, 115;

illiberal values, conflict between, 111–13, 120, 123, 146
liberty: equality, conflict between, 112
List experiment technique, 124–25
loyalty, 8, 89–92, 94, 116, 147, 150

Mansbridge, Jane, 177n13
Marcus, George, 112
Meguid, Bonnie, 136
Mill, John Stuart: common sense, 93; local government, 93–94; ordinary citizens, on limitations of, 92–93; tyranny of the majority, 36
Miller, David, 109–10
Modood, Tariq, 6, 55
"Mohammad Cartoon Crisis," 17
Mohammed, 54
Mudde, Cas, 132
multiculturalism, 25; minority cultures, worth of, 38; sustaining, of minority cultures, 38
Multidisciplinary Opinion and Democracy (MOD), 177n8
Muslims, 11, 70, 106; abusive speech, as vulnerable to, 54; affirmation of, 38; anti-Islamic activists, 17–19, 28–30, 33; appraisal respect, 145; asylum seekers, 96–97; bad faith, 13–14, 116–19; bad press, 25; barriers to, 105, 109–10; civic life, 101, 104, 110; civic participation, 149–50; conflict of values, 111; critical and contemptuous speech, difference between, 66; cultural values, clash of, 130; demonization of, 3, 16–17, 19, 21–22, 24, 29–31, 33–34, 37; differences, acknowledging of, 3; differentiation, 19, 25–29, 31, 33–34; dignity of, 37, 44, 61, 144–45; discrimination against, 31–33, 90, 91, 107, 128; as disloyal, perception of, 117; dogmatism, perception of, 122; dual loyalties, charge of, 117; emulation, as worthy of, 5; exclusion of, 3, 143; as existential threat, 10; "fair game," 55, 142; far right, targeting of, 10; freedom of assembly, rejection of, 113–16; freedom of religion, 9–10, 113; generalizing about, 24; hate crimes, target of, 128; illiberal choices, 10; ill will toward, 68; inclusion, 1, 4–5, 7, 12, 18, 33–34, 141; inclusionary options, as vital to, 141; Islamophobic sentiments, 22, 24, 28–29, 33; loyalty, 8, 88–92, 94; mortal enemies, viewed as, 18; Muslim leaders, bad faith of, 13–14, 119–21, 123; Muslim

Muslims (*continued*)
  leadership, distrust of, 116–19, 122, 147; negative emotions against, 130–31; negative stereotypes about, 22, 33; offensive speech, 53, 55–64, 66–69, 143, 145; as outsiders twice, 89; political speech, as abusive to, 6; prejudice against, 2, 53, 68, 114; recognition respect, entitled to, 52; refugee crisis, 21; religious Muslim leaders and secular Muslim leaders, distinction between, 121–23; respect for, 36–37, 44–46; respect v. protect, 45–46, 50; respect v. support, 47–48; rights as citizens, as contested, 112–13; right to assembly, 32, 134–35; right to free speech, rejection of, 113; role of women, and liberal values conflicts, 135, 146–47; stereotyping of, 117; stigmatizing and rejecting of, 16, 116; stranger anxiety toward, 24; support of, 52; as terrorists, theme of, 17, 22–23, 29–30; as threatening, 129; value conflict, 9; "Western culture," conflict with, 22–24; what may be said v. what should be said, 6–7, 145; women, oppression of, 23; worth, acknowledgment of, 5, 52; worthy of respect, 35

National Front, 128, 132
national identity, 172n22; ambivalence, 138; assimilation, 4; construction of, 74–76, 79–81, 87; continuity of process, 87, 150; continuous and interrupted processes of, as pivotal, 150; diverse forms of, 7; and diversity, 8, 80, 82, 85; and inclusiveness, 77, 87; as institutionalized, 71–72, 79; national continuity, 71; national narrative, 70, 72; psychology of, 7, 70; self-narrative, 82; transmission of, 72
National Identity Construction sequence, 72, 77, 79–80, 82, 138
nativism, 2, 129, 132, 139
Neo-Nazis, 31–32, 112
Netherlands, 3, 12, 14–15, 17, 29, 31, 80, 82, 116–18, 128, 147, 178n23, 180n12, 181n26
niche parties, 136
Nordic democracies: self-image of, 94
North America, 1
Norway, 11, 14, 22–25, 29, 31, 38, 42, 44–48, 54, 79, 80, 82, 88, 96, 100–102, 106, 118, 122–23, 128, 132–33, 139, 147, 149, 181n26; asylum seekers, 97; celebrating and respecting diversity, 41; diversity in, 75–78, 138; refugee applications, 98; refugee crisis, 19, 21; school textbooks, written v. rewritten, 75
Norwegian Citizen Panel, 14–15, 21, 105, 151
Norwegian Elections Study, 133
null hypothesis, 40, 42
Nygaard, William, 54

offensive speech, 53, 67–69, 112; as acceptable, 59, 64; common decency, 66; evenhandedness, 61, 64, 66; hate speech, distinction between, 6, 58–61, 64, 145; as problematic, 58; Unreasonable and Inaccurate conditions, 62
Opening a New Chapter, 83
Oslo (Norway), 54
out-groups, 10, 16, 24, 63, 129; asymmetry, as trademark feature of, 24; reactions to, 130

Participatory Citizen hypothesis, 94, 96–97
participatory democracy, 8, 88–89, 177n13
participatory values, 94
patriarchy, 37
Patriotic Europeans against the Islamization of the West (PEGIDA), 3, 17–18
Pierson, James, 112
Piss Christ (Serrano), 55
pledging allegiance: as form of political theater, 89
pluralism, 17, 35, 109–10, 140
polarization traps, 10, 131, 139–41, 150; and inclusion, 1, 11; liberal democratic values, friction between, 1
political extremism, 2
political participation: local government, 93; and voting, 93
political tolerance, 2
political tolerance studies, 113
populism, 2, 139
prejudice, 53, 67, 107, 109, 125–27, 129, 142–44, 175n1
prejudice and politics model, 131, 142, 144, 150, 180–81n16; concurrence, 130; far right, 135; long-term affective predispositions, 129; short-term shocks, 129; similarity, 130
Progressive Party, 138
Progress Party, 133, 181n23
public affairs, 88, 92
Public Rally experiment, 9–10, 117, 120, 123–24, 146–47; controversial ideas, 114–15; four conditions of, 113; Preach conditions of, 133
public speech, 69; letters to the editor, 55–56

public sphere, 24, 145; Islamic religious and cultural symbols, and cultural ascendency, 148–49

race, 74
randomization, 29, 100–101, 115
recognition respect, 5, 14, 140; appraisal respect, distinction between, 11–12, 15, 35–38, 44, 46–50, 52, 69, 111, 142, 144, 182n2; free speech, 55
refugee crisis, 19, 21, 96, 98, 100, 149
representative democracy, 88
right to assembly, 32; transgressive groups, 29
Rushdie, Salman, 53–54

Satanic Verses (Rushdie), 53–54
Scandinavia, 94, 96, 133
Schleifer, James, 2
school textbooks, 8, 72, 176n9; changes in, as routinized, 80; and diversity, 74–82, 84, 138; revising and rewriting, 81–82; updating or expanding, 82; written v. rewritten, 74–82, 84–85
Scotland, 128. *See also* United Kingdom
Seat at the Table experiment, 101, 103–4, 146
self: and continuity, 79; and similarity, 79
September 11, 2001, attacks, 17
sequential factorials, 12–13; repeatable template, 38–40, 56–57
Serrano, Andres, 55
Skam (series), 28
Smith, John Maynard, 12
Sobolewska, Maria, 178n23
social dominance orientation, 4
Socialist Left Party, 181n23
social sciences: crisis of replication, 13
speech: acceptable and unacceptable, 57
Speech sequence, 54, 56, 59, 64
Stop the Islamization of Europe (SIOE), 17–18
Storhaug, Hege, 26, 173n14
Stouffer, Samuel, 112
substantive continuity, 7
Sullivan, John, 112
survey experiments, 19, 151, 176n14; statistically significant difference, 30
Sverigedemokraterna, 128
Sweden, 15, 29, 31–32, 88, 91, 94, 174n22;

diversity, valuing of, 90; refugee crisis, 19; as tolerant, 90
Sweden Democrats, 132
Swiss People's Party, 132
Switzerland, 128, 181n26
Symbolic Declaration, 90
symbolic goods, 144
Syria, 19, 21, 28, 133
system justification, 4

Tocqueville, Alexis de, 2
tolerance, 1, 12, 50, 53, 85, 107, 109, 113, 117, 134–35, 147; and diversity, 84; free speech, 58, 67; and inclusion, 2, 111–12, 150; inclusionary options, 49; intolerance, converging of, 115–16, 119–20, 124; and respect, 35; rethinking of, 143; rights of others, accepting of, 144; what may and should be said, 57–58
Traunmüller, Richard, 174n23
True Finns, 132
Trump, Donald, 17, 128

UK Independence Party (UKIP), 132
United Kingdom, 11, 14–15, 38, 46–48, 80, 82–83, 121, 123, 128, 133; public affirmation of diversity, 43. *See also* Scotland
United States, 2, 9–10, 12, 15, 18–19, 26–27, 38, 40, 42–43, 46–47, 55, 70, 133, 176n9; anti-Islamic activism in, 17, 29; diversity, 74; race, as defining feature, 74

valence framework, 131, 137, 142, 150; intergroup attitudes, 130
value conflict, 9
Vlaams Belang, 133. *See also* Vlaams Blok
Vlaams Blok, 133. *See also* Vlaams Belang

Waldron, Jeremy, 144, 182n2
what may and should be said, 6–7, 12, 58; and dignity, 145; distinction between, 57, 62–64, 66, 69; free speech, 142; and intolerant, 67; irony of, 68; liberal democratic ideals, friction inherent in, 142
white supremacists, 17
Wilders, Geert, 3

xenophobia, 27, 128

www.ingramcontent.com/pod-product-compliance
Lightning Source LLC
Chambersburg PA
CBHW051357290426
44108CB00015B/2055